African Americans on Stamps

African Americans on Stamps

Mack Bernard Morant

FOREWORD BY MACGORINE CASSELL

McFarland & Company, Inc., Publishers

Jefferson, North Carolina, and London

Library of Congress Cataloguing-in-Publication Data

Morant, Mack Bernard.
African Americans on stamps / Mack Bernard Morant ; foreword by
MacGorine Cassell.
p.   cm.
Includes bibliographical references and index.

ISBN 0-7864-0948-7 (illustrated case binding : 50# and 70# alkaline paper)

1. African Americans on postage stamps.   I. Title.
HE6183.A35M669   2003   769.56'42 — dc21   2002015003

British Library cataloguing data are available

Designed by Virginia Tobiassen

Manufactured in the United States of America

*McFarland & Company, Inc., Publishers
Box 611, Jefferson, North Carolina 28640
www.mcfarlandpub.com*

In memory of my Mama, Jannie Gilmore Morant;
Virgie Lee Brown (Big Auntie); Aunt Jessie Lee Davis;
Aunt Maggie Morant; a special person, Yvonne A. John;
and my cousins, Margaret Brown Stevenson, Helen Brown Johnson,
and Mary Brown Randolph. And in memory of Dr. Ellis Odom,
who served as chairman of my dissertation committee at the
University of Massachusetts, Amherst.

To my Daddy, Mack Morant; Mrs. Vashti Julan Cassell,
a very special Mama of Liberia, Africa;
and to my daughters, Jeanette Nicole Morant and
Jordain Nortosha Searles, and to Bernice Franklin, my godddaughter.

Acknowledgments

To complete a book of this size and maintain high quality is a tremendous task that requires the input of others. It would have been impossible to bring to closure fifteen years of research and writing without the help and advice of many people.

I first want to acknowledge those who were the pioneers in providing valuable information on African Americans on United States and international stamps. Those individuals and organizations include Earnest A. Austin, M.D., F.A.C.S., author of *The Black American Stamp Album* (1988); Clement A. Wells, Jr., who documented extensive research in an article titled "Black Americans on Stamps" published in the *American Topical Time Journal* (1987); and the Ebony Society of Philatelic Events and Reflections, known as ESPER (named after its founder, Ms. Esper Hayes, a New Jersey stamp enthusiast), and Standford Byrd.

I wish to thank that giant of philately, Scott Publishing, for the information they have made available on stamp issues for more than 150 years. Completion of this book would have been impossible without their *Standard Postage* volumes, which are published annually.

MacGorine Cassell, a native Liberian, is a friend and brother who gave me much advice and information on Liberia. His wife, Rosa Jones Cassell, provided my first basic computer lessons as I organized the early stages of this book. I also had help from James Lafayette Toles, Jr., a great friend whom I came to know and respect while we were at South Carolina State University (Orangeburg) and Virginia State University (Petersburg).

I thank my sister Gloria Morant James, who provided valuable input, special editorial contributions and support during the writing of this book. Thanks, too, to my brother-in-law Irby James, my brothers, Percy and Joseph Morant, my sister Virgie L. Morant James, and Sharon Morant Garland, for their support.

I am grateful for the help of William Harvey, my old Voorhees College roommate and friend, who worked with the biographies in the early stages of this manuscript; Marilyn Irving, who provided valuable information and special editorial material and advice; O.C. Bobby Daniels, a longtime friend whom I met at the University of Massachusetts; Reggie Jamerson, a superb artist and longtime friend, who advised me in the early stages on strategies for the layout of this book; my old friend and roommate Michael Ivy (at the University of Massachusetts); Cassandra Williams, whom I met at South Carolina State

University, who helped me with the typing when I was beginning this fifteen-year task; and my favorite friends from Voorhees College, Alfonso Montgomery, Leslie Floyd, Azell C. Smith, and James Swindell.

My thanks also go to Minnie Prince and Sarah Hawkins Turner, for their basic concepts and editorial input; Gwendolyn Sides St. Julian, coauthor with Eugene Jackson of *Eugene "Pineapple" Jackson: His Own Story*, for her support and positive reinforcement and very helpful hints; Mary Aiken Walker, for her continuous support and input; Jimmy Lee Franklin, Lin S. Amaker, Sammuel Bonaparte, Joseph Fuller, Frank Wolfe, Chris Robinson, Dillard Haley, Akinniyi Savage, Alonzo Stevens, Delearn Allen, Bruce Watts, Mr. William C. Marshall (Voorhees College professor), Ms. Serena Staggers (Voorhees College professor), Suzanne Reid-Searles, Neselyn Chambers-Reid, Dexter Divine Jones and Beverly Coleman who advised and supported me while writing this book.

Barbara Blackwell, another friend, provided positive input and advice. Charlotte Orange, a longtime friend and a most creative person, gave me advice in the early stages. Special acknowledgment goes to the Richmond County Library staff of Augusta, Georgia, for their professional help, support, and keen insight which supplied me with the information I needed to complete this book, Karen Riddle who edited a portion of the biographies, and the faculty, students, staff and Blackville Hilda High School in Blackville, South Carolina.

It is impossible to mention all of those others who along the way provided advice or gave a word of positive reinforcement. You know who you are, and I thank you.

Table of Contents

Foreword

BY MacGorine Cassell

The general intent of *African Americans on Stamps* is to offer the neophyte philatelist a comprehensive look at the hobby, as well as to provide the established enthusiast more in-depth sources from which to gain greater enjoyment and profit. In both cases the book offers the distinct pleasures of exploring a comprehensive compilation of stamps featuring African American visages and themes. To this end, I am proud to pen this foreword, not only because the book is the product of the hard work of a great intellect and avid stamp collector, but also because that mind belongs to a person I have been proud to call my best friend for over twenty years. In addition to *African Americans on Stamps*, Dr. Morant is the author of *Teacher/Student Work Manual: A Model for Evaluating U.S. History Textbooks*. Additional publications include several other books and various articles for journals. All of his works offer enlightenment in a style that is easy to read and comprehend.

The publication of *African Americans on Stamps* at the beginning of a new millennium is extremely timely, not only because it recognizes, honors, and confirms the achievements of African Americans, but also because it establishes the significant impact of African Americans on the history of the United States, as well as on world history.

African Americans on Stamps is the resource that will help citizens of the 21st century to discover black Americans on stamps. It is the only book that conveys such comprehensive knowledge of stamps on African Americans. Each stamp is individually identified, and Dr. Morant provides a concise biography of the personality the stamp represents. He also provides information helpful to both the new and the experienced stamp collector. For example, a reference number identifies each stamp, the country from which the stamp originated, the date of issue, the face value, and other comments that are significant to the reader and collector.

This African American stamp book has several special features. Beginning with a basic guide to collecting stamps, it then discusses the five distinct groups or types of African American stamps, providing the reader with a broader perspective and a clearer understanding of African American stamp issues. Within this discussion is an interesting and unique story on the historical connection and relationships between the United States of America and Liberia, West Africa (the African nation founded for former slaves who were sent to Liberia during President Monroe's administration).

To make this reference book even more complete, it identifies men and women of African descent who were born in America; who were born in America then moved to another country; and who came to America from another country and made significant contributions to American culture. All the stamps that pay tribute to African Americans in the United States and abroad (even commercial stamps that are in some cases not used for postage) are recognized in this source. The only exception is Cinderellas (stamps that are created for fun, for protest, or for other reasons by an individual or organization). From this wide array, collectors can choose stamps suitable for his or her own purpose.

Dr. Morant spent over fifteen years studying the historical and philatelic background of the stamps found in this book. He began his research with only the United States in mind, but he soon discovered that the U.S. represented only a small portion of the philatelic history relating to African Americans on stamps. Other countries had given honor to African Americans on the faces of their stamps long before America.

Dr. Morant's research involved attending stamp shows around the United States and spending many hours with local and state stamp dealers. Years, too, were spend contacting significant stamp dealers in the United States, Canada, and Europe through direct mail to acquire information through memberships and subscriptions such as *The American Philately Society, Inc.*, *Scott's Standard Postage Stamp Catalogue*, *Topical Association*, *The Stamp Collector*, and *The Black American Stamp Album: A Philatelic Study of Black Americans, World Wide*.

No other work on this topic is as comprehensive as this one. Similar resources that do exist are listed in the bibliography of this book.

If you are interested in a unique view of American history, a general reference source on stamp collecting, a topical source on African American stamps, or a new challenge in collecting, this book will give you the information you need, and a rewarding experience altogether.

This is a time of great promise and hope for Africans in the Diaspora. In *African Americans on Stamps*, the reader will revel in the inspiring biographies that Dr. Morant has provided, as well as the variegated designs with which more than fifty countries have transformed African American history into visual art. For the avid collector, the book offers an incisive literary "chatroom" platform from which to launch a variety of discussions.

All in all, *African Americans on Stamps* is the kind of book that I urge you to enjoy and use to the fullest advantage. Although the privilege has been mine to write this foreword, the pleasure will be all yours as you leaf through the information and stamps in this fascinating book.

Introduction

A guide to the recognition of African Americans on United States and international stamps is reference material long overdue. To begin this journey into collecting stamps on the African American, we must pinpoint when and where stamps were used for mailing letters and honoring significant persons and events.

While organized messenger services existed in the ancient world, the adhesive postal stamp first appeared in England in 1840. The idea is credited to British educator Rowland Hill, who proposed it in an 1837 pamphlet on postal reform. Hill advocated the adoption of a single rate for delivery (regardless of distance) and the use of stamps that could be purchased and affixed to letters to show that the sender had paid the delivery charge. Hill's proposals were so popular and successful in England that other countries around the world were soon producing postage stamps for their own use.

In 1903, fifty-six years after the issue of Britain's first postage stamp, Garretson Wilmot Gibson, an African American and the eighth president of Liberia, West Africa, was honored on a Liberian postage stamp. This marked the first time ever in the world that an African American was honored on a postage stamp. Matilda New-port was recognized on a stamp of Liberia in 1947, making her the first African American woman to receive the honor. America followed Liberia's 1923 Joseph Roberts stamp seventeen years later with the first U.S. stamps ever recognizing an African American. The noted African American was Booker T. Washington, who was born a slave and became one of America's greatest educators, as well as a model for African Americans and others all over the world.

Since the introduction of Garretson Wilmot Gibson, Maltilda Newport, and Booker T. Washington on stamps, more than eighty-five countries have issued stamps paying tribute to individual African Americans or African American themes, recognizing the contributions of African Americans in education, science, engineering, human and civil rights, the arts, sports, and other fields. Not only do stamps recognizing African Americans indicate great honor, but they are also evidence of African Americans' impact on U.S. and world history. For example, the Reverend Dr. Martin Luther King, Jr., has been depicted on postage or commemorative stamps in more than 50 countries. The Middle Eastern nation of Ajman was the first country to issue stamps recognizing Dr. King (1968). The United States of

America recognized him as recently as September 17, 1999. Even though one must be dead for eleven years to appear on a United States stamp, the Independent Postal Service of America issued a stamp in King's honor in 1968. Jesse Owens, who won four gold medals in the 1936 Olympics, was the first African American with no political ties to have a stamp issued in his honor by a foreign country, the Dominican Republic (1957). On September 14, 1960, Mildred McDaniel, another Olympic star, became the first African American woman with no political ties to be so recognized, by a stamp issued in Panama. Nineteen years later, Harriet Tubman, the former slave who led many other slaves to freedom through the Underground Railroad, was the first African American woman to appear on a U.S. stamp. That stamp, issued in 1978, introduced the Black Heritage Series, which recognizes a significant African American annually. Twenty-four African Americans have so far been recognized in the Black Heritage Series.

It might surprise you to know that the West Indian nation of St. Vincent in 1985 issued nine colorful postage stamps paying honor to Michael Jackson. Tanzania and Lesotho as recently as the 1990s have paid tribute to Bill Cosby, Eddie Murphy, Sammy Davis, Jr., and many other black entertainers. You will find many similar stamps recognizing African Americans in countries throughout the world.

Even though African Americans have been recognized on stamps by countries around the globe, numerous Americans, even many avid stamp collectors, are not cognizant of these unique miniatures of art depicting black Americans. The aim of this book is to serve as a major reference source for African American stamp issues through December 31, 1999; to provide interesting information about those African Americans who are recognized on stamps in the United states and internationally; and to introduce both general and topical stamp collectors to African Americans on stamps. Whether you are a collector, a history buff, or just an avid reader who likes discovering new facts, you will find this book interesting (often fascinating), useful and practical, adding a new and exciting twist to stamp collecting. (If you are new to stamp collecting, the general information that follows this introduction may prove helpful.) And who knows? This book may even enhance your opportunities to discover the next "sleeping" collectible.

This reference guide provides information on hundreds of stamp issues. Issues featuring African Americans are increasing annually. Few people can boast that they have a complete or even half-complete collection of African Americans on stamps—but this book can point everyone in the right direction. Collecting these stamps is a wonderful hobby and more. The stamps are unique to American and African American heritage; they provide an excellent challenge (many are rare), as well as an opportunity to increase one's knowledge of history (and perhaps of one's investments in stamps).

It is of utmost significance that those who get involved with this book or use it as reference material feel free to forward information or make the author aware of important facts about African American stamps that may have been either omitted or incorrectly included. Even with careful research, mistakes are inevitable, and much is likely still to be discovered by readers of this book. Therefore, the author welcomes your comments, information, and other materials for improvement. (Please write in care of the publisher.) With readers' help, this book can be one of the best resources available on African Americans on U.S. and international stamps.

A Basic Guide to Collecting Stamps

Stamp collecting is one of the most fascinating activities to choose as a hobby. Not only is it fun, it is therapeutically relaxing; a learning tool for history, geography, and politics; and even a way of investing. However, if you are new to the hobby, it is wise to learn as much as possible before making a financial commitment. Make it your first rule of thumb not to spend one cent on stamps, materials or tools until you have a clear understanding of the basic concepts. Too often new collectors end up investing too much money in stamps or coins— money that they will never recoup in a lifetime. This mistake is largely due to the lack of knowledge. Not knowing what to buy, where to buy, when to buy or how to buy and other basic pitfalls can be avoided to a great degree if you acquire as much basic information as possible previous to your involvement.

Impatience is a common human failing. Most of us do not like to wait, even if our impatience causes us to spend money unnecessarily. When we are excited about involving ourselves with such a fascinating hobby as stamp collecting, many times our first instinct is to buy stamps without taking into account the cost.

This section is an introduction to the basic concepts of stamp collecting with a practical "how-to" approach. It discusses terminology associated with the hobby, offers information on tools and materials needed, and provides the names and addresses of some related organizations and associations. It also includes tips for buying internationally, other basics on stamp collecting, and some pointers on topical collecting, using African American–themed stamps as a model that will prove interesting to both new and seasoned collectors.

The hobby of stamp collecting—formally known as *philately*— is divided into two major categories, *general* and *topical* collecting.

General collecting is the saving of many kinds of stamps. The experts suggest that a beginner should start with general collecting until he or she becomes familiar with philately. General collecting allows the newcomer the opportunity to experience new ideas and to develop a good feel for the hobby while learning about different kinds of stamps. General collecting is also less expensive than topical collecting because a person can collect many stamps at little or no cost. Stamps for a general collection can be acquired through family, friends, neighbors, local businesses, organizations, or others who receive many letters.

Topical collecting is the saving of a specific kind of stamp. An example of topical collecting would be the saving of bird stamps only, flower stamps only, or even a specific species of a bird or flower — in short, a specific category that the collector finds interesting. The collection of African American stamps is an example of topical collecting.

It can sometimes be more expensive to collect or search for a specific kind of stamp for a particular topic. However, it's still possible to ask family, friends, and others to save a special kind of stamp for a topical collection until one learns how to buy economically.

In addition to understanding the definition and the categories of philately, it is of equal importance to note that stamps are classified according to how they are used. *The Postal Service Guide to U.S. Stamps* lists and defines U.S. stamps as follows:

Definitive Stamps: On most mail these are found in denominations ranging from 1 to 5 cents. Their subjects frequently are former presidents, statesmen, other prominent persons, and national shrines. Printed in unlimited quantities for specific postal rates, definitive stamps are available for several years. Examples of people pictured on definitive stamps are Abraham Lincoln, George Washington, and Dr. Charles Drew.

Commemorative Stamps honor important people, events or special subjects of national appeal and significance. They usually are larger and more colorful than definitive stamps. Printed in limited quantities, commemorative stamps are available

for only two to three months at most post offices and for about one year by mail order from the Postal Service's Philatelic Sales Division.

Special Stamps include issues that supplement the regular stamps, such as Christmas stamps, "love" stamps, and others.

Airmail Stamps are used for sending mail overseas.

Booklet Stamps are issued in small folders containing one or more panes of 3 to 20 stamps each. A stamp may have one straight and three perforated sides; two straight and two perforated sides; or three straight and one perforated side.

Coil Stamps are issued in rolls. Each stamp has two straight and two perforated edges.

The United States Postal Service is one of the best sources of information on philately, for both new and seasoned stamp collectors. The U.S. Postal Service has been in the business of stamps since it bought out City Dispatch Post, a private carrier service in New York City run by Alexander Greig for six months in 1840. Since the U.S. Postal Service purchase of the business, it has consistently published, produced and disbursed materials to keep the American public and the world informed of the hobby of philately.

One of their most practical and informative publications is *The Postal Service Guide to U.S. Stamps*, mentioned above. This guide has very carefully outlined the basic terminology, tools, organizations, associations, publications, philatelic centers and other services to meet the needs of the philatelist. This book is published and upgraded annually by the U.S. Postal Service and is an excellent tool for the fledgling philatelist. It is particularly recommended to those who are interested in collecting U.S. stamps.

A Practical and Economical Approach to Collecting Stamps

In order to avoid costly mistakes in collecting, it is necessary to understand how value is assessed. The value or cost of a stamp depends on three important factors:

(1) the rarity of the stamp
(2) the condition of the stamp
(3) the importance of the stamp to the prospective buyer (for completing a collection, perhaps, or for sentimental reasons).

In many instances one can determine the rarity of a stamp by its cost. But the condition of a stamp also plays a significant part in assigning a value or cost to a stamp. For example, if a stamp is extremely rare *and* is in fine to mint condition, the value or cost will be greater than if it was rare but not in good condition. The *Postal Service Guide to U.S. Stamps* further advises that collectors should look for the following to determine the condition of a stamp:

(1) Examine the front of the stamp, and check to see if colors are bright or faded.
(2) Check to observe if the stamp is dirty, stained or clean. Torn stamps are not considered "collectible" (unless they are extremely rare).
(3) Check the design in the center of the stamp, to observe if it is a little crooked or off to the side.
(4) Check to see if the edges are in good condition, or are some of the perforations missing.
(5) Check the back of the stamp to check for thin spots in the paper, which may have been caused by careless removal from an envelope or a hinge.

It is important to understand that evaluating the condition of a stamp is in most cases a subjective process—which simply means that it often depends on an individual's personal assessment. What one collector or dealer might consider a stamp of superb condition, another individual might consider fine. There are no exact guidelines for determining the condition of a stamp, and the price and value are usually decided by individual agreement at the time of the transaction. There is, however, a commonly accepted set of descriptive terms: superb, very fine, fine, good, light cancel, medium cancel, heavy cancel. It is useful to have a general understanding of these terms, as defined below.

Superb: A stamp in superb condition is in the same condition as it was when purchased from the post office. This is a mint condition stamp. There are few or no detectable flaws.

Very Fine: A stamp that has not been canceled, or has been only lightly canceled. It may not have any gum on it, or it may be a little off-center on one side or slightly off-center on two sides.

Fine: A stamp in fine condition may be either canceled or not canceled, but it may have been hinged, or the design may be clearly off center.

Good: A stamp considered in good condition may have light, medium or heavy cancel marks with other problems such as off-center design or faded color.

Look carefully at stamps that you buy from the post office and canceled stamps that you observe on envelopes and postcards. Try to decide which of the descriptions above best matches each one's condition.

It will help you to evaluate the condition of a stamp if you read other criteria that are set by such giants as *Scott Standard Postage Stamp Catalogue*, talk to dealers and others in the field, and most of all, work with the stamps you come in contact with. Observe and study them carefully. You will continue to learn, and you'll acquire the skill of judging what to look for in a stamp. This skill will help you select the best stamps you can afford.

Tools and Protective Storage Materials for the Hobby

Stamps are very delicate pieces of art that require special handling and storage to preserve their beauty and value. Stamps should not be handled with the hand. Even when hands are clean, natural skin oils can distort the beauty of a stamp. To avoid contact with the naked hand, philatelists use a tool called *tongs*, a metal grasping device with flat ends similar to tweezers. Tongs are inexpensive, costing between $1.50 and about $7.50 depending on type of metal, style, and other characteristics. The flatter and rounder the ends of the tongs, the easier it is to lift stamps from various surfaces.

Another tool used by the philatelist is the *magnifying glass*, which enlarges the picture on the stamp to allow closer study of the design or damages. Many flaws, as well as much beauty, that cannot be seen by the naked eye can be observed through a magnifying glass.

A *perforation gauge* is an instrument used to measure the jagged cuts or little holes, called perforations, along the edges of stamps. The size and number of perforations are sometimes used to identify stamps. The gauge also helps you to set up an even and exact layout of various stamps.

A *watermark tray* and *watermark fluid* are used to make more visible the designs or patterns (called watermarks) that are pressed into some stamp paper when it is manufactured. Use only recommended fluids for identifying watermarks. An ex-cellent recommended fluid will show the watermark immediately and will dry fast without any damage to the stamp. The stamp should be dipped in the watermark fluid for just a moment. A local dealer or longtime collector can offer good advice on the use of watermark fluid.

A *stamp catalog* is a must for the beginning stamp collector. It is handy reference material with illustrations of various stamps to help you identify them. These reference catalogs also provide information about the estimated cost of unused and used stamps.

It is also necessary for your stamps to be properly stored to protect them from climatic conditions such as humidity, sunlight and mold. For example, if stamps receive too much sunlight, moisture, mold or fungus, fading could result, destroying a valuable stamp. To protect your stamps from the conditions described, there are many storage types of materials available. If you have not yet decided on how you are going to organize and store your stamps, *glassine* (glass-een) envelopes are excellent for temporary use. Glassine is a special thin material that protects stamps from grease, dirt, air and foreign matter that might cause damage. These glassine envelopes are recommended only for temporary storage.

Following is excellent advice as to the protection, storage and organizing of your collection (1989 Edition *Price Guide to United States Stamps*):

It's safer and also easier to work with stamps kept in albums or stock books which are like scrapbooks but with pages that have pockets, so that part of the stamp is exposed and the items can be quickly and easily moved around with tongs. Albums can be purchased or made by hand, and beginners may want to make their own albums just to get a feel for arranging a collection, or, maybe you will want to arrange your material in a certain way for which no standard album exists. You can buy blank album pages, made of acid-free paper (or not), and just use an ordinary ringed binder to make a very nice personalized album. Stamps can be fastened into albums either with small squares of gummed glassine adhesives called "hinges," or by using special stamps mounts, little plastic envelopes of various sizes that have self-adhesive backing to attach to pages. Using mounts keeps the stamp in the same condition in which you acquired it, with no extra glue from a stamp hinge. Mounts come in a variety of sizes to fit stamps and covers both large and small. Never use cellophane tapes on or around your stamps—not even the so-called "magic" tapes that do not seem as sticky as some of the other kinds. Both the plastic part of the tape and, especially, the sticky part, can cause great damage over time to stamps and covers. Do not use cheap papers such as colored construction paper to make albums—this pulpy paper with large quantities of coloring is a true hazard to have around stamps. Don't take chances with items that you have spent time and money acquiring! It seems very foolish to spend a considerable amount of money to buy some stamps, and then to store them in a cheap and unsafe way. Plastic can be the worst offender—especially in page protectors that have leached their softeners and other additives onto the pages and the stamps they contain. The adhesive part of plastic mounts may have migrated onto the faces or backs of the stamps they hold, and some kinds of hinges signal their presence on the back of the stamp by making rectangular stains on the front. Damage is almost irreversible; "prevention is the best cure"! Buying something new on the market is no guarantee of safety; ... there are modern items that are even worse than old ones.

Try to choose materials that are known to be safe because they have been tested and used by libraries and museums and similar places where long-term safekeeping is the most important matter. Acid-free papers and cardboard and plastics such as mylar and polypropylene perform well in archival uses, and can be found in philatelic products.

As you become more sophisticated and artistic in your approach to organizing, categorizing and displaying your collection, you will probably look for more sophisticated devices for storing and displaying your stamps. These display and protective folders and mounting sheets of various sizes can be very expensive. You should spend time with local stamp dealers, attend local stamp shows, and compare prices of various mail order companies that sell philatelic supplies. The latter will be discussed later in more detail.

Removing Stamps from Canceled Envelopes, Postcards, and Other Items

Every stamp collector needs to understand the simple skills of removing canceled or used stamps from envelopes, postcards, packages, and so on. But a word of warning (1989 Edition *Price Guide to United States Stamps*, p. 7): "Postal historians want the entire piece of mail—the stamps still 'on cover.' This is something to consider if you come across a batch of old letters and your first thought is to soak off all the stamps. Think again, and then get some advice, as even some very common stamps are of great interest (and perhaps monetary value) if they are on their original cover, with all the markings intact."

In the process of moving a canceled stamp from a cover, follow these procedures:

(1) Tear or cut very carefully around the used stamp(s) in the upper right hand corner of the envelope (the envelope is also called a "cover").

(2) Use a medium size or small flat pan, depending on number of stamps.

(3) Fill the pan half full with cold water.

(4) Place the stamp(s) face down in the pan of cold water.

(5) Let the stamps soak face down for five or more minutes.

After the stamps have soaked face down, they will automatically separate from the cover and sink to the bottom of the pan. You may now spread paper towels where you will place your stamps to dry. With your tongs, remove each stamp from the pan of water and carefully lay the stamps face down on the paper towel. Then spread paper towels on top of the face-down stamps and apply pressure with a heavy flat object such as a book. The heavy object flattens the stamps while they are drying. Leave the stamps under this condition overnight or for at least for six hours.

Sometimes, when stamps separate from their covers in the water, you will find they have retained more glue than usual. When this occurs, you should place the stamps face down, but let them dry without the top layer of paper towels and without a heavy object to press them flat. This procedure will keep stamps with glue from sticking to the paper towel or the object that is pressing them. Of course, when this method is used, the stamps will curl after they have dried. However, you may apply the heavy flat object to the dry stamps. Leave them under the object for six hours or overnight and they will flatten.

The Final Steps

Throughout this section you have been encouraged to learn as much about the hobby of philately as possible. Here now are some final steps to prepare you for the hobby of philately.

(1) Become a member of the American Philately Society, Inc. It is the oldest stamp collecting society in America. The society provides you with many of the basic needs of the hobby; it keeps you in touch with the current trends in philately; you receive a monthly magazine; and you have access to a library — the largest in the world. The monthly magazine and library services provided by the society are worth more than the annual membership fee. For a membership application write to the American Philatelic Society, P.O. Box 8000, State College PA 16803.

(2) If you are interested in topical collections, it is a must that you become a member of American Topical Association (ATA). The association specializes in providing information on almost any topic associated with stamps, both U.S. and foreign. You automatically receive a monthly copy of their stamp journal, *Topical Time*. For more information write to ATA, P.O. Box 630, Johnstown PA 15907.

(3) Subscribe to a weekly or monthly newsletter or newspaper for stamp collectors. They keep you in tune with what is going on in the U.S. and internationally. *Stamp Collector* is an excellent weekly paper. To subscribe write to *Stamp Collector*, Box 10, Albany OR 97321-0006. They will provide you with a free sample copy if you send a large self-addressed, stamped envelope.

(4) Join your local philatelic club if one is available.

(5) Attend local, state or national stamp shows as often as possible. Information providing places and dates for stamp shows can be found in your local stamp shops, through local clubs, stamp newspapers, newsletters, and magazines. The shows are listed by state and address in the *Weekly Stamp Collector*.

(6) Learn how to use *Scott Standard Postage Stamp Catalogue* volumes.

The Scott catalogs include numerous comprehensive volumes. These catalogs list almost all stamps known in the U.S. and other countries of the world. It would have been impossible to complete this book without the use of *Scott Standard Postage Stamp Catalogue* volumes. The volumes are updated annually, and monthly updates are provided in other Scott sub-catalogs. These Scott volumes are the "bible" for the stamp collector or dealer. These volumes also provide updated information on stamp collecting and almost any service or product you might need to improve the sophistication of your stamp collection. You can buy individual volumes, but if you buy the whole set, many dealers will give you a discount. You may also borrow these volumes from APS if you are a member.

If you are a serious stamp collector and have particular interest in world stamps, the Scott volumes are a must. A serious collector would not be without them. Write to Scott Publishing Co., 911 Vandemark Road, Sidney OH 45365, or contact your favorite stamp dealer or book chain.

(7) Pick up a copy of *Postal Service Guide to U.S. Stamps.* It illustrates in color every stamp that has been issued in America and provides both how-to information for collecting and a basic price guide to U.S. stamps. The guide is updated annually and is perfect for those whose major interest is U.S. stamps. The guide sells for approximately $10.95 and you can find it at your local U.S. Post Office. It can also be ordered from the United States Postal Service, Philatelic and Retail Services Department, 475 L'enfant Plaza SW, Washington DC 20260-0700. You may also write to the postal service for U.S. stamps and all other postal materials such as first day issues.

(8) Make contact and build relationships with dealers through mail order. There are many excellent companies that will allow you the opportunity to examine stamps before you buy them at no cost to you. Kenmore is an excellent company of this nature. Their ordering catalogue is one of the best, listing stamps of many topical subjects and for the general collector along with products that will meet your needs as a collector. Write to Kenmore, 119 West Street, PO Box 331, Milford NH 03055-0331.

Jamestown Stamp Company, Inc., is such a company also. They have what is known as the approval stamp system, which they describe as follows: "You are under no obligation. If you like them, buy what you want. If you don't want them, or don't need them, you return them in the postage paid or self-addressed return envelope." You may write to Jamestown Stamp Company, Inc., Jamestown NY 14700-0019.

Please note that many companies of this type can be found in classified ads in *Topical Time, American Philatelic Society, Stamp Collector* and other journals, newspapers, and so on which offer stamps on the approval program. Beware of very high costs. Compare prices. It is also wise to build relationships with companies that sell stamps at wholesale prices. Wholesale allows you the opportunity to buy in bulk at a low cost, and the experience and satisfaction of reviewing many stamps to decide on whether you want to begin a general or topical collection. Paul Engelson provides worldwide stamps from various countries by the pound at reasonable cost. Write to Paul Engelson, Wolvertone E-20806, Boca Raton FL 33434. Check other sources for similar deals.

(9) Make contact with companies that sell philatelic supplies and accessories. There are philatelic suppliers available to meet your every need, from simple albums for storing and displaying your stamps to the most advanced technological instruments. For a complete illustration and pricing of supplies of all kinds, write to SAFE Publications, Inc., P.O. Box 283, Southampton PA 18966. They provide you with first-hand information in a colorful catalog that depicts and explains the tools and materials of the hobby.

(10) This final step is especially geared to those who are interested in collecting

African American subjects on U.S. and international stamps. It is relatively easy to obtain the 100 or more United States postage and commemorative stamps issued on African Americans. In most cases it is just a matter of visiting your local stamp dealer or writing to one of the many American mail order stamp dealers. However, the challenge is likely to be quite different, and more costly, when it comes to acquiring the more than 1000 stamps issued on African Americans in more than 85 foreign countries. The following tips will be helpful to you in collecting African American–themed stamps:

• Become an ESPER (Ebony Society of Philatelic Events and Reflections) member. For more information about ESPER, write to Manuel Gilyard at 800 Riverside Drive, Apartment 4H, New York NY 10032-7412, call 212-928-5165, or try their Web site www.slsabyrd.com/esper.htm. This Web site carries not only stamps but other postal memorabilia on African Americans, such as first day issues.

• Become a member of the Black American Philatelic Society. Write to the society at 9101 Taylor Street, Landover MD 20785-2554.

• Become a member of the Black Memorabilia Collectors Association, 1121 University Blvd. W. #1206, Silver Spring MD 20902. For an annual membership fee, they offer a one-year subscription to *Black Ethnic Collectibles* and more than ten other valuable benefits. If you are not knowledgeable about African American collectibles, even one issue of the magazine is well worth the membership fee.

• Lloyd A. de Vries Unusual First Day Material carries a *Black History List of Postal Information*. Write to Lloyd A. de Vries, P.O. Box 145, Dumont NJ 07628-0145, or call (201) 967-7160.

• Research for this book suggests that Ernest Austin was the first to publish a U.S. and international photo stamp album on African American subjects. Austin sells copies of his *Black American Stamp Album* and also sells rare stamps on African Americans. The album is excellent and is updated annually. If you are serious about collecting stamps featuring black Americans, the photo album is excellent for both beginners and seasoned collectors. Write to Austin Enterprises, PO Box 3717, Cherry Hill NJ 08034-0541.

• Besides the ESPER Web site already mentioned, other Internet sites provide special information on African Americans on stamps.

Most of the prominent stamp dealers in America do not carry African American–themed stamps as a normal item. However, if you provide them with the Scott catalog and other reference numbers (e.g., Minkus, Michel, Stanley Gibbons) they may be able to help you with some of the stamps. Two companies that do provide excellent service on African American stamps are Mini Arts (403 First Avenue, North Estherville IA 51334) and Westminster Stamp Gallery Ltd. (P.O. Box 456, Don Palazzo, Foxboro MA 02035.

The associations, societies, and other organizations mentioned in this section are only a few of the many who offer services to the philatelist. In no way is it being suggested that a collector use only these sources. It is worth every collector's time and effort to seek out organizations that provide excellent services to their customers.

Getting involved with at least one philatelic organization will help you develop a discriminating taste for buying what you need in the way of philatelic supplies. You should subscribe to a philatelic newsletter, magazine, newspaper or journal. Once you are involved with at least one or more aspects of philately, you will receive many good benefits. For example, you will meet people who collect stamps, people with whom you can share thoughts and discuss questions. If through various philatelic subscriptions you respond to various articles and advertisements, you will be surprised how quickly you some-how find yourself on an exclusive mailing list that keeps you informed of trends in the world of philately. And please do not forget the Internet. Start your research using search engines on the World Wide Web and you are bound to find more information on the art of philately than you expect.

Collecting African American Topical Stamps

When the U.S. Postal Service issued a commemorative stamp in 1940 to recognize Booker T. Washington for his contributions to education, it was the first time an African American was depicted on a U.S. stamp of any kind. Recognizing Washington was a step forward for the federal government, a step offering some hope that African Americans would begin to gain the national recognition they deserved. Almost eight years would pass, however, before another great African American would be depicted on a U.S. stamp. On January 5, 1948, a stamp honored Dr. George Washington Carver as a distinguished scientist. This was the first time a black American was recognized on a U.S. stamp for having made a major contribution to science. It was another breakthrough that helped make the American people more aware of the contributions of African Americans.

Worldwide, the first African American to appear on the face of a stamp was Garretson Wilmot Gibson, president of Liberia 1900–1904, followed by Joseph Roberts, the first President of Liberia (1848–1856 and 1872–1876). Gibson was recognized in 1903 on a surcharge semi-postal of Liberia.

In 1957 the Dominican Republic issued the first stamp recognizing Jesse Owens. Owens was the first African American to be honored on a stamp internationally without having any political ties to a foreign country. Three years later the Dominican Republic issued the first stamp ever recognizing an African American woman, Mildred McDaniels, a track star in the 1950 Pan-American Olympic Games. Dr. George Washington Carver sixteen years later would again be recognized as a scientist, but this time in a foreign country. Ghana of West Africa issued a commemorative acknowledging Dr. Carver for his contributions to science. After the Dominican Republic and Ghana, many foreign countries followed. Annually, one or more foreign countries recognize African Americans on their stamps.

Many African Americans have been recognized on stamps for their musical and athletic abilities. Such giants as Louis Armstrong, Duke Ellington, Jesse Owens, Mildred McDaniels and others have appeared on stamps the world over.

Nineteen years after honoring George Washington Carver, the United States issued another stamp recognizing an African American. On February 14, 1967, a stamp was issued in honor of Frederick Douglass under the Prominent Americans Issue. The Civil Rights Movement was at its peak, but change was slow to come for the postal service. Nevertheless, the Douglass stamp was another step forward.

After the Douglass issue, U.S. stamps recognizing African Americans began to appear more frequently. Henry Ossawa Tanner, who left America in the early 1900s to gain appreciation for his artwork and became well known in France as a painter of religious subjects, was issued a U.S. stamp in his honor on September 10, 1973, under the American Arts Issue. Thereafter, at least 1 to 2 stamps were issued annually in the United States in honor of African Americans. For example, in 1978 the Black Heritage Series was launched to pay tribute to significant black Americans annually. This series introduced the Harriet Tubman stamp, the first U.S. issue recognizing an African American woman.

Today, stamps recognizing African Americans can be divided into five basic groups:

Group I: African Americans of Liberia (see color section) includes those stamps issued by the government of Liberia in honor of African American–Liberians. These are the sons and daughters of slaves who were allowed to leave the United States under President James Monroe's administration. The Americans who financed these ex-slaves were the Colonization Society and the Monroe administration. They wanted to help these people begin a new life in Liberia, Africa. Free blacks during this period (early 1800s) went to Africa hoping for a better life. It is of utmost importance to understand that many of these African Americans had

spent 30 to 40 years living in America. Additionally, they had been a part of the slave system for many generations and had clearly adopted the Euro-American ways. They will therefore be treated as African Americans in the presentation of this book as it relates to stamps and historical facts. To illustrate, the first nine presidents of Liberia were born in America (each of these presidents appears on a stamp; see their biographical entries in the main text for more information). In the *American Philatelic Journal*, 1991, page 339, Henry B. Fleishman presents historical documents showing that many of the ex-slaves had spent most of their lives in America and were freed on condition that they leave for Liberia and stay in Liberia for the rest of their lives:

I John M. Preston of Abingdon in Washington County and State of Virginia have this day liberated the following servants to wit. Lucinda aged about fifty years, Mary her daughter aged about thirty-three and Henry son of Mary and grandson of Lucinda aged seventeen last fall on the special condition that they the above named Lucinda Mary and Henry emigrate to Liberia. And on no other condition do I liberate them. It is now understood that a vessel will sail from Norfolk in the state of Virginia some time next month which is to take to Liberia all emigrants that are willing and ready to leave the United States and it is expected the said Lucinda Mary and Henry will go. I have also furnished the said Lucinda Mary and Henry, with one hundred and fifty dollars to defray their necessary expenses to Liberia, and should either of them die before reaching the coast of Africa, then the residue of the money or property belonging to such deceased one is to belong to the survivors or survivor, and should it so happen that all three of the above named Lucinda Mary and Henry die on the voyage before reaching the coast of Liberia then the money and property belonging to them is to go to the benefit of the Colonization Society. In witness whereof I have hereunto set my hand and affixed my seal at Abingdon in the county and state aforesaid this thirteenth day of April in the year of our Lord one thousand eight hundred and forty-two.

Witness John M. Preston (seal)

  A copy

I hereby certify that I copied the above on the day and date mentioned therein.

Leonidas Baugh.

Group II: Prominent African Americans includes those stamps issued in the United States to recognize prominent African Americans who made major contributions in education, human rights, music, the arts, medicine, diplomatic relations, and other areas of importance in U.S. and world societies. The first tribute was to Booker T. Washington in 1940.

Group III: African American Images and Events encompasses U.S. and world stamps depicting various African American events, humanistic and political messages, and other images. The earliest example of such a stamp was issued in 1956 when an unidentified African American was included in a group with a diversified group of people from around the world. The theme of the stamp was "Friendship the Key to World Peace." There are no recognizable faces of African Americans in any of the stamps in Group III. The stamps do, however, feature images and historical events which had significant impacts on the lives of African Americans throughout the world.

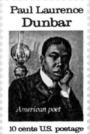

Prominent African Americans (examples)

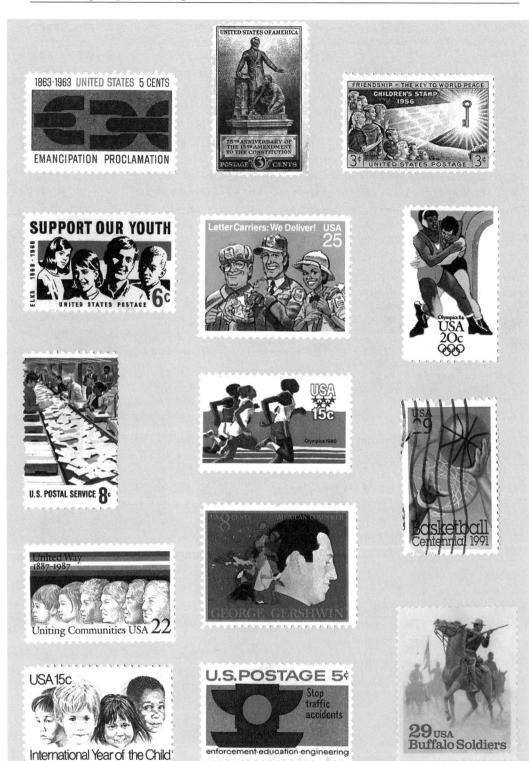

African American Images and Events (examples)

Group IV: Foreign Issues on African Americans consists of those stamps issued to recognize African Americans in countries other than the United States. Since the Dominican Republic honored Jesse Owens in 1957, more than 85 foreign countries have recognized African Americans on stamps. Foreign countries have honored African Americans for their contributions to science, human and civil rights, music and most fields of human endeavor.

Group V: The Black Heritage Series (see color section) is a United States series begun in 1978. From that date through December 31, 1999, twenty-two stamps were issued in recognition of African Americans, and the series continues today. This series includes the first U.S. stamp recognizing an African American woman, Harriet Tubman (1978). It also includes a stamp honoring Dr. Martin Luther King, Jr. (1979).

Many Americans are not aware of the number of U.S. and international stamps honoring African Americans, simply because the information has not been readily available or easy to find in libraries nor even through the American Philatelic Society Library. The lack of information has probably kept many of America's estimated 19 million stamp collectors from getting involved. The general lack of awareness has also kept book values rather low, compared to values on stamps recognizing white Americans. Consider, for example, some stamps issued during the same period (1940s) as the U.S. Booker T. Washington stamp, with the same face value of 10 cents and approximately the same quantity issued. Alexander Graham Bell has a value of $11.00 in mint condition; Frederick Remington, $1.65 in mint condition; and Booker T. Washington in mint condition, $1.25. Such price differences are the result of supply and demand,

and demand can only happen when people are aware of a product or service.

Even with the demand not very high, African American stamp issues have been a good investment. A person who bought 1000 mint condition stamps issued on Booker T. Washington on April 7, 1940, at 10 cents a stamp ($100.00), would by now have gained $1150 — not a bad return. With the demand for African American memorabilia on the rise, there is a lot of potential for investment growth. For many of the African American issues beginning as early as the 1967 issue of Frederick Douglass, values have increased by almost 85 percent. The stamp issued on Douglass in 1967 has a face value of 25 cents and sells for 55 cents in mint condition, an increase of 120 percent. Within one year after U.S. stamps have been issued on African Americans, their value has increased by approximately 85 percent or more.

The potential is even greater for foreign issues on African Americans. More than 1,500 stamps have been issued recognizing significant and prominent African Americans in the U.S. and foreign countries. Even though far more of these stamps have been issued in foreign countries than in the United States, they are more rare and often more striking in color and design. One reason for their rarity is that they are likely issued in smaller quantities. It is difficult, however, to accurately compare the quantities issued by the United States and by foreign countries. To illustrate, U.S. postal documents indicate that when the 1940 Booker T. Washington stamp was issued, 14,125,580 stamps were printed. In contrast, there is no record showing the quantity of the Dominican Republic's Jesse Owens issue in 1957. This holds true with most foreign issues with the exception of stamps issued by Canada and Ghana.

The attributes discussed above are all the more reason for choosing African American stamps as a topical collection.

Foreign Issues on African Americans (examples)

Not only do they provide excitement and fascination in the hobby of philately, they have excellent potential for investment growth. African American stamps are a rarity, a "sleeper" in the field of philately.

According to *Black Ethnic Collectibles*, an educational magazine on black memorabilia (January/February 1989, Vol. 2 No. 5), the lack of interest in these rare stamps is especially unfortunate among black

Americans: "Market research shows there are over 19 million Americans who collect stamps. Less than one percent of the collectors are Black Americans. Hopefully Black Americans will not repeat their history of buying collectibles after they become fashionable, expensive and/or unobtainable."

This simply means that the door is open for getting involved in collecting African American stamps before the sleeping giant awakens. Even though rare, African American stamps are still relatively inexpensive, particularly those illustrated in Groups II, III, and V. Many foreign issues of African American topics can be had for as little as 10 cents, though the range may extend as high as $1,500 for a single stamp. These stamps will become higher in price as they become more scarce and more popular with philatelists in the United States and the world over. Now is the time to become involved with African American stamps and the art of philately.

How to Read
the Stamp Listings

Each of the hundreds of stamps listed in this book helps to bring to life the characters, events and images of African American history. Each entry attempts to provide sufficient information to acquaint the reader with both the stamp and the person or event represented. Information is presented in the following format:

• A bio-sketch or brief description of the individual, image or theme that the stamp represents.

• An identifying number, usually from the Scott Catalogue, a major reference number used to identify stamp issues worldwide. Stamp collectors use the Scott numbering system to identify stamps when buying, selling, trading, or organizing their collections. Each stamp issued by a country has a unique number assigned by Scott. For example, the first Hank Aaron stamp issue listed below is identified as S#1671b or Scott number 1671b. This number is used to identify only this particular Hank Aaron stamp. Other stamps honoring Aaron have different Scott numbers.

Other catalog reference numbers include Official, Michel, Minkus, and Stanley Gibbons. These other catalog numbers are used to identify African American Stamps in this text only when a Scott number is not available or has not yet been assigned by Scott Publishing Company.

If none of the catalogs listed above provides a reference number for a stamp, no identification number will be present in the entry.

• The name of the country that issued the stamp.

• The date of issue, e.g., 1/16/99 (or 1999, if the complete date is not known).

• The quantity issued, i.e., the total number of stamps printed at the time of issue.

• The face value, i.e., the cost that has been printed on the face of the stamp by the issuing country. Please note that the face value doesn't necessarily represent the book value, that is, the actual cost of the stamp today. The stamp could be worth less than or more than face value depending on the monetary value of the particular country, the rarity and condition of the stamp, and so on. Because prices depend on so many factors and can change so quickly over time, this book does not attempt to estimate book values for the stamps. Current stamp catalogs are the best source of that information.

In some entries, the information just listed will be followed by some comments on the stamp — a few words of description, notes about errors on the stamps, and so forth. If the stamp is not described, the reader can assume it features a portrait of the person named in the entry.

Most stamps in this book are not only described but pictured. Stamp illustrations are grouped several to a page. An illustration number under each pictured stamp allows the reader to match it to the stamp description in the book. A page of illustrations is usually placed near the text that describes the stamps on that page. An ex-ception is the pages reproduced in full color, which are grouped together in a section of sixteen pages. When a stamp is pictured in the color section, the stamp description includes the words "See color section," and the illustration number includes the letter C (C1, C2, etc.).

Some stamps were not available for reproduction or could not be reproduced because of some special feature, such as a 3D illustration. These stamps are not pictured in the book. In such cases the identifying number in the description is followed by the words "Not pictured."

In some cases the author has heard of stamps representing certain African Americans but has not been able to confirm the existence of such stamps. In such cases the person's name is listed with the information that no description of a stamp honoring this person could be located.

AFRICAN AMERICANS ON STAMPS

Aaron, Hank

Baseball player Henry Louis Aaron, better known as Hank, was born in 1934 in Mobile, Alabama. Hank Aaron left many baseball records on the books, and he holds more batting records than any player.

Hank Aaron made baseball history when he broke Babe Ruth's home run record on April 8, 1974. While playing with the Atlanta Braves, Hank hit his 715th home run against a pitch from the Los Angeles Dodgers. Aaron ended his baseball career with a home run record of 755.

When Hank began his professional career as a baseball player, it was difficult for black Americans to get into the major leagues. Aaron, like most other black ballplayers of his time, started in the Negro leagues, taking a berth with the Indianapolis Clowns in 1952.

Aaron was called to the majors in 1954. He was harassed and endured many racial insults from fans as well as fellow players. He withstood the insults and stayed with the National League for 23 years. Hank Aaron to this day is a part of the Atlanta Braves, working in management and public relations. Even though he has been long retired, he still works in his community and with National League baseball in helping to bring racial harmony to baseball and sports in general.

He has also been a strong advocate for increasing minority coaching and executive jobs in baseball, and presently serves on the board for Turner Broadcasting Systems. He has been recognized on stamps internationally.

11/28/88. Grenada. Quantity unknown. 30 cents. S#1671b. (See color section.) *Illus. C1.*

11/9/92. St. Vincent. Quantity unknown. 2 dollars. S#1734. (Not pictured.) Issued in recognition of Aaron being inducted into the Hall of Fame in 1992.

1/23/97. St. Vincent and the Grenadines. Quantity unknown. 1 dollar. S#2380g. (Not pictured.) Besides Hank Aaron (S#2380g), this issue, titled "Black Baseball Players," recognizes the following black baseball players: Frank Robinson (S#2380a), Satchel Paige (S#2380b), Billy Williams (S#2380c), Reggie Jackson (S#2380d), Roberto Clemente (S#2380e), Ernie Banks (S#2380f), Roy Campanella (S#2380h), Willie McCovey (S#2380i), Monte Irvin (S#2380j), Willie Stargell (S#2380k), Rod Carew (S#2380l), Ferguson Jenkins (S#2380m), Bob Gibson (S#2380n), Lou Brock (S#2380o), Joe Morgan (S#2380p), and Jackie Robinson

(S#2380q). These stamps come in a souvenir sheet of 17 stamps valued at $16.50 per sheet. Perf, 14×14.5. These are multicolored stamps with a unique portrait of each player.

Abdul-Jabbar, Kareem

Kareem Abdul-Jabbar was born in New York City in 1947. His birth name was Ferdinand Lewis Alcindor. Abdul-Jabbar is an American professional basketball player. He was six-time National Basketball Association (NBA) champion and six-time winner of the Most Valuable Player award.

Abdul was educated at the University of California at Los Angeles. He led the university's basketball team to three consecutive National Collegiate Athletic Association championships (1967–1969). During his years as a student he became a member of the Black Muslim faith and changed his name in 1971 to Kareem Abdul-Jabbar.

From 1969 through 1975 he played center for the Milwaukee Bucks of the NBA and led his team to the NBA championship for the 1970-1971 season. In 1975 the 7 ft. 1⅜-in. player was traded to the Los Angeles Lakers; he led the Lakers team to five NBA championships. Abdul-Jabbar also developed a high-percentage signature shot known as the "skyhook," which was difficult for opponents to block. When he retired in 1989, he was the all-time NBA leader in points (38,398) and games played (1,560). Following Abdul-Jabbar's retirement, the Lakers team did not win another national championship until 2000.

7/15/93. Tanzania. Quantity unknown. 100 shillings. S#1074c. (See color section.) This stamp is in a perforated souvenir sheet that also includes Florence Joyner, Jesse Owens, Jack Johnson, Daley Thomas (British), and Jackie Robinson. *Illus. C2.*

African American Images (Miscellaneous)

Some stamps depict unnamed African Americans, sometimes in connection with African American history and sometimes in connection with other topics such as sports, children, or veterans (to name but a few).

On December 15, 1956, America presented its first stamp depicting an unnamed African American face. This stamp paid tribute to children of the world, presenting them as symbols of the key to friendship and peace. In 1950s America, depicting an African American in a group with other races was an unusual move indeed. Thereafter, however, slowly but surely, more African American faces and images began to appear on U.S. and international stamps.

Sometimes the figures honored on stamps were people who offered artistic portrayals of African American culture as they perceived it — regardless of the accuracy of those perceptions. For example, Al Jolson (4/20/87), who is not of African American descent, is best known for blackface, minstrel show–type performances in early sound films like *The Jazz Singer* (1927). Joel Chandler Harris, a white author famous for his stories about the black character Uncle Remus, was honored on a stamp (12/9/48). So was George Gershwin, whose music was influenced by African American jazz, and who wrote the musical *Porgy and Bess*; the Gershwin stamp (2/28/73) includes a depiction of African American characters from that musical.

The following list offers many other examples of miscellaneous African American–related stamps.

1923. Liberia. Quantity unknown. 2 cents. S#210. (See color section.) Liberia issued this stamp for its centennial in celebration of the ex-slaves who came from America to Africa. This stamp depicts the first settlers landing at Cape Mesurado in their ship, the *Alligator*. *Illus. C3.*

12/9/48. United States. 57,000,000. 3 cents. S#980. (See color section.) Joel Chandler Harris, the white American author who made the black character Uncle Remus famous. *Illus. C15.*

4/12/49. Liberia. Quantity unknown. 3 cents. S#311. Celebrating the landing of the first former slaves to arrive in Liberia from the United States. *Illus. C4.*

4/12/49. Liberia. Quantity unknown. 5 cents. S#312. (See color section.) Celebrating the Republic of Liberia, Jehudi Ashmun, and the defenders of Liberia. *Illus. C5.*

4/12/49. Liberia. Quantity unknown. 25 cents. S#C63. (See color section.) Features a map of the country and portraits of its people. *Illus. C6.*

12/15/56. United States. 100,975,000. 3 cents. S#1085. (See color section.) "Children's stamp, 1956": First stamp in the United States to depict an African American with other races on the same stamp. *Illus. C7.*

5/1/67. United States. 147,120,000. 6 cents. S#1342. (See color section.) "Support our youth" and "Elks 1868–1968." Depicts an African American child along with three white children. *Illus. C9.*

1968. Yemen. Quantity unknown. 4 riyals. (See color section.) This stamp was issued in Yemen in recognition of the 1932 Olympic Games. It depicts an African American boxer in front of an American flag. *Illus. C13.*

5/19/72. Liberia. Quantity unknown. 20 cents. S#595. (See color section.) Honors the Olympic Games in Munich, 1972. Depicts an African American athlete performing the long jump. *Illus. C16.*

1973. Umm-Al-Qiwain. Quantity unknown. 1 riyal. (See color section.) Photograph of the United States Olympic Basketball Team in action. *Illus. C18.*

1973. Umm-Al-Qiwain. Quantity unknown. 1 riyal. (See color section.) This stamp is a smaller version of the previous entry. *Illus. C19.*

2/28/73. United States. 139,152,000. 8 cents. S#1484. (See color section.) Depicts George Gershwin and a scene from his *Porgy and Bess*, an opera featuring a black cast. *Illus. C8.*

3/30/73. United States. 48,602,000. 8 cents. S#1493. (See color section.) Honors the U.S. Postal Service. Shows two postal workers, one of whom is African American. *Illus. C10.*

3/30/73. United States. 48,602,000. 8 cents. S#1490. (See color section.) Honors the U.S. Postal Service. Portrait of a letter carrier, who is an African American. *Illus. C11.*

3/30/73. United States. 48,602,000. 8 cents. S#1491. (See color section.) Honors the U.S. Postal Service. Shows numerous workers sorting mail. At least two of the workers are African Americans. *Illus. C12.*

3/30/73. United States. 8 cents. S#1495. (See color section.) Honors the U.S. Postal Service. Depicts workers in electronic letter routing, including an African American. *Illus. C14.*

3/14/75. Liberia. Quantity unknown. 10 cents. S#700. (See color section.) In recognition of international Women's Year (1975). Shows Eleanor Roosevelt with children of several races. *Illus. C20.*

9/5/79. United States. 162,535,000. 15 cents. S#1772. (See color section.) Commemorates the International Year of the Child (1979). Includes an African American child among other races. *Illus. C22.*

9/5/79. United States. 67,195,000. 10 cents. S#1790. (See color section.) Celebrating the 1980 Olympic Summer Games. Depicts an African American throwing a javelin (part of the Decathlon, which the stamp honors). *Illus. C23.*

9/28/79. United States. 46,726,250. 15 cents. S#1791. (See color section.) Depicts African American runners in the upcoming 1980 Olympic Summer Games. *Illus. C21.*

11/1/79. United States. 47,200,000. 31 cents. S#C97. (See color section.) Celebrates the upcoming 1980 Summer Olympics. Depicts an African American high jumper. *Illus. C25.*

12/28/79. Central African Republic. Quantity unknown. 50 francs. S#403. (See color section.) In 1979, the Central African Republic issued a number of stamps celebrating the "pre–Olympic year" (Année Preolympique). These stamps featured photographs of basketball games between the national teams. African American players are shown in the stamps listed here. S#403 shows a player from the men's team. *Illus. C26.*

12/28/79. Central African Republic. Quantity unknown. 125 francs. S#404. (See color section.) Shows U.S. women's basketball team. See S#403 above for more comments. *Illus. C27.*

12/28/79. Central African Republic. Quantity unknown. 200 francs. S#405. (See color section.) Shows U.S. women's basketball team. See S#403 above for comments. *Illus. C28.*

12/28/79. Central African Republic. Quantity unknown. 300 francs. S#406. (See color section.) Shows U.S. men's basketball team. See S#403 above for comments. *Illus. C29.*

12/28/79. Central African Republic. Quantity unknown. 500 francs. S#407. (See color section.) Shows U.S. men's basketball team. See S#403 for comments. *Illus. C30.*

11/12/80. Central African Republic. Quantity unknown. 50 francs. S#425. (Overprint; see color section.) In November 1980 the Central African Republic issued a series of overprints of the 1979 "Pre-Olympic" stamps. The overprints honored the winners of Olympic medals in basketball. S#425, an overprint of S#403, reads, "Medaille or Yougoslavie" (gold medal Yugoslavia). *Illus. C31.*

11/12/80. Central African Republic. Quantity unknown. 125 francs. S#426 (Overprint; see color section). Overprint of S#404 reads, "Medaille or URSS" (gold medal USSR). *Illus. C32.*

11/12/80. Central African Republic. Quantity unknown. 200 francs. S#427. (Overprint; see color section). Overprint of S#405 reads, "Medaille or URSS" (gold medal USSR). *Illus. C33.*

11/12/80. Central African Republic. Quantity unknown. 300 francs. S#428. (Overprint.) Overprint of S#405 reads, "Medaille argent Italie" (silver medal Italy). *Illus. 1.*

11/12/80. Central African Republic. Quantity unknown. 500 francs. S#429 (Overprint.) Overprint of S#407 reads, "Medaille bronze URSS" (bronze medal USSR). *Illus. 2.*

3/14/82. Tanzania. Quantity unknown. 1 shilling. S#218. Celebrating "Commonwealth Day, 14 March 1982." Shows blacks running and boxing. Many believe one of the boxers is Muhammad Ali. *Illus. 7.*

7/27/82. Grenada and the Grenadines. Quantity unknown. 30 cents. S#499. Celebration of the 100th anniversary of Franklin D. Roosevelt's birth. Honors both Roosevelt's New Deal and his soil conservation program. FDR is depicted surrounded by African Americans. *Illus. 3.*

7/27/82. Grenada. Quantity unknown. One dollar and ten cents. S#1108. Celebrating the 100th anniversary of Franklin D. Roosevelt's birth. Depicts FDR signing the 1941 Fair Employment Act as African Americans look on. *Illus. 4.*

7/27/82. Grenada. Quantity unknown. 3 dollars. S#1109. Celebrating the 100th anniversary of Franklin D. Roosevelt's birth. Honors the Farm Security Administration. Roosevelt is shown observing African American farm workers. *Illus. 5.*

4/5/83. United States. 114,290,000. 20 cents. S#2037. Celebrates 50 years (1933–1983) of the Civilian Conservation Corps. At least one of the three workers appears to be African American. *Illus. 6.*

4/8/83. United States. 63,573,750. 40 cents. S#C105. Pictures an African American shot-putter in the upcoming 1984 Olympics. *Illus. 9.*

5/17/83. United States. 111,775,000. 20 cents. S#2043. (See color section.) Issued in recognition of physical fitness. Shows three runners, one of them African American. *Illus. C24.*

6/7/83. United States. 42,893,750. 28 cents. S#Cl03. Depicts an African American basketball player in the upcoming 1984 Olympics. *Illus. 10.*

7/28/83. United States. 98,856,250. 13 cents. S#2051. Pictures Olympic boxers. One is African American. *Illus. 8.*

5/4/84. United States. 78,337,500. 20 cents. S#2083. Depicts an African American long jumper in the upcoming 1984 Olympics. *Illus. 11.*

5/4/84. United States. 78,337,500. 20 cents. S#2084. Depicts two wrestlers, one an African American, in the upcoming 1984 Olympics. *Illus. 12.*

8/84. Ghana. Quantity unknown. 1.40 cedis. S#934. Celebrates the 1984 Olympics in Los Angeles. A black boxer is pictured. The words "U.S. Winners" are printed over his portrait in gold. *Illus. 13.*

1/7/85. Central African Republic. Quantity unknown. 60 francs. S#C303. (See color section.) Honors the 1984 Los Angeles Olympics and the American winners at the 400m relay. Photograph depicts two U.S. runners. *Illus. C17.*

10/15/85. United States. 120,000,000. 22 cents. S#2164. "Help End Hunger" stamp. Depicts three faces. The boy on the right is black. *Illus. 14.*

4/20/87. Mali. Quantity unknown. 550 francs. S#C536. Celebrating the 60th anniversary of the film *The Jazz Singer*, this is a rare stamp

portraying Al Jolson, who performed in blackface in that film's minstrel-style number. This stamp is done in litho ink. Al Jolson is also recognized by the U.S. Postal Service in an issue (S#2849) titled "Popular Singers Issue" (9/1/94) with such great popular singers as Nat "King" Cole, Ethel Waters, Bing Crosby, and Ethel Merman. *Illus. 15.*

4/28/87. United States. 157,995,000. 22 cents. S#2275. "Uniting Communities" is the slogan on this stamp honoring the United Way. People of several races, including African Americans, are pictured. *Illus. 16.*

8/30/89. United States. 188,000,000. 25 cents. S#2420. A stamp honoring letter carriers. The three letter carriers in the drawing include an African American female. *Illus. 18.*

7/12/91. United States. 34,005,129. 29 cents. S#2555. 1992 Summer Olympic Games issue. Depicts Women Sprinters, including African Americans. *Illus. 22.*

7/12/91. United States. Quantity Unknown. 33 cents. S#2557. (Not pictured.) Shows a colorful background of women running hurdles (Olympic track and field).

8/28/91. United States. 149,260,000. 29 cents. S#2560. Honors the 100th anniversary of basketball. Shows two hands reaching for the ball; one hand is that of an African American. *Illus. 20.*

10/25/91. Canada. Quantity unknown. 40 cents. S#1343a. Commemorates the 100th anniversary of basketball. Three players are shown, at least one of whom is black. Sheet of three: $3.00. *Illus. 27.*

1992. Lesotho. Quantity unknown. 16 lisente. Commemorates the 1992 Barcelona Olympics. Pictured is a United States contender in the Men's Triple Jump. *Illus. 19.*

6/1/92. United States. 30,000,000. 29 cents. S#2640. 1992 Summer Olympic Games issue. Depicts an African American boxer. *Illus. 21.*

2/25/93. United States. Quantity unknown. 29 cents. S#2748. (Not pictured.) Honors the World University Games.

3/25/93. Gambia. Quantity unknown. 3 dalasis. S#1349g. A scene from the movie *Major League* includes an African American. This stamp comes from a series centering around American-made movies. A souvenir sheet is available. *Illus. 17.*

7/14/93. United States. 129,000,000. 29 cents. S#2767. This stamp, from the legends of American Music series, depicts black characters from the musical *Show Boat*. This musical was unique for its African American characters and its exploration of racism and other serious issues. *Illus. 23.*

7/14/93. United States. 129,000,000. 29 cents. S#2768. This stamp from the legends of American Music series depicts characters from George Gershwin's *Porgy and Bess*, which featured a black cast and African American–influenced music. *Illus. 24–5.*

5/26/94. United States. 269,000,000. 29 cents. S#2962. Shows an African American female softball player. *Illus. 26.*

5/26/94. United States. Quantity unknown. 50 cents. S#2836. (Not pictured.) Depicts World Cup soccer.

5/2/96. United States. 324,000,000. 32 cents. S#3068c. Commemorates the 1996 Centennial Olympic Games. Shows a female African American runner. *Illus. 28.*

5/2/96. United States. 324,000,000. 32 cents. S#3068m. Commemorates the 1996 Centennial Olympic Games. Shows a male African American sprinter. *Illus. 29.*

5/2/96. United States. Quantity unknown. 32 cents. S#8068p. (Not pictured.) African American male hurdlers (1996 Olympics).

5/2/96. United States. 324,000,000. 32 cents. S#3068t. Commemorates the 1996 Centennial Olympic Games. Shows a male African American basketball player. *Illus. 30.*

10/6/96. United States. Quantity unknown. 32 cents. S#3109. (Not pictured.) Depicts a black family decorating their Christmas tree.

1/23/97. St. Vincent and the Grenadines. Quantity unknown. Two dollars. S#2377a. (Not pictured.) A multicolored stamp depicting a portrait of the African American character Tuvok in the television *Star Trek Voyager.* Other characters featured in the *Star Trek Voyager* issue are Kes (S#2377b); Lt. Paris (S#2377c); the Doctor (S#2377d); Capt. Janeway (S#2377e); Lt. Torres (S#2377f); Neelix (S#2377g); Ens. Kim (S#2377h); and Cdr. Chakotay (S#2377i). They are done in litho, and are perforated. They can be bought in souvenir sheets of 9.

17

18

19

20

21

22

23

24-5

26

27

28

29

30

31

32

33-4

2/18/97. United States. 122,000,000. 32 cents. S#3125. (Not pictured.) This stamp is in recognition of "Helping Children to Learn." It depicts an image of an African American father teaching his child to read.

7/28/97. United States. Quantity unknown. 32 cents. S#3151a. A stamp from the Classic American Doll issue. The dolls shown here are the "Alabama Baby" and a doll by Martha Chase; both are black. *Illus. 32.*

7/28/97. United States. Quantity unknown. 32 cents. S#3151j. (Not pictured.) Another in the Classic American Doll issue (see S#3151a above), this stamp shows a black Babyland Rag Doll.

10/18/97. United States. Quantity unknown. 32 cents. S#3174. From a series celebrating women and men in the military: "Hometowns honor their returning veterans, 1945." The six military personnel shown include one African American. *Illus. 33–4.*

1998. United States. Quantity Unknown. 33 cents. S#3185b. From the Celebrate the Century series (1930s). Shows First Lady Eleanor Roosevelt with black girl. *Illus. 35.*

2/3/98. United States. Quantity unknown. 32 cents. S#3183j. (Not pictured.) From the Celebrate the Century series (1910s). Honors scouting.

2/18/99. United States. Quantity unknown. 33 cents. S#3186j. (Not pictured.) From the Celebrate the Century Series (1940s). Shows a big band playing and young people dancing.

5/26/99. United States. Quantity unknown. 33 cents. S#3187. From the Celebrate the Century series (1950s). "Movies Go 3-D." Shows a movie audience in 3-D glasses. One audience member appears to be African American. Note: This stamp can be viewed through 3-D glasses for a 3-D effect. *Illus. 37.*

6/18/99. United States. Quantity unknown. 33 cents. S#3316. (Not pictured.) Commemorates the California Gold Rush. Background picture shows Gold Rush miners.

9/10/99. United States. Quantity unknown. 33 cents. S#3287f. From the Celebrate the Century series (1950s). Represents the desegregating of American public schools during the mid-twentieth century. Shows three children, one of them African American in a schoolroom setting, pledging allegiance to the flag. *Illus. 36.*

Alexander, Archer

Archer Alexander is described as the last fugitive slave under the laws of America. He escaped from slavery in the state of Missouri, was captured, and was then freed under the Emancipation Proclamation. Archer Alexander was born in the state of Virginia, but his master Delany, who inherited Archer, took him to Missouri. It is said that this statue was built almost entirely with the funds donated by former slaves. The statue depicts Archer Alexander on his knees while Abraham Lincoln reads the Emancipation Proclamation.

To learn more about Archer Alexander read the electronic book *The Story of Archer Alexander from Slavery to Freedom March 30, 1863*, by William G. Eliot, a member of the Western Sanitary Commission. The web site address is www.sonaco.com.

10/20/40. United States. 44,389,550. 3 cents. S#902. (Not pictured.) A stamp honoring the Thirteenth Amendment. This stamp is done in shades of purple. It is further described under "Emancipation" and is pictured with stamps celebrating the Emancipation Proclamation.

1960. Liberia. Quantity unknown. 5 cents. S#422. (Not pictured.) A stamp honoring the Thirteenth Amendment to the United States Constitution.

Ali, Muhammad

"The people's champ" and one of the most famous men in the world, Cassius Marcellus Clay, an African American boxer, adopted the Muslim religion and changed his name in 1964 to Muhammad Ali, the name by which he is best known. He was born in Louisville, Kentucky, to Marcellus and Odessa Clay on January 17, 1942. He is one of three children. Ali has been married four times and is the father of five children.

He is considered the most colorful, graceful and controversial champion in boxing history. Ali began training at the

35

36

37

38

39

40

41

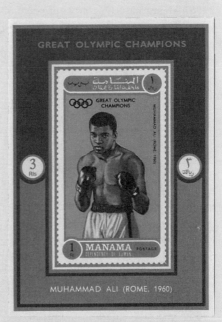

42

43

44

age of twelve. He won the light heavyweight Gold Medal in the 1960 Olympic Games, the same year in which he won the Amateur Athletic Union light heavyweight and the Gold Gloves heavyweight crowns. On Feb. 25, 1964, he became the heavyweight champion of the world at the age of twenty-two. It wasn't until March 8, 1971, after being out of the ring for three and one-half years, that the champ lost his first professional match to Joe Frazier by unanimous decision in a fifteen-round bout at Madison Square Garden in New York City in what was billed the super fight of the century.

Over a period of twenty years, Ali dominated the world boxing scene. The champ retired from the ring in 1979 to pursue other ventures, which keep him busy to this day. Ali is perhaps one of the most recognized men in the world, as the great amount of recognition on international stamps makes clear.

1967. Mahra State. Quantity unknown. 100 fils. This stamp honors Ali's 1960 Olympic win. His name is misspelled as "Cascius" Clay. This same stamp was also overprinted with the words "GOLD MEDAL" in 1968. This overprint stamp is not pictured. *Illus. 39.*

1971. Manama. Quantity unknown. 3 riyals. This is the same stamp as Minkus#611, but perforated and not shown in the souvenir format. *Illus. 43.*

1971. Manama. Quantity unknown. 3 riyals. Minkus#611. (Imperforate souvenir sheet.) Although this stamp was issued in 1971, it honors Ali as a 1960 Olympic champion and should therefore refer to him as Cassius Clay, his name until 1964. Instead the stamp uses the name Muhammad Ali. This is a souvenir imperforate stamp. The previous stamp (described above) is the perforated version of the same stamp. *Illus. 42.*

1971. Manama. Quantity unknown. 10 riyals. Minkus#627. (Perforated souvenir sheet, not pictured.) Celebrates "Great Olympic Champions." This stamp pictures Joe Frazier, the 1964 Olympic heavyweight champ, and Muhammad Ali, the 1960 champ (as Cassius Clay), in their bout of 1971. *Illus. 58.*

1971. Fujeira. Quantity unknown. 10 riyals. Minkus#699. (Imperforate souvenir sheet.) A perforated version also exists. The stamp celebrates the 1971 world championship match between Muhammad Ali and Joe Frazier. *Illus. 53, 54.*

1971. Ajman. Quantity unknown. 15 riyals. Minkus#1150. (Imperforate souvenir sheet, not pictured.) Hard to find stamp. Celebrates Ali's 1960 Olympic win. *Illus. 57.*

7/20/71. Fujeira. Quantity unknown. 2 riyals. Minkus#697. Honors Ali as 1971 world champion. Relatively difficult to find. *Illus. 40.*

7/20/71. Fujeira. Quantity unknown. 3 riyals. Minkus#698. This stamp and Minkus #697 came together (perforated). *Illus. 41.*

1972. Equatorial Guinea. Quantity unknown. 250 + 50 pesetas guineanas. Minkus#627. (Imperforate souvenir sheet.) *Illus. 56.*

9/25/75. Zaire. Quantity unknown. 0.01 ziare. S#809. (Overprint.) This stamp and the four that follow (S3810, 811, 812, and 813) depict a match between Muhammad Ali and George Foreman. *Illus. 45.*

9/25/75. Zaire. Quantity unknown. 0.4 zaire. S#810. (Overprint). *Illus. 46.*

9/25/75. Zaire. Quantity unknown. 0.06 zaire. S#811. (Overprint). *Illus. 47.*

9/25/75. Zaire. Quantity unknown. 0.14 zaire. S#812. (Overprint). *Illus. 48.*

9/25/75. Zaire. Quantity unknown. 0.20 zaire. S#813. (Overprint). See also George Foreman, S#804-808, for more stamps of Zaire depicting Muhammad Ali. *Illus. 49.*

1/7/77. Senegal. Quantity unknown. 60 francs. S#440. Rare and hard to find; only a poor-quality copy is pictured. *Illus. 50.*

1/7/77. Senegal. Quantity unknown. 150 francs. S#441. Like S#440, an extremely hard to find stamp pictured here only in a poor quality copy. *Illus. 51.*

7/2/84. Liberia. Quantity unknown. 62 cents. S#1003. Like Minkus#611, this stamp makes the error of referring to the 1960 Olympic Gold Medalist as Muhammad Ali. In 1960 his name was still Cassius Clay. *Illus. 44.*

7/27/84. Togo. Quantity unknown. 500 francs. S#C491. Reproduced here in a poor-quality copy, this is a difficult issue to find on Muhammad Ali.

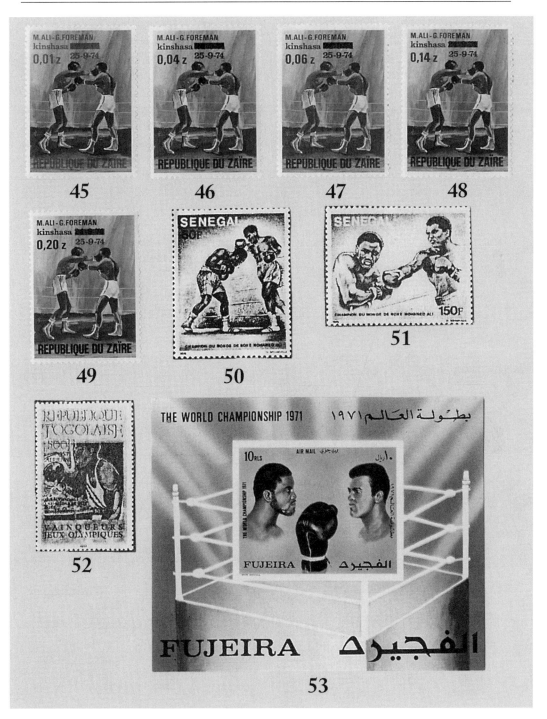

45   46   47   48

49   50   51

52   53

This stamp has been overprinted several times. *Illus. 52.*

7/27/84. Togo. Quantity unknown. 250 francs. S#491. Commemorates the 1984 Summer Olympics. *Illus. 55.*

2/6/93. Sierra Leone. Quantity unknown. 200 leones. S#1611c. (Not pictured.) A multicolored portrait of Ali.

7/15/93. Tanzania. Quantity unknown. 500 shillings. S#1080. (Souvenir sheet.) *Illus. 59.*

54

55

56

10/31/94. Nicaragua. Quantity unknown. 3.50 cordobas. S#2047. (Not pictured.) Muhammad Ali is depicted boxing.

7/16/99. Senegal. Quantity unknown. 300 francs. S#1360. (Not pictured.) Depicts Muhammad Ali with arm raised by referee. Senegal also did nine other issues of Ali (S#1362 a–h) showing various portraits of Ali in color.

Allen, Marcus

A stamp is said to exist on Marcus Allen, an African American professional football player, but no information on such a stamp is presently available.

Allen, Richie

Richie (Richard Anthony) Allen is an American baseball player. Allen, an infielder, was born March 8, 1942, in Wampum, Pennsylvania. He was the rookie of the year in 1963 and MVP in 1972 in the American League. Allen played in the major leagues for fifteen seasons (1963–1977) with five different teams, and retired with a lifetime batting average of .292 and 351 home runs. Allen had his best season in 1972 while playing for the Chicago White Sox, when he led in home runs with a total of 37 and runs batted in totaling 113.

11/20/89. St. Vincents. Quantity unknown. 30 cents. S#1271d. *Illus. 38.*

Andrew, Maynard

A stamp is said to exist on Maynard Andrew, an African American boxer, but no information on such a stamp is presently available.

Angelou, Maya

Maya Angelou is considered one of America's greatest poets and writers of the twentieth century. Maya Marguerite Johnson Angelou was born on April 4, 1928, in St. Louis, Missouri. In 1970 Maya displayed her superb and colorful writing skills in her biography, *I Know Why the Caged Bird Sings.* When her parents divorced, she and her brother were taken to Stamps, Arkansas, by her father, Bailey Johnson, Jr., to live with their maternal grandparents. The idea of sending his daughter to Missouri was also a part of helping Angelou to heal from a rape she had suffered at age eight, committed by her mother's boyfriend.

As a young person growing up in Missouri, Angelou attended segregated public schools. Later she moved in with her mother in San Francisco and became the first female streetcar conductor, before giving birth to her only child, Guy Johnson.

Angelou became interested and active in the Civil Rights Movement during the 1960s. She worked closely with Dr. Martin Luther King, Jr., and served as northern coordinator for the Southern Christian Leadership Conference. She did this while she pursued her writing and acting career. She traveled extensively in Europe and Africa. She served as an administrator in the music department of the University of Ghana.

Angelou has played many roles on television including her Emmy-nominated performance in the miniseries *Roots*. She has written many books, plays, and poems. She has been asked by presidents of the United States to share her skills and experiences with them and the American people. Those presidents include Jimmy Carter, who appointed her to the commission of the International Women's Year, and President Bill Clinton, who in 1992 requested that she compose a poem for his inauguration, which she delivered wonderfully. She is still very active to this day in civil rights for all people, and is a professor of American studies at Wake Forest University.

57

58

3/25/98. Ghana. Quantity unknown. 350 cedis. S#2027a. (Not pictured.) This stamp is included in an issue honoring African American writers of the twentieth century. Alex Haley (S#2027b); Charles Johnson (S#2027c); Richard Wright (S#2027d); Toni Cade Bambara (S#2027e); Henry Louis Gates, Jr. (S#2027f) and Rita Dove (S#2027g), all issued 3/25/98.

Armstrong, Desmond

A stamp is said to exist on Desmond Armstrong, an African American soccer player, but no information on such a stamp is available.

Armstrong, Louis

Louis Daniel Armstrong, known by many as the "King of Jazz," was a trumpeter, band leader, showman, actor, comedian, philanthropist, diplomat, humanitarian, entrepreneur, and civil rights activist. Louis Daniel Armstrong was also called by several names—Louie, Gatemouth, Satchelmouth, Pops, Dipper—but probably most recognized by the name Satchmo. He was born in New Orleans, Louisiana (the home of jazz), in the "redlight" district of Storyville, on July 4, 1900, to Willie and Mary Armstrong. He had one sister. Louie was married four times (Daisy

Parker, Lillian Hardin, Alpha Smith, and Lucille Wilson). There were no children.

It was during his teenage years (age thirteen), while detained for 18 months in a juvenile detention home for boys, that Louis began to seriously pursue an interest in jazz. Under the direction of a music teacher, he developed his beautiful tone, his unique technique, and his gruff, throaty tenor voice, which he acquired while singing in the church choir. Satchmo played the bugle, guitar, tambourine, cornet, and alto horn, but it was the trumpet that he truly mastered.

Louie moved to Chicago, Illinois, at twenty-two years of age. There he played with such greats as Joe "King" Oliver's Creole Jazz band and eventually started his own groups over a relatively short period of time.

Louis Armstrong's music took him around the world, and he left the world with a form of jazz that will be here to enjoy forever. Louis Daniel Armstrong died at the age of 71 in New York City on July 6, 1971.

Following are the many recognitions given to Louie Armstrong on stamps from around the world. These tributes are evidence of the love and admiration for Louie and his jazz music.

10/20/71. Chad. Quantity unknown. 100 francs. S#C91. Not an easy stamp to find. *Illus. 60.*

11/27/71. Senegal. Quantity unknown. 150 francs. S#Cl06. Not an easy stamp to find. *Illus. 61.*

12/6/71. Mali. Quantity unknown. 270 francs. S#C139. Hard to find stamp. Only a poor copy is included here. *Illus. 62.*

12/6/71. Niger. Quantity unknown. 100 francs. S#C168. Issued in honor of American jazz musicians. *Illus. 63.*

12/6/71. Niger. Quantity unknown. 150 francs. S#169. Tribute to jazz musicians. *Illus. 64.*

5/17/72. Upper Volta. Quantity unknown. 45 francs. S#270. Hard to find stamp. *Illus. 66.*

3/12/73. Rwanda. Quantity unknown. 30 cents. S#487. Honoring the fight against racism ("Lutte contre le racisme"). *Illus. 68.*

12/15/73. Upper Volta. Quantity unknown. 250 francs. S#C176. (Souvenir sheet; see color section.) *Illus. C34.*

4/3/89. Dominica. Quantity unknown. 2 dollars. S#1096. In recognition of jazz musicians and entertainers. *Illus. 65.*

11/3/89. St. Vincent. Quantity unknown. 3 dollars. S#1148. (See color section.) *Illus. C35.*

1990. Guyana. Quantity unknown. 50 dollars. S#2679i.(See color section.) *Illus. C41.*

1991. Senegal. Quantity unknown. 10 francs. S#943.(See color section.) Part of a series (S#943–946) commemorating the twentieth anniversary of the death of Louis Armstrong. *Illus. C36.*

1991. Senegal. Quantity unknown. 145 francs. S#944. (See color section.) See S#943. *Illus. C37.*

1991. Senegal. Quantity unknown. 180 francs. S#945. (See color section.) See S#943. *Illus. C38.*

1991. Senegal. Quantity unknown. 220 francs. S#946. (See color section.) See S#943. *Illus. C39.*

2/15/92. Tanzania. Quantity unknown. 75 shillings. S#811e. (See color section.) Recognition of jazz and other musical entertainers. *Illus. C40.*

9/1/92. Gabon. 100 francs. S#297. Quantity unknown. *Illus. 67.*

11/18/94. Madagascar. Quantity unknown. 550 francs. Pictures United States President Bill Clinton playing sax and Louis Armstrong playing trumpet. *Illus. 70.*

9/1/95. United States. Quantity unknown. 32 cents. S#2982. (See color section.) *Illus. C42.*

7/25/96. The Gambia. Quantity unknown. 4 dalasis. S#1786. In recognition of musicians. *Illus. 69.*

10/12/98. Gambia. Quantity unknown. 4 dalasis. S#2049e. (Not pictured.) Gambia's Famous People of the 20th Century series: Jazz Musicians. This stamp depicts a portrait of Armstrong. Others recognized in this series are Sidney Bechet, Duke Ellington, Charlie "Bird" Parker and Ella Fitzgerald.

59

60

61

62

63

64

65

66

67

68

10/12/98. Gambia. Quantity unknown. Face value unknown. S#2049f. (Not pictured.) This stamp shows Armstrong playing his trumpet.

Ashe, Arthur

Author Robert Ashe, Jr., was born in Richmond, Virginia, in 1943. In 1968, Ashe became the first African American and first United States tennis player since 1955 to win the United States Men's National Singles Championship. In that same year, he played on the first winning United States Davis Cup Team since 1963. In 1975, Ashe became the first black man to win the Wimbledon singles championship in England.

Ashe's career was cut short by a heart condition that forced his retirement from professional tennis in 1979. Later Ashe developed AIDS from a transfusion that accompanied a heart operation. Always active in the political and social arenas (he protested apartheid in South Africa and campaigned for other causes in the United States), he turned his attention to the fight against AIDS, establishing a foundation that raised money for AIDS research. Ashe was well respected in America and around the world and he was recognized on stamps both before and after his death in 1993.

11/18/88. Lesotho. Quantity unknown. 1 maloti. S#680. Tennis champions: This stamp series includes the great players Jimmy Connors, Althea Gibson, Chris Evert, and others. Ashe's name is misspelled as "Ash." *Illus. 71.*

7/15/93. Tanzania. Quantity unknown. 20 shillings. S#1079a. From an issue celebrating black athletes. (Other athletes in the issue have entries elsewhere in this text.) *Illus. 72.*

10/28/98. Grenada. Quantity unknown. 45 cents. S#2799. (Not pictured.) From an issue celebrating tennis players. Others recognized are Martina Hingis, Chris Evert, Steffi Graf, Arantxa Sanchez Vicario, Martina Navratilvoa, and Monica Seles.

10/28/98. Dominica. Quantity unknown. 45 cents. S#2040g. (Not pictured.) From an issue celebrating famous twentieth century athletes:

This stamp shows Ashe playing tennis and holding the Wimbledon Trophy.

10/28/98. Dominica. Quantity unknown. 60 cents. S#2040h. Issued with S#2040g (see above).

Ashford, Evelyn

A stamp recognizing Evelyn Ashford, an African American track and field athlete, is said to exist but no information on such a stamp is available.

Attucks, Crispus

It is mentioned in history that Crispus Attucks shed the first blood in the struggle for American independence: "The first to defy and the first to die." Many historians have discussed Attucks as a lead voice in the Boston Massacre, and some have said that he was drunk and just happened to have been on the scene when the massacre occurred. Whatever the situation, on the night of March 5, 1770, he died along with others. This historical event sparked the beginning of the American Revolution and the development of an independent nation. Years later, John Adams wrote, "On that night the foundation of American independence was laid." The death of Attucks and several others on that night became known as the Boston Massacre.

Not much is known about Attucks, other than that he was born in Framingham, Massachusetts, and had escaped from his master twenty years earlier. He worked as a seaman. An account of his burial in *The Gazette and Country Journal* refers to him as a stranger. The *Gazette* further described him as "six feet two inches tall, short curl'd hair, his knees nearer together than common, and was known to the towns people as the mulatto."

As a symbol of resistance to tyranny, Attucks's death placed him among the immortals. The names of Attucks and five others who died that night are carved in the monument of granite erected in their honor. Attucks has also been honored on

69

70

71

72

73

74

75

76

77

78

79

80

81

stamps internationally for this historical event.

2/22/73. Nicaragua. Quantity unknown. 40 centavos. S#C828. Depicts the Boston Massacre in front of the state house. The stamp celebrates events leading up to ("preludes and causes of") the American Revolution. *Illus. 73.*

1975. Equatorial Guinea. Quantity unknown. .30 pesetas guineanas. S#7551. Commemorating the U.S. bicentennial, this stamp reproduces a Paul Revere print of the Boston Massacre. *Illus. 75.*

4/16/75. Nicaragua. Quantity unknown. 5 centavas. S#982. Commemorates the U.S. bicentennial. Shows a print of the Boston Massacre. *Illus. 76.*

5/6/75. Grenada. Quantity unknown. 1 cent. S#629. In honor of the U.S. bicentennial. *Illus. 78.*

1/20/76. Western Samoa. Quantity unknown. 7 sene. S#428. (Not pictured.) Has the same background scene as S#7551 and S#982.

7/26/76. St. Christopher-Nevis/Anguilla. Quantity unknown. 20 cents. S#324. Commemorates the U.S. bicentennial. *Illus. 77.*

1977. Guinea-Bissau. Quantity unknown. 5 pesos. S#7701. This stamp, which commemorates the United States' bicentennial, was taken from the original perforated souvenir sheet. Attucks's name is misspelled as "Attuck." *Illus. 74.*

Audubon, John James

John James Audubon was born April 26, 1785, in Saint-Domingue, West Indies (now Haiti). He gave several accounts of his ancestry and birth, but records discovered in France in the early 1900s established that he was the illegitimate son of a French planter and a Creole woman who worked on the planter's sugar plantation. Audubon's real mother died within a short time after his birth, and the boy was taken back to France, where Captain Audubon and his legal wife adopted him.

To cover his illegitimate birth, Audubon gave different stories to persuade people to believe he was born in Louisiana or was the son of Louis XVI, the king of France. A book titled *I Who Should Command All* leans heavily on the belief that Audubon was the Lost Dauphin who disappeared from the tower during the French Revolution. Earnest Austin (1988), in his book *Black Americans on Stamps*, says, "Audubon was the son of a white French sea captain and his black mistress, who died shortly after his birth."

When Audubon was a teenager, his father sent him to manage his plantation near Philadelphia. It was here that Audubon met and married his wife, Lucy, whose support was critical in achieving his success. During his early married years he was unsuccessful in business and attained fame as an artist only after many troubled years.

Audubon succeeded only because he went to England, where his work was appreciated and subscribers made possible the long publication of his 435 prints (1826 to 1838). In the 1830s Audubon also wrote his *Ornithological Biography* which described the habits of the birds he drew. He interspersed these bird biographies with episodes on life in America during this turbulent period. His writings are now considered a literary treasure and should be explored by any serious Audubon collector. It is said that few men of Audubon's time enjoyed the travels he experienced. He would spend days and weeks in the woods studying birds and animals; and his spectacular drawings, which were criticized by some, were scenes he actually witnessed. Audubon traveled to Paris to publish and sell his book, but he would never accept an offer to buy a single print from the book; he insisted that the book be sold intact. This is one of the reasons why his prints are so rare to this date. Audubon died January 27, 1851.

Founded in 1905, the National Audubon Society is the oldest and largest conservation organization in North America. By virtue of the extensive reproductions of Audubon's paintings on stamps throughout the world, he is the most frequently honored American of black ancestry who is on stamps in the U.S. and internationally. In this book, however, we include only the stamps depicting Audubon himself.

11/8/40. United States. 59,000,000. 1 cent. S#874. *Illus. 79.*

4/23/85. United States. Quantity unknown. 22 cents. S#1863. *Illus. 80.*

7/12/85. St. Helena. Quantity unknown. 11 pence. S#438. *Illus. 81.*

Babers, Alonzo

Alonzo Babers is a track and field athlete. He won the 1984 Olympic 400m run and 4×400m-relay gold medal. Babers was born in Montgomery, Alabama, on October 31, 1961. Babers's father was a career air force officer. Babers grew up in Kaiserlauten, West Germany. He attended the Air Force Base High School in Kaiserlauten. Barbers graduated from the Air Force Academy in 1983. He became the fifth fastest man ever in the 400 meter event with a time of 44.27.

It is unfortunate that Alonzo didn't get to be known to most for his athletic abilities. In his first season of international competition he was seventh in the world and placed fourth in the National Collegiate Athletic Association and fifth at the Athletic Conference as a quarter miler. The same year he achieved a personal record of 45.07 at Zurich, and beat Bert Cameron. (This was Cameron's only loss in 1983.) Babers also ran for the United States 4×400m relay at Helsinki and won a gold medal at the Pan Am Games (where he led off the relay team with 45.21).

Babers has also served time in the United States Air Force as a jet pilot. He has flown a variety of aircrafts. His name may not be widely recognized, but most certainly he has paid his dues as a great athlete and American citizen. He is highly worthy of recognition on an international stamp.

12/15/84. Ivory Coast. Quantity unknown. 200 francs. S#C88. Recognizes Baber's 1984 gold medal win in the Olympic 400 meters. *Illus. 82.*

Baines, Harold

Harold Douglass Baines was born on March 15, 1959, in St. Michaels, Maryland. He is an American baseball player. The Chicago White Sox drafted Harold Baines in the first round in June 1977, making him the first player picked in the nation that year. He was an outfielder for the Chicago White Sox in 1980. He led the American League (AL) record with 22 game-winning RBIs in 1983. Harold also began his 1997 season with the Chicago White Sox, hitting .305 with 12 homers in 93 games. He was then traded to the Orioles on July 29, 1997. He hit .301 in games for Baltimore and .353 in the League Championship Series against Cleveland.

11/28/88. Grenada. Quantity unknown. 30 cents. S#1668d. From a sheet of 9 stamps honoring U.S. baseball players. *Illus. 83.*

Baker, Josephine

Josephine Baker was a dancer, singer, comedienne, musician, nightclub owner, actress, World War II spy, and philanthropist. Ms. Baker was born June 3, 1906, in St. Louis, Missouri, to musician Eddie Carson and dancer Carrie McDonald.

Fleeing poverty, rejection, and child abuse, she left home at the age of eight to join the vaudeville circuit. By the time she was fifteen years of age she was appearing on Broadway in New York City. She left the United States in 1925 to live in France. She eventually became a citizen of France—in fact, one of the country's most popular citizens. She carried with her to France America's most popular dances such as the Charleston, tango, black-bottom, fox trot, hucklebuck, and cakewalk. During her professional life, Josephine also developed different dancing styles of her own. She became a na-

82

83

84

85

86

87

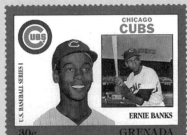
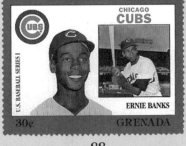

88

89

90

91

92

tional star in France, the nation's queen of dance and entertainment.

Josephine also served as a spy during World War II for the French Resistance against Germany. For her efforts, France awarded her with the highest Medal of Honor as a war hero.

Inspired by humanitarian feeling and her love for children (brought on by her childhood abuse), she adopted twelve orphans from various racial backgrounds and devoted 100 percent of her time and money to the renowned "Rainbow Family." Over a period of several years with no money coming in and all she earned going toward the care of the children, her finances went rock bottom. She was forced back to the stage to survive the financial crisis. On April 12, 1975, she died in poverty; 20,000 people attended her funeral. Josephine has not been forgotten for her humanitarian and entertainment contributions to the world. A movie titled *Josephine Baker* was produced by HBO in the 1990s. One stamp has so far been issued in her honor.

9/8/88. Dominica. Quantity unknown. 35 cents. S#1092. *Illus. 84.*

Ball, William

William Ball, an African American, is given credit for participation in the battle at Cowpens, South Carolina, during the American Revolutionary War, but no evidence has been found in the author's research. In fact, no place or date of birth or other biographical facts are available on Ball, yet he is considered a major African American figure associated with the battle at Cowpens.

An article titled "Patriot Minorities at the Battle of Cowpens" (http://www.nps. gov/cow/minority.htm, 12/30/99) suggests that there are other African Americans who were mentioned, but offers nothing confirming that William Ball was at that battle in Cowpens. The article states that

the National Park Service confirms the following African Americans were at Cowpens: James Anderson (or Asher Crockett), Julius Cesar, Lemerick Farr, Andrew Ferguson, Fortune Freeman, Gideon Griffen, Morgan Griffen, Drury Harris, Edward Harris, Allen Jeffers, Berry Jeffers, Osborne Jeffers, Andrew Peeleg, Dick Pickens, and Record Primes (Primus Record). The article added, however, that there was little or no information on these persons.

It is a historical fact that the Cowpens Battle took place during the Revolutionary War. It is also a fact, confirmed by the National Park Service, that African Americans were there. Therefore, the stamp recognizing the Battle of Cowpens offers recognition to African Americans who fought at Cowpens, including, perhaps, the forgotten or lost contributions of William Ball.

On the other hand, the article suggests that Ball did exist: "Is nothing known about Ball/Collins/Collin, Washington's waiter, depicted in the William Ranney "Battle of Cowpens?" The article still indicates further that if one were to carefully view the painting done by the famous artist William Ranney, depicting "Banastre Tarleton sword fight in which Washington's servant rode up and saved Washington's life by firing a pistol at the British officer," one might recognize that the servant could be William Ball. And since most waiters and valets were black, Ranney painted him that way.

1/17/81. United States. Quantity unknown. 10 cents. UX87. (Not pictured.) Depicts a scene at the Battle of Cowpens, South Carolina.

Bambara, Toni Cade

Toni Cade Bambara, an American fiction writer, scriptwriter, essayist, and community leader, was born in New York City on March 25, 1939. Bambara completed her undergraduate degree in 1959 at Queens College in New York City. Her first short story, "Sweet Town," was published in 1959 in *Vendome* magazine. Toni studied abroad and received her master's degree from City College of New York in 1965. Bambara also became involved in community projects and various other activities; for example, she was a social worker in the New York Department of Social Welfare. She also served as director of the psychiatry department at Livingston College in North Carolina.

She edited and published an anthology titled *The Black Woman* in 1970. The anthology included such prominent writers as Nikki Giovanni, Alice Walker, and herself. She is also credited with writing movie scripts. One of her well known scripts, *Tar Baby* (based on a novel by her friend Toni Morrison), is well known. Bambara has been recognized for her numerous articles, essays, and anthologies along with books of literary criticism. Ghana paid tribute to her on a 1998 postage stamp as one of the great African American writers of the 20th century.

3/25/98. Ghana. Quantity unknown. 350 cedis. S#2027e. (Not pictured.) Depicts a portrait of Bambara. It is part of a series honoring great African American writers of the twentieth century. See Maya Angelou, S#2027a, for more information.

Banks, Ernie

Ernie Banks is an American professional baseball player. He established a major league record in 1955 by hitting five grand-slam home runs in a single season. He also became the first player in the National League (NL) to be named most valuable player two years in a row (1958, 1959). Ernie spent all 19 years (1953–71) of his major league career with the Chicago Cubs, and earned the name "Mr. Cub."

Born in Dallas, Texas, Banks excelled in high school baseball, basketball, and track and field. He signed with the Kansas City Monarchs of the Negro American League in 1950. He left the Monarchs and served in the U.S. Army from 1951 to 1953. When he left the army, he finished the 1953 season with the Monarchs. During that 1953 season he signed a contract with the Chicago Cubs, making him that team's first black player.

In Chicago Banks became a favorite among fans in 1955 when he hit 44 home runs—a major-league record for a shortstop. Three years later he broke his own record by hitting 47 home runs. For four consecutive years (1957–60) he hit more than 40 home runs, ending his career with a total of 512.

Banks was also among the best defensive baseball players. In 1959 his fielding average set a NL season record for shortstops. In 1969 (having moved to first base in 1962) his fielding average led all NL first baseman.

A popular figure among fans, Ernie possessed an infectious enthusiasm for the game and was known for his favorite saying, "Let's play two today!" He was elected to the Baseball Hall of Fame in 1977 and has been honored on several international stamps.

7/23/89. St. Vincent. Quantity unknown. 2 dollars. S#1215. Recognition for induction in the Hall of Fame, 1977. *Illus. 87.*

12/12/99. Grenada. Quantity unknown. 30 cents. S#1667a. *Illus. 88.*

Banneker, Benjamin

Born November 9, 1731, Benjamin Banneker was a free black farmer and self-educated intellectual. Benjamin Banneker modified and completed the survey and plans for the layout of Washington, D.C. Originally, Pierre Charles L'Enfant was selected by President George Washington as chief planner and architect. But the arrogant L'Enfant did not follow through with the directives he had been given and was dismissed. Washington, assisted by Thomas Jefferson, then called upon Benjamin Banneker, who had to complete the layout of the capital from raw memory, for L'Enfant had left with all the detailed maps and plans. But all was not lost. Banneker was able to accurately reconstruct the plans from memory.

In 1791 Banneker published an almanac illustrating the results of his observations and calculations of astronomy. He sent a copy to Thomas Jefferson, who was then the U.S. Secretary of State, along with a letter defending the rights and equality of Negroes. Jefferson was sufficiently impressed by the almanac to send a copy to the French Academy of Sciences. Banneker also constructed one of the first working wooden clocks in America. This clock kept accurate time for many years. He continued to publish his almanac, which appeared regularly, until 1802. A United States Black Heritage Stamp was issued in his honor in 1980.

2/15/80. United States. 160,000,000. 15 cents. S#1804. *Illus. 85.*

5/31/82. Turks and Caicos Islands. Quantity unknown. 35 cents. S#523. Commemorates the 250th anniversary of George Washington's birth. Features portraits of Washington and Banneker, against a background of an early map of Washington. *Illus. 86.*

Baptiste, Kirk

Baptiste was an American field and track athlete. He won the silver medal in the 1984 Olympic 200m run.

Kirk Baptiste was born on June 20, 1963, in Beaumont, Texas. He ran the 200 and 400 meters and ranked fifth among American high school students in the 440 yards in 1980. Baptiste attended the University of Houston, where he majored in hotel and restaurant management. A highlight of Baptiste's career was at the 1984 Los Angeles Olympics where he ran the 200 in 19.96 and was credited with the sixth fastest time ever to win the silver medal. His teammate Carl Lewis won the gold.

Baptiste also ranked second in the world in the 200 in 1984 and first in 1985. He lost the IAAF Grand Prix Final to Calvin Smith in 1985 and suffered the ignominy of a disqualification after a fairly comfortable win in the World Cup 200. Nevertheless, he won both the NCAA and the Athletic Conference half-lap titles at the 1985 World Cup. In the 100 he was ranked number 3 in the world in 1984 and fourth in 1985 by *Track & Field News.* Baptiste's personal record in the 400, achieved in 1986, is 45.95.

Together with Harvey Glance, Calvin Smith, and Dwayne Evans, Baptiste ran an outstanding time of 38.10 to win the sprint relay at the 1985 World Cup in Canberra, Australia. Kirk Baptiste has twice defeated Carl Lewis, once in 1985 when he beat him in a post–Olympic 300-meter race in London with a world best 31.70.

The recognition of Baptiste on several international stamps has been a reminder of a great American athlete.

8/85. Togo. Quantity unknown. 500 francs. S#C521. This is an overprint of an earlier issue honoring Jesse Owens (S#496). The overprint reads in French: "Kirk Baptiste United States Silver Medal." Only a poor-quality copy is shown here. *Illus. 89.*

Barkley, Charles

Charles Wade Barkley was born in Leads, Alabama, in 1963. He is perceived as one of the great stars of professional basketball. His basketball career began during his tenure at Auburn University, where he was named basketball player of the year in the Southeastern Conference in 1984. He left college early and entered the NBA (National Basketball Association) draft and was chosen by the Philadelphia 76ers.

Barkley's achievements with the 76ers included becoming a starter his second year with the team and being named the NBA Eastern Conference All Star second team (1986–87) and the first team for several years following (1988–92). In the 1991-92 season, Barkley was once again named a first team All-Star. In 1992 he joined the Phoenix Suns and led them to the NBA's best win-loss record during the 1992-93 season. He was named the Most Valuable Player during that same season. He also helped lead the American "Dream Team" to win the gold medal at the 1992 Olympics in Barcelona, Spain. From 1996 through 2000 he played for Houston.

Charles Barkley can be ultimately remembered as an outspoken top scorer and rebounder for the National Basketball Association. He and other "Dream Team" members were recognized for winning the 1992 Olympic Gold Medal for the United States of America.

12/22/92. St. Vincents. Quantity unknown. 2 dollars. S#1745b. *Illus. 90.*

Basie, Count

A piano player, bandleader, composer, arranger, entrepreneur, and actor, Count Basie was born William Basie on August 21, 1904, in Red Bank, New Jersey. His desire for music developed early, and he dropped out of junior high school in order to pursue his musical career. His earliest involvement with bands was with the Oklahoma City Blue Devils Band and the Bennie Moten Band. It was here that he began playing his big band style music.

Basie organized the Count Basie Orchestra in 1936 and earned the title "Kansas City Swing King." His nickname list includes Willie, Bill, Billy, Base, Bateman, Nuts, and Count. The one nickname that is most recognized is "Count," for he opted to have it replace his real name.

His musical career extends for almost fifty years and is filled with awards. Among those recognitions, he was honored in 1981 with the Kennedy Center Performing Arts Award. The Black Music Association made a tribute to him in 1982. Basie died on August 16, 1984, in Hollywood, Florida.

3/5/73. Congo. Quantity unknown. 160 francs. S#146. Honoring "the great black musicians." Only a poor-quality copy is shown here. *Illus. 91.*

4/3/89. St. Vincents. Quantity unknown. 5 dollars. S#1151. (Perforated souvenir sheet.) Basie is shown with Billie Holiday on this souvenir sheet. *Illus. 93.*

9/11/96. United States. 92,000,000. 32 cents. S#3096. *Illus. 92.*

Beamon, Bob

Bob Beamon was born on August 29, 1946, in Jamaica, New York. He was one of the greatest record setters and record breakers in track and field. He began his amateur athletic career as a student athlete at Jamaica High School. Even through his studies at Adelphi University, he continued to run track. Throughout his career he set records in field events such as the indoor long jump, triple jump and outdoor long jump. Some of those record-setting performances included AAU and UCAA track and field events, the Pan Am Games, the NAIA Championships, and the Olympic Games. His feat of winning the 1968 Olympic long jump gold medal by breaking Ralph Boston's world record by an incredible 1'9¾" (0.55 m.) is considered to be the single greatest performance in Olympic history.

Beamon further established his accomplishments as a great African American by sharing his history, proving to young people that growing up in a ghetto does not prevent people from making great achievements. He opened a youth center for other ghetto youngsters and also worked for the Parks and Recreation Department of Miami, Florida.

12/15/68. Ajman. Quantity unknown. 2 riyals. Minkus#289. Honors Beamon's win in the 1968 Olympics in Mexico. *Illus. 94.*

12/15/68. Manama. Quantity unknown. 2 riyals. Minkus#157. Design is similar to Minkus #289. *Illus. 95.*

93

94

95

96

97

6/30/69. Chad. Quantity unknown. 1 franc. S#202. This stamp has been overprinted several times recognizing various athletes. *Illus. 99.*

7/7/69. Mauritania. Quantity unknown. 70 francs. S#C88. Honors Beamon's 1968 Olympic win. *Illus. 100.*

5/25/72. Equatorial Guinea. Quantity unknown. 50 pesetas guineanas. Minkus#625. This is an issue commemorating the 1972 Olympic Games in Munich, but it features a portrait of Bob Beamon in his gold medal long jump in Mexico (1968). *Illus. 96.*

7/27/84. Togo. Quantity unknown. 500 francs S#C497. *Illus. 97.*

8/6/84. Burundi. Quantity unknown. 5 francs. S#627. This stamp comes in a souvenir sheet recognizing other athletes. Honors Beamon's 1968 Olympic win. *Illus. 98.*

7/10/92. Palau. Quantity unknown. 50 cents. S#306. (Perforated souvenir sheet.) Reads in English, "Palau salutes the Olympian innovators." This stamp was issued to commemorate the 1992 Olympics in Barcelona. *Illus. 101.*

Bechet, Sidney

Sidney Bechet was born in New Orleans, Louisiana, on May 14, 1897. He was a jazz saxophonist and composer. Bechet began playing clarinet as a child and by the time he was 17 had performed with every major New Orleans jazz band. Bechet is given credit for being the first jazz musician to make serious use of the soprano saxophone. He is also recognized as a pioneer in long, fluid, intensely melodic improvisations and for his unique vibrato tone, which made everything he played recognizably his own. He was highly acclaimed in Europe. He was considered to have been the master of the soprano saxophone. Bechet played with many of the great jazz artists during his time, including King Oliver, Louis Armstrong, Duke Ellington and others. He was also a superb clarinet player.

In 1959 Sidney Bechet died on his birth date in France, where he had spent most of his life as a professional jazz musician. He

has been recognized on several international stamps.

10/20/71. Chad. Quantity unknown. 50 francs. S#C89. In recognition of African American Jazz Musicians—This is a hard to find stamp. *Illus. 102.*

9/1/72. Gabon. Quantity unknown. 60 francs. S#296. Hard to find stamp. *Illus. 103.*

3/12/84. Mali. Quantity unknown. 470 francs. S#C493. Issued in recognition of jazz singers and musicians. Extremely hard issue to find. Only a poor quality copy is shown here. *Illus. 104.*

4/8/89. St. Vincents. Quantity unknown. 15 cents. S#1143. Comes with a set (Scott numbers 1142–1149). *Illus. 105.*

10/12/98. The Gambia. Quantity unknown. 4 dalasis. S#2049a. (Not pictured.) Portrait of Bechet. See Louis Armstrong, S#2049e, for more comments.

Beckwourth, James P.

Until recently, American history has not paid much mind to the roles African Americans played during the westward expansion. Now, historians are paying tribute to the thousands of African-American men and women who were part of that movement west. One of the most famous mountain men was James P. Beckwourth (sometimes Beckwith), a Virginia-born (1798) mulatto blacksmith, who, in 1823, joined General William H. Ashley's Rocky Mountain Fur Company in St. Louis Missouri. He left this expedition in 1825 to live with the Crow Indians. During his years with the Crow tribe, he developed a reputation as both a warrior and a horse thief. His actions further promoted him to a chief in the Crow tribe. In 1844 he joined Kearny's forces in California. He participated in the Mexican War (1846–1848), joined the Colorado gold rush in 1859, and fought in the Cheyenne Wars of 1864. He later died in 1867 near Denver, Colorado, while on a peace mission.

James B. Beckwourth was one of many

98

99

100

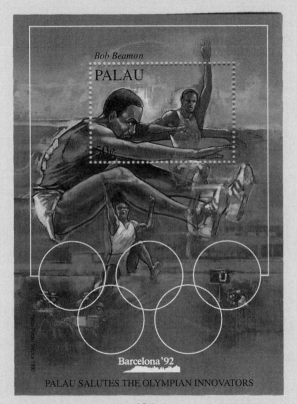

101

102

103

104

105

106

African Americans who played vital roles in the U.S. westward expansion. He is one of the most famous mountain men to have lived.

10/18/94. United States. 20,000,000. 29 cents. S#2869g. *Illus. 106.*

Belafonte, Harry

Harry Belafonte was born Harold George Belafonte in the Harlem section of New York City in 1927. His mother took him to Jamaica, her native country. After living in Jamaica for five years he returned to Harlem. Here he studied acting in the late 1940s at the Dramatic Workshop of the New School for Social Research. He later received a Tony Award for his appearance in *John Murray Anderson's Almanac* (1953).

Belafonte's first big break as a singer came with an extended engagement at Broadway's Royal Roost nightclub, where he began specializing in the music of the West Indies. His first great success was the 1956 album *Calypso*, which included "Banana Boat Song," along with such songs as "Matilda" and "Brown Skin Girl." The album sparked a surge of interest in calypso music.

As an actor, Belafonte appeared in several motion pictures, including *Island in the Sun* (1957), *Uptown Saturday Night* (1974), *First Look* (1994), and *The Player* (1992). He won an Emmy award for his 1960 television special, *Tonight with Belafonte*, becoming the first black man to win the award.

Belafonte played a significant role during the 1960s civil rights movement in the United States. He is considered a great humanitarian and activist. He also helped to organize the recording session for the album and video *We Are the World*, which supported African famine relief projects; for his effort he received a Grammy award. Additionally, he was appointed a United Nations Children's Fund (UNICEF) Good-will Ambassador, and in 1988 the Peace Corps presented him with its Leader for Peace Award. Belafonte's interest in the plight of Africans suffering under apartheid inspired his critically acclaimed album *Paradise in Ganzankulu* (1988).

Belafonte is still very active making movies and directing.

1995. Grenada and the Grenadines. Quantity unknown. 90 cents. (See color section.) *Illus. C44.*

Bell, George Harold

George Antonio (Harold) Bell was born October 21, 1959, in San Pedro De Macorís of the Dominican Republic. His contributions to history are seen in the sport of baseball. In 1981 he came to America and played baseball as an outfielder for the Toronto Blue Jays. In 1983 he led the American League in RBIs. In 1987 he was the American League MVP. His accomplishments in baseball were many. He established club records in no fewer than seven offensive categories. He was the first Toronto Blue Jay ever to be in the All-Star Game. This honor was mostly due to the fact that he tied records in the American League as well as the National League. His 28 road homers tied an earlier American League record set by Harmon Killebrew in 1962.

Bell is characterized as being a free swinger at the plate, but his .290-plus career average suggests that he knows how to hit the ball as well.

12/1/88. Grenada. Quantity unknown. 30 cents. S#1665d. (See color section.) From the "U.S. Baseball Series 1," a sheet of 9. *Illus. C43.*

Benson, Stephen

Stephen Benson was born a slave in the state of Maryland. He settled in Liberia, Africa, around the early or middle 1800s. Little is known about Benson's life in America, but in Liberia he became the nation's second president following Joseph

Jenkins Roberts. Benson served two terms (1956–1864). His biggest accomplishment as president was the annexation of the Colony of Maryland, now Maryland County, into the Republic of Liberia in 1857. He also obtained recognition for Liberia from the following countries: Belgium, 1858; Denmark, 1869; United States and Italy, 1862; Norway and Sweden, 1863; and Haiti, 1864.

1948–1950. Liberia. Quantity unknown. 2 cents. S#435. (See color section.) *Illus. C45.*

1958 and 1960. Liberia. Quantity unknown. 2 cents. S#372. (See color section.) *Illus. C46.*

Berry, Chuck

Chuck Berry (full name Charles Edward Anderson Berry) was born on October 18, 1926, in St. Louis, Missouri. He is recognized as an American singer and composer. He is also given credit for being one of the first musicians to bring the influence of rhythm-and-blues music to mainstream rock and roll. He learned to play guitar in high school and spent some time in a reform school.

Chuck wrote many popular songs during the 1960s, including "Rock 'n' Roll Music," "Johnny B. Good," and his first hit, "Maybellene," which was one of the first songs to rise to number one on three separate Billboard charts: rhythm and blues, pop, and country and western. His complex runs and energetic dancing turned the audiences on to great excitement. His famous dance was called the "duck walk." Waddling low, knees sharply bent, he played the guitar at the same time, to the delight of his audience.

He is considered one of the great pioneers in American rock and roll music, and he influenced many rock and roll musicians during the 1950s and 1960s.

During his lifetime Berry has received many honors and awards, including a Grammy lifetime achievement award in 1984. He has been recognized on several stamps around the world.

11/19/92. Grenada. Quantity unknown. 90 cents. S#2158a. (Not pictured.) From a series recognizing gold record award winners. Others recognized are Cher, Michael Jackson, Elvis Presley, Dolly Parton, Johnny Mathis, Madonna, Nat King Cole, James Brown, and Janis Joplin.

12/1/95. Tanzania. Quantity unknown. 250 shillings. S#1414a. (See color section.) From a series recognizing rock and roll musicians. *Illus. C47.*

1998. The Gambia. Quantity unknown. 3 dalasis. S#1670i. (See color section.) *Illus. C48.*

Bethune, Mary McLeod

Mary McLeod Bethune's parents were former slaves. Mary was able to receive an education at the Moody Bible Institute in Chicago, from which she graduated in 1895. She taught in the Southern Mission Schools until 1903.

In 1904 she founded the Daytona Normal and Industrial Institute for Girls in Daytona Beach, Florida. Mary was headmaster for almost twenty years. In 1923 the school merged with the Cookman Institute. The newly organized institution was known as Bethune Cookman College, which still exists. Bethune was president of Bethune-Cookman College until 1942.

She went on to found the National Council for Negro Women and directed the Division of Negro Affairs of the National Youth Administration from 1936 to 1944.

During World War II, she was appointed special assistant to the Secretary of War, Henry L. Stimson, to aid in the selection of officer candidates for the Women's Army Corps (WAC). As an educator, Bethune was well qualified for her assignment. She also served as a special consultant on interracial affairs at the San Francisco Conference of the United Nations Organization in 1945, working with Eleanor Roosevelt.

Bethune-Cookman College today has an enrollment of more than 1,700 students. It is a private Methodist coeducational college.

Bethune received many honors and awards. She is recognized on the United States 1985 Black Heritage issue and on other stamps around the world.

7/27/82. Grenada. Quantity unknown. 10 cents. S#1106. (See color section.) Commemorates the 100th anniversary of the birth of Franklin D. Roosevelt. Bethune is shown standing beside Roosevelt. On the stamp are the words "Mary McLeod Bethune appointed director of Negro Affairs in 1942." *Illus. C50.*

3/15/85. United States. 120,000,000. 22 cents. S#2137. From the Black Heritage series. *Illus. C49.*

11/22/85. Grenada. Quantity unknown. 50 cents. S#1338. (See color section.) Commemorates the International Women's Year and the 40th anniversary of the United Nations. *Illus. C51.*

Biggs, Tyrell

Tyrell Biggs was an American boxer who competed in the 1984 Olympic Games, where he won the super heavyweight boxing gold medal. Tyrell Biggs was born on December 22, 1960, in Philadelphia, Pennsylvania. He attended West Philadelphia High School and then Virginia's Hampton Institute, where he excelled on the basketball court. His boxing record is documented by James A. Page in *Olympic Medalists* as follows: "He won the 1984 Olympic trials and the 1983 U.S. Amateur and Pan Am trials and finished third at the Pan Am Games. Biggs was world amateur champion; he won his first global title in 1982 and was three-time U.S. champion. Biggs had 6 losses in 109 fights, with 40 or 45 knockouts."

3/15/84. Niue. Quantity unknown. 58 cents. S#435. (See color section.) Commemorates the boxing matches of the 1984 Summer Olympics. Tyrell's name is done in gold on this stamp,

printed over an ancient Grecian illustration of two boxers. *Illus. C52.*

Black, Larry

Larry Black was born in Miami, Florida, on July 20, 1951. According to James A. Page's *Olympic Medalists*, "Larry Black had a fine collegiate season in 1971 at North Carolina Central University. He won the NCAA, NAIA, and NCAA (College Division) all in the same year. He also ran a 440-yard relay leg in 43.8 seconds at the 1972 Penn Relays. Black led off the Olympic 4×100-meter relay team that gained the world record. He twice ran 20.0 before the Munich Games, but lost the Olympic title to Valery Borzov of the USSR by 2 meters. Larry Black later became director of Miami's Parks and Recreation Department."

1973. Umm-al-Qiwain. Quantity unknown. 5 riyals. (See color section.) Commemorates the 20th Olympic Games (Munich, 1972). Recognizes the gold medal winners of the 4×100m relay: African Americans Larry Black, Edward Hart, Robert Taylor, and Gerald Tinker. *Illus. C53.*

Blake, Eubie

Born to former slaves in Baltimore, Maryland, on February 7, 1883, James Hubert "Eubie" Blake showed his musical talent early. By the time he was six years old he was already playing his family's pump organ. He began piano lessons at age six and soon began jazzing up church hymns with syncopated rhythms. As a young man he would slip away from home at night to hang out and play in honky-tonks, bars and brothels, developing his ragtime style in the 1890s.

During the 1920s Blake teamed up with Noble Sissle to form a vaudeville act. The two of them produced the Broadway musical *Shuffle Along*, which provided opportunities for other black Americans to perform on Broadway. *Shuffle Along* featured such performing artists as Josephine Baker, Florence Mills, and Paul Robeson, who later became popular stars.

Blake traveled widely, playing his music around the world. He retired briefly after World War II, but returned to performing in the 1950s when ragtime became popular again. In his performances he played ragtime and told interesting stories about his life.

Eubie Blake received numerous honorary degrees and awards, including the Presidential Medal of Freedom in 1981. He remained active as a jazz pianist and composer until his ninety-ninth year. The death of his second wife, Marion, to whom he had been married since 1946, led to a decline in his own health. Eubie Blake died on February 12, 1993, in Brooklyn, New York, only five days after his hundredth birthday.

9/16/95. United States. Quantity unknown. 32 cents. S#2988. (See color section.) From the Legends of American Music series. *Illus. C54.*

Bluford, Guion

Guion Stewart Bluford, Jr., was born in Philadelphia, Pennsylvania, on November 22, 1942. Guion Bluford was the first African American astronaut assigned a space mission. Lt. Col. Bluford acted as mission specialist (a designation used by astronaut-scientists) on the third flight of the space shuttle *Challenger* in August 1983.

Bluford graduated from the aerospace engineering program at Pennsylvania State University in 1994. He joined the U.S. Air Force and saw extensive combat in Vietnam. He earned a doctorate in aerospace engineering from the Air Force Institute of Technology in 1978, and in that same year he was accepted in the astronaut program.

Bluford is also the second black man to have flown in space. The first was Cuban cosmonaut Arnaldo Tamayo Mendez, who was aboard the USSR's Soyuz 38 in 1980.

Bluford's contribution to aerospace technology earned him recognition on an international stamp.

5/26/85. Equatorial Guinea. Quantity unknown. 200 shillings. S#931. Only a poor copy of this stamp is shown here. *Illus. 107.*

Bolden, "Buddy" Charles

A stamp of African American musician "Buddy" Charles Bolden, generally considered the first bandleader to play the improvised music that later became known as jazz, is said to exist. No information on such a stamp is available.

Bonds, Barry

Barry Lamar Bonds is an American professional baseball player who in 1992 signed a six-year, $43,750,000 contract with the San Francisco Giants—the most lucrative contract in the history of major league baseball at that time.

Bonds was born in Riverside, California. His love of baseball was no doubt inspired by his father, outfielder Bobby Bonds, and his godfather, Hall of Fame member Willie Mays. Both his father and godfather also played for the Giants. Bonds began his major league career as a Pittsburgh Pirate. He led National League (NL) rookies in home runs (16), runs batted in (48), stolen bases (36), and walks (65). He was also voted the NL's most valuable player (MVP) and was *Sporting News's* Player of the Year. He earned his second MVP title in 1992 and received his third consecutive *Sporting News* Gold Glove for fielding excellence that same year. He helped lead the Pirates to three consecutive NL championship series (1990, 1991, and 1992).

In 1994 Bonds became a free agent. His marketability as a player was proven when he signed his highly publicized contract with the Giants. In 1993, at the end of his first season under the new contract, Bonds earned his second consecutive MVP

107

108

109

110

111

112

113

114

115

116

117

award, his third in four years, after leading the Giants to a second-place finish in the National League West Division behind the Atlanta Braves.

11/30/89. St. Vincent. Quantity unknown. 30 cents. S#1270a. From the "U.S. Baseball Series 2," a sheet of 9. *Illus. 108.*

Breland, Mark

A stamp of Mark Breland, an African American boxer, is said to exist but no information on such a stamp is available.

Brisco-Hooks, Valerie

Track and field champion Valerie Brisco-Hooks was born July 6, 1960, in Greenwood, Mississippi. She began to show her excellence as a short sprinter at Locke High School in Los Angeles, California. She continued running at California State University. There she was an AIAW champion and a runner-up in the 200 meters in the AAU division. She constantly broke records whenever and wherever she ran. She clocked a best of 23.16 and earned a world ranking of ten. She set an American record of 49.83 in the 400 meter relay at the TAC Championships. She also broke the Olympic record in the same relay at a time of 48.88 that was set by East German Marita Koch in 1980. She became the fourth fastest of all time in the event. She also became the first Olympian ever to win in both the 200 and 400 meter relay. She became the first female U.S. track and field athlete to win three gold medals since Wilma Rudolph conquered the feat in 1960. Brisco-Hooks went on to be ranked second in the 200 meter relay in the world in 1985. In 1986 she finished third in the 200 and 400 meter relays and fifth in the 100 meter relay in 1986. She has several records that still remain unbroken.

12/3/84. Ghana. Quantity unknown. 1 cedi. S#445. *Illus. 109.*

Brooks, Hubie

Hubie Brooks was born in Los Angeles, California, on September 24, 1956. Today his home is Chatsworth, California. He presently plays with the Expos and has accumulated the following record based on his times (50) at the plate: percentage on base .317, slugging .404, and strikeout 5.5.

11/28/88. Grenada. Quantity unknown. 30 cents. S#1669h. *Illus. 110.*

9/24/90. St. Vincents. Quantity unknown. 60 cents. S#1344a. Hubie Brooks shown with Orel Hershiser. *Illus. 111.*

Brown, James

No one can talk about rhythm and blues, funk music, or rock without mentioning James Brown, known as the "hardest working man in show business." James Brown's influence on American popular music has been of seismic proportions.

James Brown was born in Barnwell, South Carolina, on May 3, 1933. He moved to Augusta, Georgia, with his family at the age of four. The family was in hard circumstances, and various relatives raised Brown. These events only made the boy more determined to make a success of himself. He picked cotton, washed cars, and shined shoes—but he also earned money by dancing on the streets and at amateur contests. These were the early signs of the career that he would soon embark upon.

At the age of 15, Brown quit school in order to dedicate himself to his musical career on a full time basis. He sang with religious groups such as the Swanee Quartet and the Gospel Starlighters. He also sang and played drums with R&B bands.

In 1956, the founder of King Records, Syd Nathan, noticed James Brown's talents. He signed Brown up with the Federal label, a subsidiary of King Records. This contract brought forth Brown's first release, "Please, Please, Please." The following year he recorded "Try Me," which became a top 50 pop hit. While on the road promoting his songs, Brown polished his stage act and singing ability.

The "James Brown Sound" had now been established. His 1965 hit, "Popa's Got a Brand New Bag," earned him a Grammy for best rhythm and blues recording. He repeated this in 1986 with his release of "Living in America."

Brown's career has remained successful despite negative publicity on his personal life. He has been inducted into the Rock and Roll Hall of Fame. He received the Ray Charles Lifetime Achievement Award from the Rhythm and Blues Foundation as part of the organization's Pioneer Awards program in 1993. He has been awarded for his lifetime achievements at the Black Radio Exclusive Awards Banquet in Washington, D.C. A bridge in Steamboat Springs, Colorado, has been named after him as well as a street in his hometown of Augusta, Georgia. Further honors will likely come.

Many of his recordings are still being reissued. The humanitarian Brown provides toys, food, and clothes to deprived children in his hometown. He presently lives in Beach Island, South Carolina. The title of "the hardest working man in show business" still follows him today. His explosive stage energy and intense vocal impressions of gospel and R&B have earned him several titles as well as his place in the history of music.

11/19/92. Grenada. Quantity unknown. 90 cents. S#2158b. (Not pictured.) See Chuck Berry, S#2158a, for more information on the series that included this stamp.

Brown, Sterling A.

A stamp of the great twentieth century writer Sterling A. Brown is said to exist but no information on such a stamp is available.

Brown-Fitzgerald, Benita

Benita Brown Fitzgerald was born on July 6, 1961, in Dale City, Virginia. She is a noted track and field athlete. She won a gold medal in the 100-meter hurdle relay at the 1984 Summer Olympics. Although her excellence is mostly noted in sports, she is highly intelligent. She graduated from Garfield High School as a member of the National Honor Society and graduated from the University of Tennessee with a B.S. in industrial engineering. She excelled in track and field in both high school and college. Her specialty was in sprinting and hurdling. Her athletic achievements were many. She was state champion 1976–79, USA Jr. National Champion 1978–79, a 15 time All-American collegiate record holder, and a collegiate champion. Her best season was in 1983, when she recorded 12.84 seconds in the hurdle relay and won national titles. She placed eighth at the world championships and was ranked tenth in the world in 1983. She currently lives in Dale City, Virginia, with her husband, Laron Brown.

8/21/85. Uganda. Quantity unknown. 5 shillings. S#458. This stamp commemorates the 1984 Olympics. It features a portrait of Ruth Kyallisiima, "Uganda Sportsman of the Year 1983," but it is overprinted in gold with "Gold Medalist Benita Brown-Fitzgerald USA." *Illus. 112.*

Buchanan, Buck

A stamp of Buck Buchanan, an African American football player, is said to exist but no information on such a stamp is available.

Buffalo Soldiers

Buffalo Soldiers was the name the Native Americans gave to African-American cavalrymen during the Indian Wars in the post–Civil War American West. A white commander, Col. Robert G. Shaw, trained the initial all-black regiment, the 54th Massachusetts. The regiment suffered heavy casualties in a heroic, yet unsuccessful, attempt to capture Fort Wagner in the harbor of Charleston, South Carolina, in July of 1863. After the Civil War Congress authorized two cavalry regiments and four infantry regiments of black troops who were trained and led by white officers to control "hostile" Indian tribes in the West for 25 years. One company of the 9th regiment fought in the last battle of the

Indian Wars at Wounded Knee, South Dakota, in December of 1890. Despite racist treatment by other military officers and open racism displayed by many civilians in frontier towns, the Buffalo Soldiers performed effectively. Many Americans for a long time didn't even realize that the Buffalo Soldier existed, and many to this day do not know about them.

Black troops continued to use the "Buffalo Soldiers" name through World War II, but many Americans still didn't realize that the Buffalo Soldiers existed. The U.S. Postal Service recognized them on a stamp issued in 1994.

4/22/94. United States. 186,000,000. 29 cents. S#2818. *Illus. 116.*

Bunche, Ralph Johnson

Ralph Johnson Bunche was born on August 7, 1904, in Detroit, Michigan. Faced with early obstacles in life, he still made amazing achievements. His father was a poor Detroit barber and his mother was an amateur musician. Both of his parents died before he reached his teens, and his grandmother and several aunts in California raised him.

Bunche won an athletic scholarship to the University of California, but he still had to pay for some expenses by working as a campus janitor. Friends and neighbors also raised money for his living expenses until he won a tuition scholarship to Harvard University one year later.

Bunche was named chairman of the political science department of Howard University in 1927. In 1938 he collaborated with the Swedish economist Gunnar Myrdal to complete a comprehensive study of the American Negro. Their work was consolidated in the book *American Dilemma*, which was published in 1945.

In 1942 Dr. Bunche worked in the Office of Strategic Services as a research analyst of material relating to Africa. In 1946 he was

promoted to the position of Associate Chief of the State Department's Dependent Areas Section. After leaving this position, he became head of the United Nations Trusteeship Department and became a personal representative of the United Nations Secretary-general in the Arab-Israeli dispute.

Dr. Bunche made considerable contributions to the entire world in the name of peace. His more than forty honorary degrees are testament to this. Many have said that if Bunche were of a different hue, he would have been an American president. He died December 9, 1971. Bunche was paid tribute in 1982 on an American stamp, and as early as 1966 he was recognized on foreign issues.

1966. Yemen. Quantity unknown. Face value unknown. Stanley Gibbons#381. (Not pictured.) Hard to find stamp.

10/23/81. St. Lucia. Quantity unknown. 2 dollars. S#528. *Illus. 113.*

1/12/82. United States. Quantity unknown. 20 cents. S#1860. *Illus. 114.*

11/22/85. Grenada and the Grenadines. Quantity unknown. 5 dollars. S#711. (Perforated souvenir sheet.) The stamp shown here (in photocopy) was taken from the original perforated souvenir sheet. *Illus. 115.*

10/18/95. Grenada. Quantity unknown. 1 dollar. S#2488b. (Not pictured.) In recognition of Nobel Peace Fund Establishment.

Burton, Levar

A stamp of Levar Burton, an African American actor, is said to exist but no information on such a stamp is available.

Calhoun, Lee Quency

Lee Quency Calhoun was born in Laurel, Mississippi, in 1933. He was an excellent track and field athlete. He was the first athlete to win the 100-meter hurdles relay twice. He was victorious in the same event at the AAU indoor and outdoor, the NAIA, and the NCAA in 1956. He successively defended all four titles in 1957. He won a third AAU outdoor championship in 1959 and also won at the Pam Am Games. He was one of the most accomplished high hurdlers of all time. After he himself finished running he dedicated his time to other track athletes by coaching at Grambling College. He later became head track coach at Yale. Since 1980 he has been coaching at Western Illinois University in Macomb, Illinois. Being elected assistant coach at the 1971 and 1972 Pan Am Games and the Montreal Games in 1976 further recognized his expertise.

1968? Equatorial Guinea. Quantity unknown. 3 pesetas guineanas. *Illus. 117.*

Campanella, Roy

Roy Campanella was born in 1921 in Homestead, Pennsylvania. He was the first African American catcher in the major leagues. "Campy," as he was called by many players, was with the Brooklyn Dodgers from 1949 to 1958. He was the National League MVP in 1951, 1953, and 1955. His career was ended by a paralyzing auto accident. Several countries have paid tribute to Roy Campanella on their postage stamps.

His account of this accident and his life story, *It's Good to Be Alive*, was published in 1959. Roy Campanella died in 1993.

1971. Ras Al Khaima. Quantity unknown. 80 dirhams. Minkus#549. Hard to find stamp. Features portraits of Roy Campanella and Japanese ballplayer Katsuya Nomura. *Illus. 118.*

Campbell, Milton Gray

Milton Gray Campbell, known as Milt, was born December 9, 1934, in Plainfield, New Jersey. He was considered a great American track and field athlete. Campbell won the decathlon silver medal in 1952 and the gold medal in 1960. Traditionally the winner of the Olympic decathlon is hailed as "the world's greatest athlete"; Campbell was the first African American to achieve that distinction.

Campbell graduated from Indiana University in 1957. In 1953 he won the AAU decathlon, and in 1955 he finished first in both the AAU and NCAA high hurdles. As a student and athlete at Indiana University, he won letters in both football and track. He also set a world record of 13.4 seconds for the 120-yard hurdles.

He won the silver medal in 1952 at age 18. His 1956 decathlon scores, totaling 7,708 points, were: 100-meter run, 10.8 seconds; 400-meter run, 48.8 seconds; long jump, 7.33 meters; javelin, 57.08 meters; discus, 48.5 meters; 1,500-meter run, 4:50.6.

Milton Campbell more recently has worked with underprivileged youth in New Jersey and is a well-known lecturer.

1956. Nicaragua. Quantity unknown. 25 córdobas. Only a poor copy of this stamp is shown here. Commemorates the 21st Olympic Games and Campbell's 1956 win. *Illus. 122.*

1957–1958. Dominican Republic. S#502 (op). An overprint of S#502. Overprinted with a globe, the words "Año geofísico internacional" (International Geophysical Year) and the year "1957–1958." *Illus. 120.*

10/3/58. Dominican Republic. Quantity unknown. 2 cents. S#502. Commemorates Campbell's 1956 win in the Melbourne Olympics. *Illus. 119.*

1972. Paraguay. Quantity unknown. 12.45 guaranis. Commemorates the Munich Olympics in 1972 and celebrates decathlon winners in Olympic history. *Illus. 123.*

1974. Paraguay. Quantity unknown. Face value unknown. (Perforated souvenir sheet.) Notice the athletes surrounding the perforated stamp. Milton Campbell is the middle picture on the right. Only a poor copy is shown here. *Illus. 121.*

Carew, Rod

Rod Carew was born on October 1, 1945, in Panama. He had the highest lifetime batting average of any player whose completed career was in the postwar era. He played faithfully and ruggedly with the Minnesota Twins (1967–78) and the Cali-

118

119

120

121

122

123

124

fornia Angels (1979–85). He accumulated over three thousand hits. This was a goal accomplished by only fifteen other players. He was Rookie of the Year in 1967 and an All Star candidate every year except 1978. Between 1969 and 1978, he won seven batting titles. Only Ty Cobb, with 12, and Honus Wagner with 8, ever won more. He won the Most Valuable Player Award in 1977, and he was elected to the Baseball Hall of Fame in 1991.

12/28/88. Grenada. Quantity unknown. 30 cents. S#1664c. From the "U.S. Baseball Series 1." *Illus. 124.*

11/30/89. St. Vincent. Quantity unknown. 30 cents. S#1271i. From the "U.S. Baseball Series 2." *Illus. 125.*

Carey, Lott

Lott Carey was born a slave in Virginia in 1780, and settled in Liberia, Africa, during the Monroe Administration to escape the bondage of slavery in America. He became the governor of Careyburg, Liberia. According to *Black Firsts* (1994, p. 307), "Lott Carey was the first black Baptist missionary to Africa. He established the first Baptist Church in what is now Monrovia, Liberia. He underwent conversion in 1807, and then purchased his freedom and his two children's in 1813. On January 23, 1821, Carey, Colin Teague, and twenty-eight others set sail for Africa. When a group of churches in Virginia, North Carolina, and Washington, DC, withdrew from the National Baptist Convention, USA, in 1897, they formed the Lott Carey Foreign Mission Convention, which is still in existence to this date."

Lott Carey played a significant role in the overall establishment of Liberia, Africa.

4/21/50. Liberia. Quantity unknown. 2 cents. S#333. Lott Carey is pictured in this stamp with Jehudi Ashmun, a white American missionary credited as one of the founders of Liberia. *Illus. 126.*

Carter, Joseph (Joe) Chris

Joseph Carter is an American baseball player. He is an outfielder for the Cleveland Indians. He led the American League in RBIs in 1986 and was one of the premiere RBI men of his day. Joe was born March 7, 1960, in Oklahoma City, Oklahoma. He had a career slugging average of .465 and strikeout ratio 6.3. Career highlights include tying the great Lou Gehrig's AL record of four 3–HR games in a career; being the first Indians player ever to achieve 100 home runs and 100 stolen bases in a career; and having 10 RBIs in a 2 game span.

11/28/88. Grenada. Quantity unknown. 30 cents. S#1670b. *Illus. 127.*

Carver, George Washington

Dr. Carver was born in Diamond Grove, Missouri, in the early 1860s. At age thirteen he was on his own. Enduring great hardships, he worked his way through Simpson and Iowa State colleges. Booker T. Washington called him to Tuskegee Institute in 1896. There a small experimental farm was set up under Dr. Carver, and the work reeducating the region's farmers began.

Many Americans to this day have not realized the impact Dr. George Washington Carver has had on their lives. Millions of people who eat peanut butter on a daily basis have no clue as to who developed this tasty product. It was Dr. Carver, who revolutionized Southern agriculture almost singlehandedly. He was a great scientist, teacher, administrator and humanitarian. Dr. Carver developed hundreds of different uses for the neglected peanut, finding ways to create meal, coffee substitute, bleach, tan remover, wood filler, metal polish, paper, ink, shaving cream, rubbing oil, linoleum, synthetic rubber, plastic and many other products from its substance. There are many to this day that merrily describe him as the "peanut man."

125

126

127

128

129

130

131

132

133

In 1894, the boll weevil threatened to destroy "king cotton," the crop on which the South so heavily depended. Furthermore, cotton had depleted the soil of vital nutrients. Dr. Carver's answer to this threat lay in the South finding some sources of income other than cotton. Carver was among the first to advocate the use of legumes to replace the nutrients in the soil. He recommended the sweet potato and peanut. Today the sweet potato and peanut are main products of the southern economy.

Dr. Carver's achievements in science have perhaps obscured the fact that he was also a painter. His paintings were sufficiently competent to merit recognition and display in the Columbian Exposition held in Chicago in 1893.

Humble and devout before God and nature, Dr. Carver was eager to see others benefit from his work and the study of science. In 1938 he donated $30,000 of his life's savings to the establishment of the George Washington Carver Foundation. Shortly before his death, he willed the remainder of his estate to the foundation, whose purpose is to discover uses for agricultural wastes and to develop food products from common crops with the aim of creating new markets for them. The gentle, amiable and self-effacing Dr. George Washington Carver died in 1943 and was buried next to Booker T. Washington, the great African American educator.

The United States Postal Service was the first to recognize Dr. George Washington Carver on a U.S. stamp in 1948. Other nations have also honored him on their postage stamps.

1/5/47. United States. 122,362,000. 3 cents. S#953. *Illus. 128.*

12/7/64. Ghana. Quantity unknown. 6 shillings. S#189. *Illus. 129.*

12/7/64. Ghana. Quantity unknown. Face value unknown. S#190. *Illus. 130.*

12/7/64. Ghana. Quantity unknown. Face value unknown. S#191a. (Imperforate souvenir sheet.) This souvenir sheet was issued for "UNESCO Week 1964." It honors Albert Einstein and George Washington Carver for their contributions to science. Stamps S#189 and S#190 appear on the sheet. *Illus. 131.*

5/3/82. Turks and Caicos Islands. Quantity unknown. 65 cents. S#524. Commemorates the 100th anniversary of the birth of Franklin Delano Roosevelt. Shows FDR meeting George Washington Carver. *Illus. 132.*

7/27/82. Grenada and the Grenadines. Quantity unknown. 40 cents. S#8221. Commemorates the 100th anniversary of the birth of Franklin Delano Roosevelt. Shows FDR meeting George Washington Carver. *Illus. 133.*

11/18/85. Antigua and Barbuda. Quantity unknown. 1 dollar. S#902. This stamp was part of a perforated souvenir sheet ($3.75/$3.75). It commemorates the 40th anniversary of the U.N. and shows a portrait of Carver. This stamp is hard to find; it is shown here (separated from the souvenir sheet) only as a copy. *Illus. 134.*

1998. United States. Quantity unknown. 32 cents. S#3183. *Illus. 135.*

Chamberlain, Wilt

Wilton Chamberlain, known as Wilt, was born in Philadelphia, Pennsylvania, in 1936. He was an American professional basketball player. He played for the Warriors in Philadelphia and San Francisco until he was traded in 1965 to the Philadelphia 76ers.

The 7-ft, $\frac{1}{16}$-in Chamberlain became a dominant figure in professional basketball. He won the NBA scoring title for seven consecutive years, and in 1962 he scored a record 100 points in one game while averaging 50.4 points per game for the season. In 1968 he was traded to the Los Angeles Lakers. In 1973 he joined the San Diego Conquistadors but was prevented from playing by a contractual dispute. He retired in 1974 and was elected to the Basketball Hall of Fame in 1978.

Chamberlain was recognized on an international stamp during his lifetime. He is still the only man who shot 100 points in one game. Wilt Chamberlain was found dead in his home in California on October 12, 1999, from heart failure.

7/26/93. Guyana. Quantity unknown. 50 dollars. S#2676h. From a famous people (sports) souvenir sheet (perforated). *Illus. 136.*

Charles, Ray

The great musician Ray Charles was born Ray Charles Robinson in 1932 in Albany, Georgia. Ray Charles lost his sight as a child and studied at the Saint Augustine, Florida, School for the Blind. He left school at the age of 15. He had his own trio and soon developed a personal rhythm-and-blues style with roots from gospel music, country blues, and elements of jazz.

Ray's singing and piano playing are admired by both jazz and rock enthusiasts, as well as urban blues audiences. Ray Charles influenced the development of popular soul music and can be seen as a direct link between modern blues styles and early country blues traditions. He has won numerous Grammy awards, including the Grammy Lifetime Achievement Award (1987). *Brother Ray* (1978) is his autobiography.

Ray Charles's musical style, pleasing and down to earth, has made him welcome the world over.

1994. Grenada and the Grenadines. Quantity unknown. 90 cents. *Illus. 137.*

Checker, Chubby

Musician Chubby Checker was born Ernest Evans on October 3, 1941, in Philadelphia, Pennsylvania. He recorded his first hit song in June of 1959. The record was titled "The Class" and it made the Top 40 hit list. Checker's songs included imitations of other great artists such as Fats Domino, the Coasters, and Elvis Presley. Checker recorded his number one hit "The

Twist" in 1960. It remained number one for fifteen weeks and inspired a major dance craze. He again topped the charts in January of 1961 with "The Pony" and November of 1961 with a reissue of "The Twist."

Between 1959 and 1965 Chubby Checker continued to release a hit every two months. He has a credit of twenty-two top 40 hits. Chubby and his band continue to delight audiences around the world at festivals, theaters, and arenas. They are even booked regularly at corporate events.

1996. Liberia. Quantity unknown. 35 cents. S#1232f. (Not pictured.) See Jimi Hendrix, S#1232h, for more comments about this issue.

Cheeseman, Joseph James

Not much is known about Joseph James Cheeseman's life in the United States or about his term as president of Liberia (1892–1896). However, it is known that he was born in the United States of America either in Maryland or Virginia, and he was one of the ruling elite in Liberia. Liberian society and political structure was arranged in layers. The most powerful were "Americo-Liberians," who were of mixed African and European ancestry. They were lighter skinned than the indigenous native blacks. The Americo-Liberians sent their children to America for high school and college. While this ruling elite prospered, they failed to include native Liberians in their power base. In fact, they took the natives' land, taxed them, and controlled their trade.

Ethnic struggles with Kru, Gola, and Grebo tribes, who resented the invasion of their land, occurred several times during Cheeseman's term. One notable uprising occurred in 1893 when the Grebo tribe attacked the settlement of Harper. Troops and the gunboat *Gorronomah* were sent to defeat the tribesmen. President Cheeseman died in office.

134

135

136

137

138

139

140

141

142

143

144

145

146

147

1948–50. Liberia. Quantity unknown. 9 cents. S#321. *Illus. 138.*

Clemente, Roberto

Roberto Clemente was born in Carolina, Puerto Rico, on August 10, 1934. He enjoyed a phenomenal baseball career with the Pittsburgh Pirates. While with the Pirates, Clemente won four National League batting titles. He was the league's Most Valuable Player in 1966 and was selected to the All Star Team twelve times. He also won twelve Golden Glove Awards as the National League's premiere right fielder. Despite being involved in a 1965 automobile accident that left him with chronic back pain, he continued to play. His World Series batting average helped the Pirates win two World Series championships.

Clemente was elected to the Baseball Hall of Fame after his death in an airplane crash. He had been making the trip in order to aid Nicaraguan earthquake survivors on December 31, 1972. Clemente has been recognized in the United States and internationally on stamps.

12/22/80. Turks and Caicos Islands. Quantity unknown. 45 cents. S#459. *Illus. 139.*

8/17/84. United States. 119,125,000. 20 cents. S#2097. *Illus. 140.*

10/25/84. Nicaragua. Quantity unknown. 1 dollar. S#1387. Comes in a set, Scott numbers 1384–1390 (3). *Illus. 141.*

12/1/88. Grenada. Quantity unknown. 30 cents. S#1665a. From the "U.S. Baseball Series 1." *Illus. 142.*

11/9/92. St. Vincent. Quantity unknown. 2 dollars. S#1733. (Not pictured.) Honors Roberto Clemente's induction into the Hall of Fame 1983. This stamp is not illustrated above. This is a multicolored stamp.

Cole, Nat "King"

Nat "King" Cole was born Nathaniel Adams Cole on March 17, 1919, in Montgomery, Alabama. The son of a Baptist minister, he grew up singing and playing the organ and piano in his father's church in Chicago, Illinois. He formed his own musical group at the age of sixteen. He was a musical talent on the stage, screen, radio, and television (Cole was the first African American to have his own television show). His vocal stylings and popularity gained him a command performance for Queen Elizabeth of England, and he also performed for United States presidents. His pop music hits included "Straighten Up and Fly Right," "Mona Lisa," "Unforgettable," "Nature Boy," "Too Young," and many more. He died February 15, 1965, in Santa Monica, California, at 45 years of age.

12/6/71. Mali. Quantity unknown. 130 francs. S#C137. From a series honoring famous American black musicians. These are hard to find stamp issues. Only a copy is shown here. *Illus. 143.*

9/1/72. Gabon. Quantity unknown. 40 francs. S#295. Issued in honor of black American jazz musicians. *Illus. 144.*

11/19/92. Grenada. Quantity unknown. 90 cents. S#2156g. (Not pictured.) Celebrates Nat King Cole as a gold record award winner. See Chuck Berry, S#2158a, for more information.

9/1/94. United States. 35,000,000. 29 cents. S#2852. From the legends of American Music series. Error: The Nat King Cole stamp gives 1917–1965 as his life dates. He actually lived 1919–1965. *Illus. 147.*

7/10/96. Uganda. Quantity unknown. 500 shillings. S#1418. Commemorating the 100th anniversary of wireless (radio) transmission, this stamp issue recognizes great radio entertainers. Others recognized are Ella Fitzgerald, Bob Hope, and Burns & Allen. *Illus. 146.*

7/25/96. Gambia. Quantity unknown. 5 dalasis. S#1797. This issue comes in a set of four. *Illus. 145.*

Coleman, Bessie

Bessie Coleman was born in Atlanta, Texas, on January 26, 1893. She was the 12th of 13 children. Despite having an il-

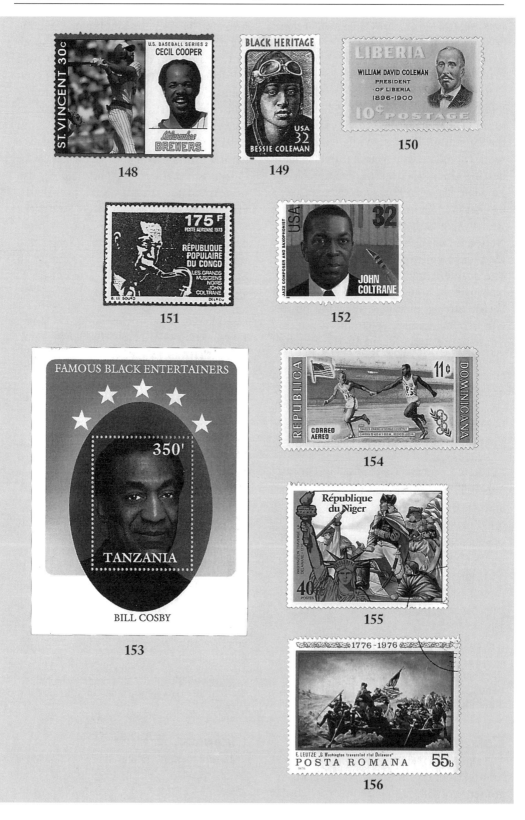

148

149

150

151

152

153

154

155

156

literate mother, Bessie Coleman managed to read by obtaining books from a traveling library wagon twice a year.

Bessie Coleman was the first female African American to receive a pilot's license. Because of both her race and sex, she had to break down many barriers to achieve her goal. Because it was harder, if not nearly impossible, for her to receive her pilot's license in the United States, Bessie Coleman had to travel overseas in order to accomplish her dreams. Through the help of Robert S. Abbott, editor and publisher of the *Chicago Weekly Defender*, she learned that she could receive her license more quickly and easily in France. She used money she earned from her manicurist's job and from a chili parlor. She learned French and made two trips to Europe. When she returned from Europe after her second trip, she returned as the World's only African American pilot.

Coleman wanted to open a flying school to teach other blacks, so she began giving flying exhibitions to raise funds. She gave lectures on aviation in movie houses and churches between her exhibitions. Her first exhibition, in 1922, was at Checkerboard Field, which is now Chicago's Midway Airport. She often refused to perform exhibitions if blacks were not permitted to use the same entrance as whites.

Bessie Coleman died performing an exhibition close to the opening date of her flying school. At the Jacksonville, Florida, Negro Welfare League on April 30, 1926, she went into a 1,500-foot nose-dive and never came out.

4/27/95. United States. Quantity unknown. 32 cents. S#2956. Part of the Black Heritage series. *Illus. 149.*

Coleman, William David

Little is known about the life of William David Coleman. However, it is known that he was an "Americo-Liberian" (see Joseph James Cheeseman, S#321, for more information on Americo-Liberians). Coleman may have been born in Virginia or Maryland. After the death in office of Liberian president Joseph James Cheeseman in 1896, William David Coleman became president of Liberia, serving out the rest of the term of President Cheeseman and another four years.

William Coleman took the office of president of Liberia with great hopes of opening up the nation's interior. He was able to establish Liberian influence in the interior northwest of the Saint Paul River. He also conducted an expedition into Gola territory. His intention was to subdue the Gola Tribe and their allies, but he was terribly defeated. The policy Coleman established was unaffected, and reports of depredations upon the natives by Coleman's commanders caused leading citizens and prominent members of the legislature to call for immediate change. Coleman resigned from office and was replaced by Garreston W. Gibson.

1948–50. Liberia. Quantity unknown. 15 cents. S#323. *Illus. 150.*

Coltrane, John

John William Coltrane was born in Hamlet, North Carolina, in 1926. He was a classic jazz saxophonist as well as composer. In fact, he is considered to be one of the greatest tenor sax players of his time and was best known for his improvisational jazz arrangements. Coltrane played with groups that were led by trumpeters such as Dizzy Gillespie and Miles Davis, and pianist Thelonious Monk, all of whom had a tremendous influence on his interesting and unique style of playing.

Coltrane's compositions include such greats as "Giant Steps," "Blue Train," A Love Supreme," and "Father, Son, and Holy Ghost." The National Academy of Recording Arts and Sciences recognized him with the Grammy lifetime achievement award.

3/5/73. Congo. Quantity unknown. 175 francs. S#C147. This is a hard stamp to find. Only a poor copy is shown here. *Illus. 151.*

9/16/95. United States. Quantity unknown. 32 cents. S#2991. *Illus. 152.*

Cooper, Cecil

Cecil Celester Cooper was born on December 20, 1949, in Brenham, Texas. He is an American baseball player (infielder). He led the American League in RBIs in 1980 and 1983. He presently plays first base for the Milwaukee Brewers.

11/30/89. St. Vincent. Quantity unknown. 30 cents. S#1267b. *Illus. 148.*

Cosby, Bill

William Henry Cosby, Jr., was one of the first African Americans to break through racial stereotypes to become a popular television entertainer. Bill Cosby was born in Philadelphia, Pennsylvania, in 1937. He was educated at Temple University and the University of Massachusetts.

Cosby's resume includes much successful work as an actor, comedian, producer, writer, and creator. He created and produced the animated series *Fat Albert and the Cosby Kids* (1972–79) and *The New Fat Albert and the Cosby Kids* (1979–84). These along with his other television specials have won numerous awards for their educational values. *The Cosby Show*, in which Cosby starred, was a family comedy featuring the life of a black doctor. The show, which was also conceived and produced by Cosby, became one of the most popular television shows of the 1980s.

3/30/90. Tanzania. Quantity unknown. 350 shillings. S#588. (Perforated souvenir sheet.) Michael Jackson and other stars were recognized in this Tanzania series with Bill Cosby. *Illus. 153.*

Courtney, Thomas

Thomas Courtney was born August 17, 1933, in Newark, New Jersey. He attended Fordham University. He won an Olympic gold medal in 1956 at the Olympics trials for 800 meters. He came in first with 1:46.4 on May 24, 1957, at a Los Angeles contest. He set a new world 880 yard record with 1:46 and took the AAU 880 yard title that year and the next.

10/3/58. Dominican Republic. Quantity unknown. 11 cents. S#C106. Commemorates the 1958 Olympics in Melbourne. This stamp shows Thomas Courtney with Charles Jenkins in the 1,600m relay. *Illus. #154.*

Cromwell, Oliver

Oliver Cromwell was born in Burlington County, New Jersey, on May 24, 1753. He joined the Second New Jersey Regiment during the Revolutionary War. He also served for six years and nine months under the immediate command of George Washington. After devoting his time to the military, he took his annual pension of ninety dollars and became a farmer. He fought in the Battle of Yorktown in 1781. He, the only black to have such an honor, crossed the Delaware River under the guidance of his commanding officer George Washington.

1976. Equatorial Guinea. Quantity unknown. 30 bipkwele. Minkus#1225. (See color section.) In recognition of the American bicentennial. Shows Washington and his men crossing the Delaware. *Illus. C58.*

1/25/76. Romania. Quantity unknown. 55 bani. S#2605. In recognition of American bicentennial. Shows Washington ad his men crossing the Delaware. *Illus. 156.*

3/3/76. Togo. Quantity unknown. 200 francs. S#273. (see color section.) Recognition of the American bicentennial. Washington crosses the Delaware River. Cromwell is rowing at the front of the boat. *Illus. C55.*

3/26/76. Liberia. Quantity unknown. 1 dollar. S#C214. (Perforated souvenir sheet.) Includes the dates "1732–1982," so probably a commemoration of the 250th anniversary of Washington's birth. A unique view of Washington and men crossing the Delaware—from the front. Most stamps showing this scene use the E. Leutze painting of 1851, which shows the boat from the side. *Illus. 157.*

4/8/76. Niger. Quantity unknown. 40 francs. S#352. In recognition of the American bicentennial. Although not very visible, Cromwell is at the helm of the boat with George Washington during the crossing of the Delaware River. *Illus. 155.*

5/6/76. Upper Volta. Quantity unknown. 200 francs. S#209. In recognition of the American bicentennial. Washington and men crossing the Delaware. *Illus. 158.*

5/27/76. United States. 2,000,000. 24 cents (each stamp). S#1688a. (Perforated souvenir sheet.) This issue is in recognition of the American bicentennial. This souvenir sheet includes 5 stamps depicting George Washington crossing the Delaware River along with his soldiers. Errors: "USA/24" omitted, Imperf—Valued at $3,500; "USA/24" omitted on "d and e" valued at $450. Cromwell is rowing at the front of the boat. *Illus. 159.*

7/4/76. Chad. Quantity unknown. 125 francs. S#Cl82. (Imperforate; see color section.) In recognition of the American bicentennial. Shows Washington and his men crossing the Delaware. *Illus. C57.*

7/4/76. Guatemala. Quantity unknown. 0.30 quetzales. S#603. (Not pictured.) In recognition of the American bicentennial. This is a multicolored stamp.

7/26/76. St. Christopher Nevis Anguilla. Quantity unknown. 1 dollar. S#327. (See color section.) In recognition of the American bicentennial. Shows Washington and his men crossing the Delaware. *Illus. C56.*

6/7/82. Lesotho. Quantity unknown. 1.25 maloti. S#371. (Perforated souvenir sheet; see color section.) Commemorates the 250th anniversary of the birth of George Washington (1732–1982). Shows Washington and his men crossing the Delaware. *Illus. C59.*

Daniels, Kal

Kal Daniels was born on August 20, 1963, in Vienna, Georgia. He played outfield for the Dodgers. Since his professional career in baseball began with the

157

158

Cincinnati Reds in 1986, he has had a batting average of more than .300 over the years. A highlight of his career came in 1988 when he led the National League in on-base percentage (.397).

8/31/89. St. Vincent. Quantity unknown. 60 cents. S#1235f. Shows Kal Daniels and Mike Marshall with the Dodgers in 1989. *Illus. 160.*

9/24/90. St. Vincent. Quantity unknown. 60 cents. S#1344d. Shows Kal Daniels and Jose Gonzalez with the Dodgers 1990. *Illus. 161.*

Davenport, Willie

Willie D. Davenport is an American track and field athlete who was born on June 18, 1943, in Troy, Alabama. He specialized in running hurdles. He attended South University in Baton Rouge, Louisiana, where he also ran track. He won the AAN outdoor title in 1964, 1965, and 1966. He tied for first place in 1969. He won the gold medal in the 110 m high hurdles at the 1968 Summer Olympics, and received a silver medal at the 1976 Summer

Olympics. He is also one of the first African Americans to participate in a Winter Olympics as member of a four-man bobsled team. He has also served as a youth director for the city of Baton Rouge, Louisiana.

9/25/68. Umm Al Qiwain. Quantity unknown. 2 riyals. *Illus. 162.* Al Qiwain also issued other stamps recognizing Davenport: 9/25/68 Minkus#186, face value 5 riyals; Minkus#187, souvenir sheet; 2/7/69, Minkus#259, face value 2 riyals (overprint); Minkus#263, face value 5 riyals (overprint). These stamps are not pictured in this book.

10/1/68. Fujeira. Quantity unknown. 2 riyals. Minkus#184. *Illus. 163.*

3/8/69. Fujeira. Quantity unknown. 2 riyals. Minkus#256. (Not pictured.)

6/30/69. Chad. Quantity unknown. 1 franc. S#201. Commemorates Davenport's 1968 win at the Olympics in Mexico. *Illus. 164.*

6/30/69. Chad. Quantity unknown. 1 franc. S#201. (overprint). This stamp is the same as S#201, but it is overprinted with the words "Munich 1972." *Illus. 165.*

7/30/96. Lesotho. Quantity unknown. Face value unknown. S#1052g. (Not pictured.) This stamp, part of a set issued in recognition of past Olympic medalists, commemorates Davenport's 110-meter hurdles win in 1968.

7/30/96. Lesotho. Quantity unknown. Face value unknown. S#1052h. (Not pictured.) This stamp, part of a set issued in recognition of past Olympic medalists, commemorates Davenport's long jump win in 1968.

Davis, Allison

Dr. Allison Davis was born in 1902. He was considered a great psychologist and educator. He was the first African American to teach at the University of Chicago. There he became the first Dewey Distinguished Service Professor of Education. Interestingly enough he was one of the first who questioned the accuracy of the IQ test, particularly as it related to individuals from low social economic backgrounds and other ethnic minority groups in America.

2/1/94. United States. 156,000,000. 29 cents. S#2816. Part of the Black Heritage series. *Illus. 166.*

Davis, Alvin

Alvin Davis was born in Riverside, California, on September 9, 1960. He was a professional baseball player for the Seattle Mariners. He led the Mariners in almost every offensive category.

11/28/88. Grenada. Quantity unknown. 60 cents. S#1665f. This stamp also comes in a sheet of 9 (1665-a-i). *Illus. 167.*

Davis, Benjamin

Benjamin O. Davis was born in 1877. General Davis began his career in the military in 1898. He was promoted to the rank of first lieutenant in the Ninth United States Volunteers shortly after he graduated from Howard University. By 1901 he had moved up to the rank of second lieutenant in the cavalry. Benjamin O. Davis remained a colonel for ten years until the pressures of World War II forced his promotion to brigadier general. After 1940, Brigadier General Davis served as a special advisor and coordinator of operations. After fifty years of outstanding service to his country, he retired in 1948. General Davis could count among his military decorations medals for service in the Philippines, the Spanish-American War, and along the Mexican Border; he could point to service medals of two world wars, including the Bronze Star, the French Croix de Guerre with Palm, and the Distinguished Service Medal. Davis died in 1970. America took pride in recognizing General Davis as one of its great war veterans on a stamp in 1997.

2/28/97. United States. 112,000,000. 32 cents. S#3121. (See color section.) Part of the Black Heritage series. *Illus. C60.*

Davis, Eric Keith

Eric Keith Davis was born May 29, 1962, in Los Angeles, California. His hometown is Woodland Hills, California. A noted baseball player, he was an outfielder for the Cincinnati Reds. He was one of several African Americans in the starting line-up of the 1987 All-Star Game. His career highlights include becoming the second player in history to hit twenty home runs and steal eighty bases in 1986. In 1984 he hit home runs in four consecutive

Washington Crossing the Delaware
From a Painting by Emanuel Leutze / Eastman Johnson

159

games. He holds the National League record with three grand slams in one month. Eric was National League All Star and Gold Glove Winner in 1987.

11/2/87. Grenada. Quantity unknown. 1 dollar. S#1552b. (Perforated souvenir sheet.) This stamp comes in a souvenir sheet. The gentleman to the left of Eric Davis is Wade Boggs. You will also find on the souvenir issue two plaques with the names of Rickey Henderson, Dave Winfield, Don Mattingly, Cal Ripkin, Wade Boggs, Terry Kennedy, George Bell, Willie Randolph, Bret Saberhagen, Eric Davis, Jack Clark, Ryne Sandberg, Darryl Strawberry, Andre Dawson, Gary Carter, Mike Schmidt, Ozzie Smith and Mike Scott. This souvenir sheet is part of the "U.S. Baseball Series 1." *Illus. 168.*

11/28/88. Grenada. Quantity unknown. 30 cents. S#1672e. Part of the "U.S. Baseball Series 1." *Illus. 169*

Davis, John

John Davis was born January 12, 1921. He was a professional weightlifter. He was a 1948 and 1952 Olympic gold medalist. He set new world records each time. He was the first to win this weight class and the

only American to win it twice during his time. He secured the world championship light heavyweight for fifteen years. His other careers included that of a garageman, correctional officer, and opera singer. Davis retired from the New York City Department of Corrections after many years of service. John Henry Davis, Jr., the man who was known as the "strongest man in the world," died on July 13, 1984.

5/25/72. Equatorial Guinea. Quantity unknown. 2 pesetas guineanas. Minkus #620. Not an easily found stamp. Commemorates Davis's Olympic wins in 1948 and 1952. *Illus. 170.*

Davis, Mike

Mike Davis was born on June 6, 1959, in San Diego, California. He considers his hometown San Ramon, California. He plays outfield for the Los Angeles Dodgers. His professional record before the 1988 All Star Break was: batting average .197, home runs 1, and RBI 11; his record after was: batting .194, home runs 1, RBI 6.

8/21/89. St. Vincent. Quantity unknown. 60

160

161

162

163

164

165

166

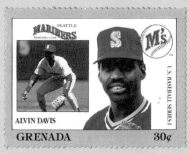

167

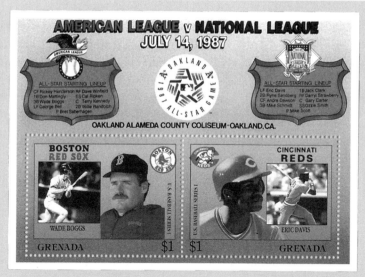

168

169

170

171

172

cents. S#1234b. Mike Davis and Kirk Gibson with the Dodgers, 1989. *Illus. 171.*

Davis, Miles

Miles Dewey Davis was born in 1926 in Alton, Illinois. A jazz trumpet player and composer, Davis was a Grammy award winner who is credited with the birth of the "cool" school of jazz. *Birth of the Cool* and *Sketches in Spain"* are among some of his best known albums. Davis played with such greats as Dizzy Gillespie, Charlie Parker, and Coleman Hawkins. In 1948 he developed a short-lived yet influential nine-piece band. The creation produced albums such as *Sketches of Spain*, *Porgy and Bess*, and *Miles Ahead*. In 1958 Davis released his album *Kind of Blue*. It was one of the first attempts to base jazz on modal rather than harmonic progression. He sparked controversy through his use of electronic instruments to produce a sound heavily influenced by rock music. Miles Davis died on September 28, 1991.

3/5/73. Congo. Quantity unknown. 125 francs. S#C144. This stamp and the other 3 from this issue are virtually impossible to find. All 4 stamps in the sheet honored musicians. Only a poor quality copy of the Miles Davis stamp is shown here. *Illus. 172.*

Davis, Sammy, Jr.

Sammy Davis, Jr., was born in December 8, 1925, in New York City, New York. He was an American actor, singer, and dancer. In fact, Sammy was considered the greatest one-man show on earth.

Sammy began his career in show business at the age of three, when he performed with the Will Mastin Trio. Despite his talented attributes, he still had to deal with racial barriers. He was drafted into World War II at the age of eighteen and displayed his talent by entertaining the troops even when racial insults and physical attacks were openly made. He began his solo recording career and performed on TV va-

riety shows after he returned from the war. He lost an eye in a near-fatal auto crash. This didn't stop his career. Two years later, sporting a glass eye, Davis won rave reviews in the semi-autobiographical Broadway musical *Mr. Wonderful* and made his film debut in *The Benny Goodman Story*. He acted in other popular plays such as *Golden Boy* (1964) and *Stop the World I Want to Get Off* (1978).

In the film industry Sammy Davis was most recognized for his portrayal of Sportin' Life in *Porgy and Bess* (1959) and his close association with the Frank Sinatra–led "Rat Pack." Some of Davis's most memorable signature recordings are "What Kind of Fool Am I," "Candy Man," and "Mr. Bojangles."

After a battle with liver disease, recovering from hip degeneration and addictions to alcohol and cocaine, Sammy died of throat cancer at age 64 on May 16, 1990. A recent TV movie, *The Rat Pack* (1998), provided a look at the life of Sammy Davis, Jr. He has been recognized on several international stamps for his contributions to world entertainment.

3/30/90. Tanzania. Quantity unknown. 200 shillings. S#586. (See color section.) *Illus. C61.*

2/15/92. Tanzania. Quantity unknown. 75 shillings. S#811b. (See color section.) Issued in a sheet of 9. *Illus. C62.*

Dawson, Andre

Andre Nolan Dawson is an American baseball player. He was born on July 7, 1954, in Miami, Florida. He was the 1976 National League Rookie of the year. In 1977 he led the National League in home runs and RBIs. He also won the Most Valuable Player Award in 1987 — an extraordinary feat for a player from a last-place baseball club.

11/22/88. Grenada. Quantity unknown. 30 cents. S#1671e. (See color section.) See Eric Davis, S#1552b (souvenir sheet), for further recognition of Andre Dawson. His name is shown on the stamp. *Illus. C63.*

Dee, Ruby

Ruby Dee was born in Cleveland, Ohio, on October 27, 1924. However, she grew up in Harlem, New York, and attended school there. In 1965, Ruby Dee became the first black actress to appear in major roles at the American Shakespeare Festival in Stratford, Connecticut. Her movie roles included *No Way Out* (1950), *Edge of the City* (1957), *Raisin in the Sun* (1963), *Purlie Victorious* (1963), and others. She is credited with helping many African Americans get their first breaks in Hollywood and on television. She is married to actor Ossie Davis.

3/25/93. The Gambia. Quantity unknown. 3 dalasis. S#1348h. (Not pictured.) This stamp is part of a series in recognition of American movies and stars.

Devers, Gail

A stamp is said to exist on Gail Devers, an African American track and field athlete, but no information on such a stamp is available.

Dillard, Harrison W.

Harrison W. Dillard was born July 8, 1923, in Cleveland, Ohio. He was an American track and field athlete. He won two gold medals each at the 1948 and 1952 Summer Olympics. He graduated from Baldwin-Wallace College in Berea, Ohio. It was in college that he became a specialist high hurdler. There were no doubts that he was the best high hurdler in the immediate postwar years. Track enthusiasts called him the best combination sprinter-hurdler who ever lived.

8/12/91. Guyana. Quantity unknown. 25 dollars. S#2393g. (Perforated Souvenir sheet; see color section.) This stamp is a part of a souvenir sheet of 8. The stamp commemorates Dillard's 1948 100 m win. *Illus. C64.*

Domino, Fats

Fats Domino sold more than 65 million records between 1950 and 1963. A pianist, singer, and composer, he had an easy-rolling boogie woogie style of music.

Antoine "Fats" Domino, Jr., was born in New Orleans on February 28, 1928. He was born into a musical family. He began performing for small change in local honky-tonks while working odd jobs to make a living. In 1949 he met Dave Bartholomew, who became his longtime producer, bandleader, and collaborator. This relationship resulted in a string of New Orleans rhythm and blues records. Between 1950 and 1963, he cracked the pop Top Forty thirty-seven times and the R&B singles charts fifty-nine times. Domino's biggest songs include "Ain't That a Shame," "Blueberry Hill," "I'm Walkin,'" "Blue Monday," and "Walking to New Orleans."

1996. Liberia. Quantity unknown. 35 cents. S#1232d. (Not pictured.) See Jimi Hendrix, S#1232h, for more comments on this issue.

Dorn, Michael

A stamp of actor Michael Dorn, known for his role as Lieutenant Worf in the popular television series *Star Trek: The Next Generation*, is said to exist, but no such stamp is available at the present time.

Douglass, Frederick

Frederick Douglass was officially born as Frederick Augustus Washington Bailey on February 7, 1817, in Tuckahoe, Maryland. The son of a slave mother, he never knew who his father was. In 1838 he fled slavery, escaping first to New York City and then to New Bedford, Massachusetts. He changed his name to Frederick Douglass out of fear of being identified by his former master. He went on to become an abolitionist, speaking for the Massachusetts Anti-Slavery Society.

Because he had illegally learned to read and write while a slave, he was able to establish the first abolitionist newspaper to be owned by an African American. The name of the paper was *The North Star*. The paper denounced slavery and prejudice against African-Americans during the 19th century.

Frederick Douglass had a remarkable life and career. He was an ex-slave, abolitionist, orator, politician, newspaper publisher, author, lecturer, diplomat, civil rights activist, and a promoter of women's rights. He relocated to Washington, D.C., and held government offices. He was a United States marshal, a police commissioner, and a recorder of deeds, and he represented the United States abroad as Minister to Haiti.

Sixty years after Douglass's death, the house in which he lived was designated a national shrine by the National Park Service. Most recently, a bridge was named in his honor. He has also been recognized on U.S. postage stamps since 1967.

2/14/67. United States. Quantity unknown. 25 cents. S#1290. (See color section.) *Illus. C65.*

6/29/95. United States. Quantity unknown. 32 cents. S#2975h. (See color section.) From an issue recognizing figures of the Civil War. *Illus. C66.*

1998. Senegal. Quantity unknown. 40 francs. S#1215. (Not pictured.) This stamp features a portrait of Douglass.

Dove, Rita

Rita Dove is an African American writer. She, along with other African Americans, was recognized as one of the greatest writers of the twentieth century. Dove was born in Akron, Ohio, in 1952. She graduated from Miami University (Ohio) in 1973 and from the Writers' Workshop at the University of Iowa in 1977. She taught at Arizona State for nearly ten years, and later joined the faculty of the University of Virginia in the English department. Dove is the author of several books, including *Yellow House on the Corner* (1980), *Museum* (1983), *Thomas and Beulah* (1986),

Grace Notes (1989) and others. Most of Dove's poetic writings concentrate on showing the beauty and importance of everyday life. Dove also had the joyous opportunity of serving as poet laureate of the United States from 1993 through 1995 (the first African American to serve in this capacity.)

Date issued unknown. Ghana. Quantity unknown. 300 cedis. S#1549a. (Not pictured.) This stamp features a portrait of Rita Dove.

Drew, Charles

Charles Richard Drew was born in Washington, D.C., on June 3, 1904. He was a student and athlete at Dunbar High School in Washington. He excelled in academics as well as in football, basketball, swimming, and track and field. He also excelled in sports and academics at Amherst College in Amherst, Massachusetts. His greatest desire was to become a medical doctor to help and inspire other African Americans to do the same. He attended McGill University Medical School in Montreal, Canada. He received his master of surgery and doctor of medicine degrees. He became a member of the Medical Society and won the Williams prize. Dr. Drew studied at Physicians and Surgeons Hospitals in New York City. He went on to become an instructor of biology and chemistry as well as the athletic director at Morgan State College in Baltimore, Maryland.

Charles Drew's most outstanding contribution was the development of efficient ways to preserve and store blood plasma, leading to the creation of blood banks. These discoveries grew from Drew's doctoral research at Columbia University Presbyterian Hospital in New York City.

Dr. Drew was one of the world's greatest medical scientists. He won the National Association for the Advancement of Colored People's Spingarn Medal for recognition of his contribution to African American progress.

6/3/81. United States. Quantity unknown. 35 cents. S#1865. (See color section.) From the Great Americans issue. *Illus. C67.*

Drexler, Clyde

Clyde Drexler was born on June 22, 1962, in New Orleans, Louisiana. In 1983 the Portland Trail Blazers selected him as a professional basketball player in the first round of their draft. He was traded from Portland to the Houston Rockets on February 14, 1995. He was a member of the 1992 American Basketball "Dream Team" that won a gold medal during the 1992 Olympic Summer Games.

12/22/92. St. Vincent. Quantity unknown. 2 dollars. S#1745e. (See color section.) Honors Drexler as an Olympic gold medalist — a member of the United States basketball team in 1992. *Illus. C68.*

Du Bois, W.E.B.

William Edward Burghardt Du Bois was born February 23, 1868, in Great Barrington, Massachusetts. He attended the public schools of the commonwealth of Massachusetts from the age of five years old. He graduated from high school at the age of sixteen. He received an undergraduate degree from Fisk University in Nashville, Tennessee. He also received a degree in philosophy from Harvard University and went on to earn a Ph.D. in philosophy from Harvard University in 1896. He was highly recognized as an educator, philosopher, and the African American most noted for changes in the attitudes of black people in America. He was an advocate of Pan-Africanism, a founding figure of the National Association for the Advancement of Colored People, and editor of the NAACP newspaper *Crisis.* After increasing problems in America because of his strong beliefs and his alignment with the Communist Party, he renounced his American citizenship and lived out the rest of his life in Ghana. He died on August 27, 1963, in Ghana, and he is buried there. Dubois has received recognition on stamps in the U.S. and abroad.

9/25/69. Cameroon. Quantity unknown. 30 francs. S#128. (See color section.) Hard to find issue. *Illus. C69.*

1/31/92. United States. 150,000,000. 29 cents. S#2617. (See color section.) Part of the Black Heritage series. *Illus. C70.*

1/3/98. United States. Quantity unknown. 32 cents. S#1312. (See color section.) Part of the "Celebrate the Century" series (1900s). Recognizes W.E.B. Du Bois as a social activist. *Illus. C71.*

Dunbar, Paul Laurence

Paul Laurence Dunbar was born June 27, 1872, in Dayton, Ohio. He was a writer of African American poetry. He was noted for his ability to capture the dialect of African Americans. He composed the school song for his high school when he graduated in 1891. His poems were first published in 1895. Until then, he earned his living as an elevator operator and spent his leisure time writing poetry. He was often invited to do readings. In 1897 he was asked to do a reading in England. When he returned, he served as an assistant at the Library of Congress for over a year. He wrote several novels, but they were not as popular as his poems.

Paul Laurence Dunbar died February 9, 1906, in Dayton, Ohio. He was honored on a U.S. postage stamp in 1975.

5/1/75. United States. 146,365,000. 10 cents. S#1554. (See color section.) American Arts issue. *Illus. C72.*

Du Sable, Jean Baptiste Pointe

Jean Baptiste Pointe Du Sable was born free in 1745 at Saint Marc, Haiti. Du Sable is given credit as founder of the second largest city in America today, Chicago, Illinois. He was an immigrant, sailor, explorer, hunter, trader, and entrepreneur. He was the only child born to Pointe De Sable, a pirate and merchant, and Suzanne Du Sable, an ex-slave.

Du Sable was married to Kittihawa, a Potawatomi Indian. She bore him two children, and there was also a granddaughter. Jean Baptiste, the Frenchman, was formally educated at Saint Thomas, a school for boys at Saint Cloud, France. When he completed his education, his father made him a partner in his business in Saint Croix, Haiti. After his father's death, Baptiste established trade with a business in New Orleans, Louisiana, but after a shipwreck and loss of his possessions en route he stayed on in America to capitalize on the many opportunities after being assisted by a Jesuit priest.

With the signing of the Treaty of Paris, New Orleans came under the rule of the Spaniards. Baptiste vowed that he would not live under Spanish rule. His fear was being recognized as a Negro and possibly enslaved. With that in mind, he moved further north to St. Louis, Missouri, which was still under French control. Here he established himself as a merchant and became friends with the Native Americans.

During his travels in the Great Lakes region, he recognized the commercial potential of establishing a trading post on the north bank of the Chicago River. Thus he founded, in 1774, the city of Chicago.

This immigrant of French and African descent, believed by many early American settlers to be a Potawatomi chief, was laid to rest in Saint Charles, Missouri, on March 28, 1818, in his 73rd year on earth. Du Sable has been honored on several international stamps.

8/27/59. Haiti. Quantity unknown. 25 centimes. S#448. (See color section.) Du Sable's house is shown in the foreground in a dark brown, with the Chicago skyline in the background rendered in blue. *Illus. C73.*

8/27/59. Haiti. Quantity unknown. 50 centimes. S#449. Shows Du Sable against a background map of American Midwest. Borders and picture of Du Sable are a dark red-orange; map is blue-green. *Illus. 173.*

8/27/59. Haiti. Quantity unknown. 75 centimes. S#450. Same as S#449 except for face value color: Du Sable portrait and borders are brown, while the map is blue. *Illus. 174.*

8/27/59. Haiti. Quantity unknown. 1 gourde. S#451. Same as S#448 for exception of face value and color: The Du Sable house is blue-green, while the Chicago skyline is rendered in purple. *Illus. 175.*

8/27/59. Haiti. Quantity unknown. 25 centimes plus 75 centimes surcharge. S#Cl45 (Overprint). Same as S#448, with overprint: "Pour le Sport." Difficult to find. Only a poor copy is shown here. *Illus. 176.*

8/27/59. Haiti. S#C146. (Overprint.) Quantity unknown. 50 centimes plus 75 centimes surcharge. Same as S#449, with overprint: "Pour le Sport." Difficult to find. Only a poor copy is shown here. *Illus. 177.*

8/27/59. Haiti. Quantity unknown. 75 centimes plus 75 centimes surcharge. S#147. (Overprint). Same as S#450, with overprint: "Pour le Sport." Difficult to find. Only a poor copy is shown here. *Illus. 178.*

8/27/59. Haiti. Quantity unknown. 1 gourde plus 75 centimes surcharge. S#C148. (Overprint.) Same as S#451, with overprint: "Pour le Sport." Difficult to find. Only a poor copy is shown here. *Illus. 179.*

2/29/60. Haiti. Quantity unknown. 50 centimes. S#C149. (Overprint.) Hard to find issue. Same as S#449, with overprint for the 1960 Olympic Winter Games in Squaw Valley, California. *Illus. 180.*

2/29/60. Haiti. Quantity unknown. 1 gourde. S#C150. (Overprint.) Hard to find issue. Same as S#451, with overprint for the 1960 Olympic Winter Games in Squaw Valley, California. *Illus. 181.*

2/20/87. United States. Quantity 143,000,000. 22 cents. S#2249. From the Black Heritage series. *Illus. 182.*

Ellington, Duke

Composer, pianist, and bandleader Edward Kennedy Ellington was born on April 29, 1899, in Washington, D.C. He earned

173

174

175

176

177

178

179

180

181

182

183

184

185

his nickname, "Duke," for his somewhat flashy clothes. Even though he began formal piano lessons before he was ten years old, he actually taught himself to play on the family piano. He attended Armstrong High School in Washington, D.C., where he developed a skill for painting and drawing. He dropped out of high school in his senior year. He abandoned a sign painting business that he had created in order to pursue a career in music.

Ellington formed a dance band, Duke's Serenaders, after taking private lessons in composition and harmony. The name of the band was later changed to the Washingtonians.

It wasn't until Ellington moved to New York City that his musical growth and individuality emerged. He and his band became internationally famous through nightclub appearances, recordings, and radio broadcasts. He composed over two thousand separate works for religion, motion pictures, television, plays, musical comedies, ballets, and opera. He was given the nation's highest civilian honor, the Presidential Medal of Freedom, on his 70th birthday. Some of his most popular tunes are "Take the 'A' Train," "Satin Doll," "Sophisticated Lady," "Mood Indigo," "Black Brown," and "Don't Get Around Much Anymore."

Edward Kennedy "Duke" Ellington, African America's most prolific composer of modern jazz, ended his fifty-year contribution to jazz history on May 24, 1974, when he died in New York City at the age of 75.

4/15/67. Togo. Quantity unknown. 15 francs. S#601. Hard to find issue. Commemorates the twentieth anniversary of UNESCO. *Illus. 185.*

4/15/67. Togo. Quantity unknown. 30 francs. S#603. Hard to find. Same artwork as S#601. *Illus. 183.*

10/20/71. Chad. Quantity unknown. 75 francs. S#C90. A difficult stamp to find. *Illus. 184.*

2/27/84. Mali. Quantity unknown. 500 francs.

S#492. (See color section.) Hard to find issue. *Illus. C74.*

4/29/86. United States. 130,000,000. 22 cents. S#2211.(See color section.) *Illus. C75.*

4/3/89. St. Vincent. Quantity unknown. 4 dollars. S#1149. (See color section.) From a sheet of 8 (S#1142–S#1149). *Illus. C76.*

10/12/98. The Gambia. Quantity unknown. 4 dalasis. S#2049c. (Not pictured.) This stamp shows Duke Ellington conducting his band. See Louis Armstrong, S#2049e for more comments. The stamp is done in litho ink.

10/12/98. The Gambia. Quantity unknown. 4 dalasis. S#4049d. It is done in litho ink. See Louis Armstrong, S#4049e, for more comments.

Emancipation

The Emancipation Proclamation is considered one of the most important decrees ever passed in America. It was of significance because it "freed" African Americans who had been enslaved for nearly 250 years. African Americans still have more than 100 years of freedom to go to equal the time they spent enslaved.

In his *Black American Stamp Album,* Ernest Austin writes that a careful examination of Lincoln's Emancipation Proclamation shows that the proclamation had little to do with the freeing of slaves in America. Lincoln's chief interest was preserving the Union, and he was prepared to take whatever action was necessary—including *not* freeing the slaves, or freeing *some*—to achieve that goal. In 1861 and 1862, he nullified proclamations by two Union generals to free slaves in Missouri and Georgia. In 1862, after having written the Emancipation Proclamation but before delivering it, he urged blacks to emigrate to Africa or Central America. The Emancipation Proclamation was written to gain support of England and France, both of which had already abolished slavery, against the Confederate states. In the Emancipation Proclamation, Lincoln decreed that "all slaves in areas still in rebellion…" were forever free. Therefore, slaves outside the areas of rebellion were not freed, and since the Confederate States of America was a hostile foreign nation at the time, the proclamation was meaningless.

Slavery was abolished only when Congress adopted the 13th Amendment to the Constitution of the United States, seven months after the end of the Civil War, eight months after Lincoln was assassinated, and three years after the Emancipation Proclamation was presented.

Nevertheless, many countries have taken the energy to carefully recognize the Emancipation Proclamation. The adoption of the Thirteenth Amendment has also been commemorated.

Issue date unknown. Honduras. Quantity unknown. 5 cents. S#C298. (Overprint; see color section.) *Illus. C80.* Same artwork as S#292. Overprinted with "In Memoriam, John F. Kennedy, 22 Noviembre [November] 1963."

10/20/40. United States. 44,389,550. 3 cents. S#902. (See color section.) Commemorates the seventy-fifth anniversary of the Thirteenth Amendment. *Illus. C77.*

1959. Honduras. Quantity unknown. 5 cents. S#C292. (Overprint; see color section.) *Illus. C81.*

1959. Honduras. Quantity unknown. 5 cents. S#298. (See color section.) *Illus. C82.*

2/12/59. Honduras. Quantity unknown. 1 Cent. S#C292. (See color section.) Commemorates the 150th anniversary of Lincoln's birth. Depicts the signing of the Emancipation Proclamation. *Illus. C79.*

1960. Liberia. Quantity unknown. 5 cents. S#422. *Illus. 186.*

8/16/63. United States. 132,435,000. 5 cents. S#1233. (See color section.) Commemorates the America celebration of the 100th anniversary of the Emancipation Proclamation. *Illus. C78.*

10/63. Togo. Quantity unknown. 1 franc. S#455. (See color section.) Commemorates the 100th anniversary of Emancipation in the United States. *Illus. C84.*

10/63. Togo. Quantity unknown. 25 francs. S#456. (See color section.) *Illus. C86.*

10/63. Togo. Quantity unknown. 50 francs. S#554. (See color section.) *Illus. C88.*

10/63. Togo. Quantity unknown. 100 francs. S#C35. (See color section.) *Illus. C90.*

2/64. Togo. Quantity unknown. 50 francs. S#473. (Overprint; see color section.). Overprinted with "En Mémoire de John F. Kennedy 1917–1963." *Illus. C89.*

2/64. Togo. Quantity unknown. 1 franc. S#474. (Overprint; see color section.) Same artwork as S#455, overprinted with "En Mémoire de John F. Kennedy 1917–1963." *Illus. C85.*

2/64. Togo. Quantity unknown. 25 francs. S#475. (Overprint; see color section.) *Illus. C87.*

2/64. Togo. Quantity unknown. 100 francs. S#C41. (Overprint; see color section.). Overprinted with "En Mémoire de John F. Kennedy 1917–1963." *Illus. C91.*

5/64. Honduras. Quantity unknown. 5 cents. C0106. (Overprint; see color section.) *Illus. C83.*

1976. Seychelles. Quantity unknown. 5 cents. S#374. (See color section.) Depicts the signing of the Emancipation Proclamation. *Illus. C92.*

Evans, Mari

A stamp is said to exist on the African American poet Mari Evans, but no information on such a stamp is available.

Ewing, Patrick

Patrick Ewing was born in Kingston, Jamaica, on August 5, 1962, and came to America with his parents when he was eleven years of age. After high school he attended Georgetown University in Washington, D.C., and was coached under the great John Thomas who became the first black coach to win the NCAA Division I Championship. Georgetown's championship win over the University of Houston, 84–75, was in many ways attributable to the skills of Ewing.

Ewing was selected by the New York Knicks in the first round (first pick overall) of the 1985 NBA draft. Ewing has had a distinguished career but has never been on a team winning the NBA Champi-

187

188

186

189

190

191

192

193

194

195

196

197

onship. He was also a member of the 1992 Olympic "Dream Team." That year (1992) he won a gold medal as a team member and was recognized for that reason on a stamp.

12/22/92. St. Vincent. Quantity unknown. 2 dollars. S#1745f. Celebrates the U.S. Olympic "Dream Team," 1992. *Illus. 187.*

Fitzgerald, Ella

Ella Fitzgerald was born in 1918 in Newport News, Virginia. She was a well-known jazz singer who was known as "The First Lady of Song." She gained international recognition in 1938 for her recording of "A-Tisket, A-Tasket," which she co-wrote. She recorded over 250 albums and was the recipient of numerous music awards, including a Grammy in 1962 as the best Female Vocalist. One of her best known songs is "How High the Moon." According to Ernest Austin's *Black American Stamp Album*, one myth about Ella should be put to rest, namely that she won an amateur talent contest at the Apollo Theater in Harlem, New York. According to Austin, "she entered such a contest, but was 'gonged' off the stage. However, Benny Carter, a jazz saxophonist, was in the audience and was so impressed with her potential that he introduced her to bandleader Chick Webb, who took her under his wings. The rest is history."

3/5/73. Congo. Quantity unknown. 140 francs. S#145. This is a hard to find stamp. Only a poor copy is shown here. *Illus. 188.*

2/12/92. The Gambia. Quantity unknown. 2 dalasis. S#1185. This "History of the Blues" stamp is in recognition of American jazz and blues singers. *Illus. 189.*

1994. Mali. Quantity unknown. 200 francs. S#621. (Not pictured.) This stamp features a colorful portrait of Ella Fitzgerald. The stamp is Mali's recognition of Ella's contributions to music.

7/10/96. Uganda. Quantity unknown. 200 shillings. S#1416. This stamp commemorates the 100th anniversary of wireless transmission. A similar stamp was issued for Nat King Cole (S#1418). *Illus. 190.*

10/12/98. The Gambia. Quantity unknown. 25 dalasis. S#2051. (Not pictured.) See Louis Armstrong, S#2049e, for more information.

Fletcher, Simon

A stamp is said to exist on Simon Fletcher, an African American professional football star, but no information on such a stamp is available.

Foreman, George

George Edward Foreman, Sr., was born on January 10, 1949, in Marshall, Texas. He was a heavyweight boxing champion from January 1973 through October 1974. He was also the heavyweight boxing champion at the 1968 Olympic games.

Foreman dropped out of high school in Houston, Texas, in 1964. He joined the job corps and began his formal boxing training. He developed boxing skills which enabled him to become famous by representing the United States of America and winning the gold medal as the heavyweight champion at the 1968 Summer Olympic games in Mexico City, Mexico. He moved to the ranks of professional boxing in 1969.

George won the world heavyweight championship title four years later in 1973 when he upset the previous champion, Joe Frazier. He lost his first professional match and the title in 1974 in Zaire, Africa, when Muhammad Ali knocked him out.

George retired from the ring in 1977 after being defeated by Jimmy Young in a championship comeback. Foreman had a spiritual calling and became pastor of the Church of the Lord Jesus Christ in Houston, Texas. He also cofounded the George Foreman Youth Development Foundation.

He came out of retirement due to his hunger for the world heavyweight boxing crown and a need for funds to operate his foundation. Since his comeback, he has won fifteen fights—all by knockouts.

Foreman is very active in commercials of all kinds. He is also a demanded figure for speaking engagements. He serves as an HBO commentator for boxing events and is considered a shrewd businessman.

11/9/74. Zaire. Quantity unknown. 1 makuta. S#804. Set of 5 $2.00 *Illus. 191.*

11/9/74. Zaire. Quantity unknown. 4 makuta. S#805. *Illus. 192.*

11/9/74. Zaire. Quantity unknown. 6 makuta. S#806. *Illus. 193.*

11/9/74. Zaire. Quantity unknown. 14 makuta. S#807. *Illus. 194.*

11/9/74. Zaire. Quantity unknown. 20 makuta. S#808. *Illus. 195.*

Franklin, Aretha

Aretha Louise Franklin was born on March 25, 1942, in Memphis, Tennessee. She spent most of her childhood in Detroit, Michigan, with her father, a well-known evangelist, preacher, and singer. Her spiritual roots and background are obvious in every song she ever recorded. Some of her recordings included "Respect" and "Dr. Feel Good." Her music appealed to pop as well as rhythm and blues fans. She has won several awards, including a Grammy Legends Award and Grammy Lifetime Achievement Award. Aretha also influenced many musicians during the early sixties and seventies. She is still going strong to this date.

12/1/96. Tanzania. Quantity unknown. 250 shillings. S#1414c. *Illus. 202.*

1998. Grenada and the Grenadines. Quantity unknown. 90 cents. *Illus. 201.*

Frazier, Joe

Boxer Joe " Billy Boy" Frazier was born on January 12, 1944, in Beaufort, South Carolina. He was a student and athlete at Robert Small High School in Beaufort. He played both baseball and football.

Frazier's amateur boxing career started when he visited a gymnasium in the inner city of Philadelphia, Pennsylvania. He was discovered at the age of eighteen, but because of his unique physique, the experts questioned his capabilities to be a world class fighter. His trainers designed a style of fighting tailored exclusively for his short, tree-stump legs and short arms.

Frazier won the gold medal for the United States as the Olympic heavyweight boxing champion at the 1964 Summer Games in Tokyo, Japan. He became a professional fighter in August 1965. He won eleven fights by knockout in his first year of fighting. Joe earned worldwide recognition and respect on March 8, 1971, at Madison Square Garden in New York City, New York, when he defeated Muhammad Ali in a fifteen round fight. He retired from the ring on January 22, 1983, at the age of thirty-nine.

Joe Frazier was inducted into the United States Olympic Hall of Fame in 1989 for his contributions to mankind and his career achievements as an Olympic boxing champion and former heavyweight champion of the world. Joe has been paid recognition on international stamps by several countries.

7/20/71. Fujeira. Quantity unknown. 1 riyal. Minkus#696. Hard to find issue. Commemorates Frazier's world championship win in 1971. *Illus. 197.*

10/71. Manama. Quantity unknown. 5 riyals. Minkus#612. Hard to find stamp. Celebrates "Great Olympic Champions" and commemorates Frazier's 1964 win in Tokyo. *Illus. 196.*

1972. Ajman. Quantity unknown. 10 dirhams. Minkus#1147. Hard to find stamp. Celebrates Olympic Boxing gold medal winners. Commemorates Frazier's 1964 win in Tokyo. *Illus. 198.*

5/25/72. Equatorial Guinea. Quantity unknown. 8 pesetas guineanas. Minkus#623. (Perforated.) Hard to find stamp. This stamp was also issued silver and green imperforated version. Also see Muhammad Ali, S#440 and

441 and Minkus 613 and 699m which portray Frazier and Ali on imperforated and perforated souvenir sheets. *Illus. 199, 200.*

Gardner, Anthony W.

Anthony W. Gardner was born in America, but little is known about his life there. He left America during the early or middle part of the 1800s to settle in Liberia, West Africa. He became president of Liberia in 1878 following James S. Payne's second term as president. During Gardner's administration (1878–83) the ruling elite in Liberia continued to have territorial disputes with the European countries of England and France. In 1883, Liberia lost the region north of the Mano River when Sierra Leone claimed that territory and was backed by Great Britain. President Gardner became very upset with the way the British had taken the territory and resigned as president in 1883.

1950. Liberia. Quantity unknown. 7 cents. S#319. This stamp shows Gardner along with President A.F. Russell of Liberia. *Illus. 203.*

4/2/79. Liberia. Quantity unknown. 5 cents. S#836. (Not pictured.) This stamp shows presidents Gardner (left) and President Tolbert (right) along with the UPU emblem. This stamp is also issued under S#837, the same design except for a face value of 35 cents.

Garner, Erroll

Erroll Garner was born in 1923 in Pittsburgh, Pennsylvania. He was a pianist, singer, songwriter, and composer. He began playing the family piano almost before he could walk or talk. His family inspired him to make a career of playing the piano. He took formal piano lessons, but his instructor gave up on him because he refused to learn to play from written music. Garner, instead, wanted to play by ear and memory. Garner mastered the piano, tuba, drums, and slap-bass. He was playing in night clubs and on radio with a small group in Pittsburgh at an early age. He played the tuba in his high school band

at Westinghouse High, but he quit high school to pursue his musical dreams. His pursuit led him to New York City, where he became an itinerant jazz club pianist.

By the time he was twenty-five years old, Erroll had organized his own trio that consisted of piano, drums, and bass. He became internationally known as the "Picasso of the Piano" because of the way he invented his own style of improvising and utilizing the keyboard to produce orchestral and band type compositions flavored with a Latin American rhythmic sound.

Garner's musical career included his winning musical awards from various nations as well as music-related polls in magazines. Much of his best music was not recorded, but some of his more famous pieces include "Laura," "Misty," "Erroll's Bounce," "Play, Piano Play," and "Cocktail Time."

Erroll Louis Garner, the guy with the pleasant disposition and smile, left a legacy, although much of his music was lost because it was not documented. Garner died at the age of 55 in Los Angeles, California, on January 2, 1977.

12/6/71. Du Mali. Quantity unknown. 150 francs. S#C138. This stamp is difficult to find. Only a poor copy is shown here. This stamp will cost many times its estimated book value — if you can find it. *Illus. 204.*

7/5/84. Gabo. Quantity unknown. 200 francs. S#567. (Not pictured.) Hard to find stamp.

9/16/95. United States. Quantity unknown. 32 cents. S#2992. (See color section.) From a vertical block of 10, Legends of American Music Series, S#2983 — 2992. *Illus. C93.*

Garrison, Zina

Zina Garrison is an African American tennis player. A stamp is said to exist on Zina Garrison, but no information on such a stamp is available.

Garvey, Marcus

Marcus Garvey was born in St. Ann's Bay, Jamaica, on August 17, 1887. He was

198

199

200

201

202

203

204

able to attract the ordinary African American as no other black leader during his time or after. He gained a following of six million people at the height of his popularity.

Garvey was a short, stocky, dark man possessing a shrewd sense of crowd psychology. He preached economic independence and the return of the Negro to Africa as a solution to the problems that his race faced in America. Despite his popularity, he was criticized for not realizing that African-Americans had become part of American society and that there were some African Americans who felt that America was their home.

Garvey was charged with fraud in connection with the sale of the Black Star Line. He was seen as a buffoon for defending himself in court and was eventually found guilty. He served two years in prison. After his release, he was deported from America. Marcus died in London, England, in 1940, a lonely and penniless man.

Even though African American intellectuals and others felt skeptical of Marcus Garvey and his teachings, he was a driving force in providing hope and positive feelings for the Negro race.

9/25/69. Cameroon. Quantity unknown. 50 francs. S#C131. (See color section.) *Illus. C94.*

3/11/70. Jamaica. Quantity unknown. 10 cents. S#300. (See color section.) *Illus. C95.*

3/21/70. Senegal. Quantity unknown. 45 francs. S#C77. (See color section.) *Illus. C96.*

12/22/80. Turks and Caicos Islands. Quantity unknown. 2 dollars. S#462. (Perforated souvenir sheet; see color section.) *Illus. C97.*

8/17/87. Jamaica. Quantity unknown. 25 cents. S#669. (See color section.) Celebrates the 100th anniversary of Garvey's birth. *Illus. C98.*

8/17/87. Jamaica. Quantity unknown. 25 cents. S#670. (See color section.) Celebrates the 100th anniversary of Garvey's birth. *Illus. C99.*

Gates, Henry Louis, Jr.

Henry Louis Gates, Jr., is recognized as a leading African American scholar and dapper academic superstar. He has been tenured at Yale, Cornell, Duke and Harvard. Recently Henry Louis Gates has been recognized on a Ghana stamp as one of the greatest African American writers of the 20th century.

Nicknamed by his Uncle Raymond from birth as "Skipper" and later "Skippy," Gates was born on September 16, 1950, in Keyser, West Virginia. Gates prides himself in being born in a middle class family with a loving mother and father who had strong beliefs in helping their children get what they wanted out of life, as well as a healthy relationship with their community and the church.

Gates encountered racism in West Virginia just as most African Americans did anywhere in America, but he didn't allow it to get in the way of his success and progress. After high school he entered Yale University and graduated summa cum laude with a B.A. in 1973. He earned an M.A. from Cambridge University in 1974 and a Ph.D. from Cambridge in 1979 (he was the first African American to receive a degree from the 800-year-old British institution).

Dr. Gates is married to Sharon Lynn Adams. They have two daughters. He has traveled extensively in Africa and written numerous books and articles. He presently serves as director of the Afro American Department and Professor of English at Harvard University, Cambridge, Massachusetts.

Ghana recognized Gates on a stamp along with other blacks as being one of the great African American writers of the 20th Century.

3/25/98. Ghana. Quantity unknown. 350 cedis. S#2027b. (Not pictured.) This stamp was done in honor of great African American writers of the twentieth century. It features a multicolored portrait of Gates. For more comments see Maya Angelou, S#2027a.

Gaye, Marvin, Jr.

Marvin Pentze Gaye, Jr., was born on April 2, 1939, in Washington, D.C. Born into a religious family, he just could not accept the doctrines of no drinking, no dancing, and no nonsense preached and practiced by both the church and his father. Marvin rebelled against his father, who was very violent and beat his children for minor and frivolous infractions. He quit high school before graduation and joined the Air Force. After his discharge he turned to music.

Gaye succeeded as a solo artist and a polished duet partner. With Motown Records, Marvin Gaye recorded such duet hits as "What's the Matter with You, Baby" with Mary Wells, "It Takes Two" with Diana Ross, and "You're All I Need to Get By," "Ain't Nothing Like the Real Thing," "You Ain't Livin' Till You're Lovin'," and "Ain't Easy to Come By," all with Motown recording artist Tami Terrel.

In 1971, Marvin Gaye declared a sudden independence. He produced his own songs, sang his own songs, and basically set his own agenda. In this way he enjoyed continued success in music, but his personal life was filled with turmoil. He developed a dependency on drugs that worsened as time went by. He lost his emotional stability and easy charm, which gave way to paranoia and fear.

Gaye's life ended on April 1, 1984, in his parents' Los Angeles home when his father fatally shot him. Marvin had physically attacked his father for verbally abusing his mother.

1996. Liberia. Quantity unknown. 35 cents. S#1232g. (Not pictured.) This is a multicolored stamp. See Jimi Hendrix, S#1232h, for more comments.

Gibson, Althea

Althea Gibson was born in Silver, South Carolina (near Sumter) on August 25, 1927. She attended Florida Agricultural and Mechanical University. At the age of 15, she became New York State's black girls' singles tennis champion. This was the first of many titles that she won.

Gibson won the Italian Championship in 1956 and 1957. She also won Wimbledon and the U.S. Open championship. She repeated her singles victories at Wimbledon and the U.S. Open in 1958 and ranked number one in the world among women players in both 1957 and 1958. The Associated Press named her Woman Athlete of the Year in 1957. In 1971 she was named in the National Lawn Tennis Hall of Fame. Her strength in her playing was found in her powerful serve and volley.

11/18/88. Lesotho. Quantity unknown. 1.55 maloti. S#679. (See color section.) Commemorating the 75th year of the International Tennis Federation. *Illus. C100.*

Gibson, Bob

Bob "Hoot" Gibson was an American baseball player. He pitched for St. Louis from 1959 to 1975. He also set World Series record for strikeouts in 1968 and won the National League Cy Young Award twice. He was MVP once and was inducted in to the Hall of Fame in 1981.

Bob Gibson was born on November 9, 1939, in Omaha, Nebraska. Gibson played both baseball and basketball for Creighton University. In 1957 he signed a contract with the Cardinals and played in the minor leagues to refine his raw pitching skills.

Gibson's best year of pitching was 1968, when he earned 22 victories, set the major league season record for lowest earned run average (1.12), and struck out what was then a league record of 268 batters. Gibson also set World Series pitching records during the 1968 series. He had the most strikeouts in a single game (seventeen) and the most strikeouts in a World Series (thirty-five), although the Cardinals lost the series to the Detroit Tigers.

11/30/89. St. Vincent. Quantity unknown. 30 cents. S#1267h.(See color section.) From the "U.S. Baseball Series 2." *Illus. C101.*

1/23/97. St. Vincent. Quantity unknown. 1 dollar. S#2380n. (Imperforated; not pictured). Sixteen other black baseball players from the U.S. are recognized in this issue. See Hank Aaron, S#2380g, for the total listing. This issue comes in a sheet of seventeen (17) and is valued at $16.90.

Gibson, Garretson Wilmot

Garretson Wilmot Gibson was born in the state of Maryland. Not much is known about Gibson's life in America. He made the decision to relocate to Liberia, West Africa, during the early or middle 1800s. He became the eighth president of Liberia and served one term (1900–1904). He was sixty-eight when he took office as president and had gained years of experience politically. He had served as secretary of the interior and secretary of state. His claim to fame as president of Liberia was the granting of rights to the Union Mining Operations to investigate the hinterland for minerals including gold and other products. Gibson is recognized as the first African American to appear on a postage stamp; that stamp was issued by Liberia in 1903.

1903. Liberia. Quantity unknown. 10 cents. S#F10 (Not pictured.)

1920. Liberia. Quantity unknown. 10 cents. S#178. *Illus. 205.*

1948–1950. Liberia. Quantity unknown. 15 cents. S#323. *Illus. 206.*

1948–1950. Liberia. Quantity unknown. 15 cents. S#374. *Illus. 207.*

Glover, Danny

Danny Glover, an African American actor, is said to have been featured on a stamp, but no information on such a stamp is available.

Gooden, Dwight

Dwight Eugene Gooden is an American baseball player (pitcher) for the New York Mets. He was born on November 16, 1964, in Tampa, Florida. His father was a semi-professional baseball coach who introduced Gooden to the sport as a child, and by high school Gooden was a star pitcher. When he completed high school in 1982, he was drafted by the New York Mets and in 1983 pitched in the minor leagues, breaking strikeout records and being selected as minor-league player of the year.

As pitcher in 1984, Gooden led the majors with 276 strikeouts (breaking a major-league rookie record). He posted a 17-9 win-loss record and was voted National League (NL) rookie of the year. In 1985 he led the NL in complete games (16) and innings pitched (277) and achieved the rare "triple crown" of pitching by leading both leagues in wins (24), earned run average (1.53), and strikeouts (268). He was unanimously voted that year's Cy Young Award winner, the youngest player to win that honor. The following year he became the first pitcher in major-league history to strike out 200 batters in each of his first three seasons; in post-season play that year he helped the Mets win both the league championship and the World Series. In 1987 Gooden's .682 win percentage led the NL, and he was the dominating force for the Mets.

Having undergone rehabilitation therapy for a substance-abuse problem in 1989, Gooden returned to the Mets' starting lineup and ended the 1990 season with 19 wins. After winning 12 games in 1991 he missed the season's last month because of shoulder surgery. He returned to the field in 1992 with 10 wins.

11/28/88. Grenada. Quantity unknown. 30 cents. S#166b. From the "U.S. Baseball Series 1." *Illus. 208.*

Gray, Johnny

Johnny Gray was the American indoor record holder of the 800m run, 880 yard run, and 1000 yard run. Gray competed in

205

206

207

208

209

210

211

both the 1984 and 1988 Olympic 800m runs.

11/30/84. Central African Republic. Quantity unknown. 500 francs. S#679f. (Perforated souvenir sheet.) This perforated souvenir sheet celebrates winners of the 1984 Olympics in Los Angeles. Gray did not win — the stamp celebrates 800m winner J. Cruz — but he is pictured among the other runners. Gray is located in the center-perforated stamp to the left of the Olympic symbol. *Illus. 209.*

Green, "Mean" Joe

"Mean" Joe Green is an African American professional football player. A stamp is said to exist on "Mean" Joe Green, but no information on such a stamp is available.

Griffey, Ken, Jr.

Ken Griffey, Jr., has been well recognized from the later 1980s through the '90s for his hitting ability. Many thought that he would be the first to break Joe DiMaggio's one-season home run record. Even though he didn't break DiMaggio's long-running record, Ken Griffey has maintained an excellent home run record since he has been playing professional baseball.

George Kenneth Griffey, Jr., was born in Donor, Pennsylvania, in 1969. He was drafted by the Seattle Mariners in 1989 right out of high school. He made history as the first to play on the same team with his father.

Griffey is recognized as one of baseball's finest for his fielding and batting abilities. He is the winner of ten consecutive Gold Glove awards (1990–1999) and is the American League's best defensive center fielder. Griffey established in 1993 an AL record for outfielder after 542 consecutive fielding chances without committing an error. He has been selected to five consecutive AL All-Star teams (1990–1994). His three hits, including a home run, earned him the Most Valuable Player award in the 1992 All-Star game, duplicating his father's home run and All-Star MVP honors in 1980.

Griffey's most notable batting feat occurred over the course of eight consecutive games (July 20–28, 1993), when he hit a home run in each game and tied the AL and major-league records for most consecutive games with a home run. His entire professional career was with the Mariners until 2000, when he was traded to the Cincinnati Reds for more than fifty million dollars.

7/23/89. St. Vincent. Quantity unknown. 60 cents. S#1225i. This is a stamp in recognition of Ken Griffey, Jr.'s rookie year. *Illus. 212.*

7/30/89. St. Vincent. Quantity unknown. 30 cents. S#1270f. From the "U.S. Baseball Series 2." *Illus. 213.*

9/6/95. St. Vincent and the Grenadines. Quantity unknown. 1 dollar. S#2204c. *Illus. 214.*

9/6/95. St. Vincent and the Grenadines. Quantity unknown. 1 dollar. S#2204d. *Illus. 215.*

9/6/95. St. Vincent and the Grenadines. Quantity unknown. 1 dollar. S#2204h. *Illus. 216.*

9/6/95. St. Vincent. Quantity unknown. 30 dollars. S#2204j. (Not pictured.) This is a gold stamp done in litho ink and embossed. This stamp comes in a set of 9 perf (Scott Numbers 2204j–2204l).

Griffin, Alfredo

Alfredo Griffin was born in Santo Domingo, Dominican Republic, on March 6, 1957. He plays shortstop for the Dodgers. Before the 1988 All Star Break he was batting an average .167; home runs 0; RBI 19. After: batting average .227; home runs 1; RBI 8.

8/31/89. St. Vincent. Quantity unknown. 60 cents. S#1235d. Griffin shares this stamp with Dave Anderson. *Illus. 210.*

1990. St. Vincent. Quantity unknown. 60 cents. S#1334h. Griffin shares this stamp with Jim Gott. *Illus. 211.*

Gwynn, Chris

Baseball player Chris Gwynn was born October 10, 1964, in Los Angeles, California. His home is Long Beach, California.

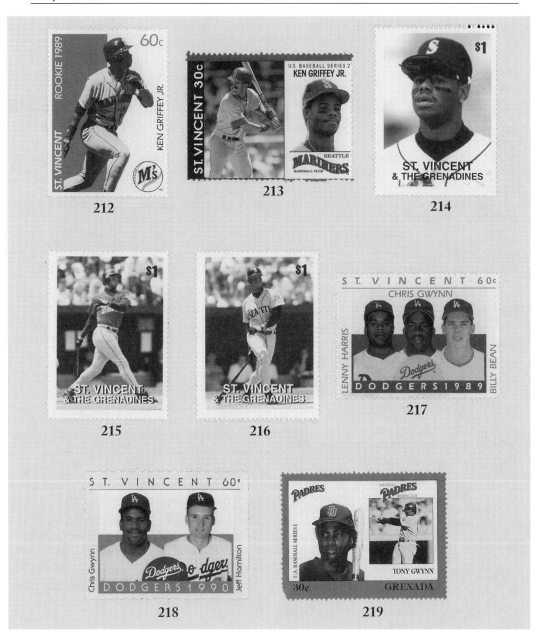

212

213

214

215

216

217

218

219

Chris Gwynn plays for the Los Angeles Dodgers. He had the best season as pro in 1988 with .299 at Albuquerque. He was the no. 1 pick of the Dodgers in 1985 and was an NCAA All-American player at San Diego State. He is also the brother of Tony Gwynn of the Padres, and batted .484 as a senior in high school.

8/3/89. St. Vincent. Quantity unknown. 60 cents. S#1235i. Gwynn shares this stamp with Lenny Harris and Billy Bean. *Illus. 217.*

9/24/90. St. Vincent. Quantity unknown. 60 cents. S#1344f. Chris is featured along with Jeff Hamilton. *Illus. 218.*

Gwynn, Tony

Anthony Keith Gwynn was born May 9, 1960, in Los Angeles, California. As a college student at San Diego State University, Tony played both baseball and basketball. He still holds the all-time record for San Diego State University in basketball assists.

The San Diego Padres, in the third round of the 1981 free draft, selected Gwynn. Even though he suffered with a sore knee, a fractured toe, a strained calf, a sore hamstring, a chipped bone in his thumb and a strained Achilles tendon and missed 35 games, when he played he could play with the best. Gwynn is still considered a master when it comes to putting the ball in play.

11/28/88. Grenada. Quantity unknown. 30 cents. S#1666h. From the "U.S. Baseball Series 1." *Illus.* 219.

7/9/89. St. Vincent. Quantity unknown. 5 dollars. S#1225. (Souvenir sheet.) Look in the right-hand (National League) column of this souvenir sheet for Tony Gwynn's name. *Illus.* 220.

Haley, Alex

Alex Haley was an American author who wrote *The Autobiography of Malcolm X* (one of the most powerful books of the twentieth century) as well as *Roots*, another powerful book, which later became a TV mini-series—the most-watched mini-series in the history of American television during the twentieth century.

Alexander Murray Palmer Haley was born in 1921 in Ithaca, New York. Six weeks after Haley's birth, his mother moved to a small town, Henning, Tennessee, with her parents. As Haley grew into a young man, he and his maternal grandmother, Cynthia Palmer, built a close relationship. He was amazed at the stories she told him about slavery. He became most taken when she told young Haley about his great-great-great-great grandfather, who was African. In later years this story set Haley on a research venture for his family genealogical roots, a search for more than ten years to Tennessee, to the

continents of Europe, to Africa and back to the United States.

Haley didn't excel at school or a university; instead, he joined the Coast Guard as messboy during World War II. He later became a journalist while serving his time in the Coast Guard. After retiring from the Coast Guard he became a full time writer. Haley became the first African American to win a Pulitzer Prize when he was awarded that honor for *Roots*.

Alex Haley died in 1992. Along with other African Americans, he was recognized on a Ghana stamp as a great writer of the twentieth century.

3/25/98. Ghana. Quantity unknown. 350 cedis. S#2027b. (Not pictured.) This stamp was in a series honoring the greatest African American writers of the twentieth century. This stamp features a multicolored portrait of Alex Haley. See Maya Angelou S#2027a, for more comments.

Hall, Arsenio

Arsenio Hall was born in 1957 in Cleveland, Ohio. He is a comedian, actor, and talk show host. He was educated at Kent State University, where he majored in speech communication. His interest in show business developed at the age of twelve when he began watching television talk shows so that he could study them as entertainment.

After college Hall worked as an opening act for the Temptations and other musical acts. He hosted *The Late Show* and *Solid Gold*. Hall appeared in two films with Eddie Murphy. They were *Coming to America* (1988) and *Harlem Nights* (1989). He became the first African-American to host his own late night talk show, *The Arsenio Hall Show*.

6/20/91. Lesotho. Quantity unknown. 4 maloti. S#824. In recognition of entertainers in films about Africa. This stamp features Eddie Murphy and Arsenio Hall in *Coming to America*. (Other film stars recognized in this issue include such greats as Clark Cable and Johnny

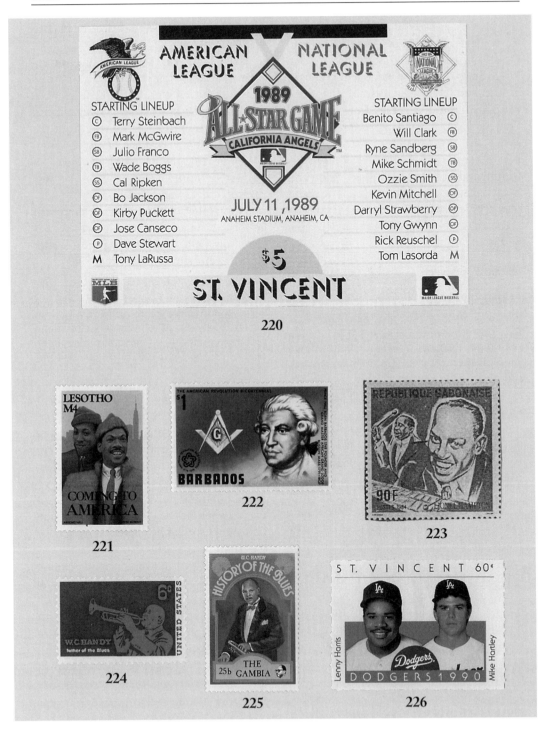

220

221

222

223

224

225

226

Weissmuller.) This stamp also comes in a sheet of nine at a price of $7.14. *Illus. 221.*

Hall, Prince

Prince Hall was born in Barbados at Bridgetown on September 12, 1748. His father was an Englishman and his mother was a free black woman of French lineage. He arrived in the American colonies at the age of seventeen. He was very sympathetic to other blacks and felt that one of the best ways for improving their condition was through cooperative economics. He became a Methodist minister and fought in the Revolutionary War.

Prince Hall was the first ever to attempt organizing black people into unitary structures. His efforts were rebuffed and all of his petitions were denied. He was persistent and turned to England. He was successful in 1787 in obtaining a charter and organized the African Lodge No. 459. He himself was installed as grand master.

Hall later took an interest in the status of Negroes in Boston and elsewhere. He urged the Massachusetts legislature to support the cause of emancipation. In 1797 he successfully convinced the city of Boston to establish schools for Negro children.

Prince Hall has been recognized all over the world for his contributions to masonry. Many towns in America have a Prince Hall Lodge controlled by African Americans.

8/17/76. Barbados. Quantity unknown. 1 dollar. S#443. This is a hard stamp to find. It celebrates the bicentennial of the American Revolution and features a portrait of Hall. *Illus. 222.*

Hampton, Lionel

Lionel Hampton was born in Louisville, Kentucky, in 1913. He was a jazz vibraphonist and composer. He became part of the first major integrated jazz bands when he joined the Benny Goodman Quartet in 1936. He formed his own big band in 1940, but he continued to perform as a soloist and a small group leader. He also plays a staccato, two-finger piano as well as drums. Some of his best known hits are "Flying Home" and "Midnight Sun."

8/5/84. Gabon. Quantity unknown. 90 francs. S#565. This is a difficult stamp to find. Only a poor copy is shown here. *Illus. 223.*

Handy, William Christopher

William Christopher Handy was born November 16, 1873, in Florence, Alabama. He was raised in a strict Methodist household. He received his formal music training in the segregated school system of Florence. He learned to sing and read music, and in church he was a member of the choir. Handy also learned to play the church organ. His family forbade him playing any other instrument.

Handy accomplished his childhood dream of becoming a teacher by becoming director of music at the agricultural and mechanical college at Normal, Alabama. This career was short lived as he became attracted to the blues. He became the first musician to actually write, compose, arrange and publish the blues style. This effort earned him the title "Father of the Blues Style." It wasn't until Handy published the internationally known "Memphis Blues" in 1912 that his style of music became accepted.

Handy gathered songs from farmhands, washerwomen, woodcutters, railroad laborers, and roustabouts for years while traveling throughout the South. By doing this, Handy helped American musical tradition. He was one of the first to bring these secular songs to the larger world.

Despite being blind by the age of 49, Handy continued to direct his own music publishing company in New York City. W.C. Handy died of pneumonia at the age of 80, on March 28, 1958.

5/17/69. United States. 128,000,000. 6 cents. S#1372. *Illus. 224.*

2/12/92. The Gambia. Quantity unknown. 25 bututs. S#1179. From a "History of the Blues" issue including 12 African American spiritual, blues, and jazz singers. Others recognized are Son House (S#1178); Muddy Waters (S#1180); Lightnin' Hopkins (S#1181); Ma Rainey (S#1182); Mance Lipscomb (S#1183); Mahalia Jackson (S#1184); Ella Fitzgerald (S#1185); Howlin' Wolf (S#1186); Bessie Smith (S#1187); Leadbelly (S#1188); Joe Willie Wilkins

(S#1189), and Billie Holiday (S#1992 souvenir sheet). *Illus. 225.*

Harris, Leonard Anthony

Leonard Anthony Harris, known as Lenny, was born in Miami, Florida, on October 28, 1964. He is an American Major League baseball player. He was chosen by the Cincinnati Reds in the fifth round of the June draft in 1983. He was a versatile player while he was with the Cincinnati Reds.

8/3/89. St. Vincent. Quantity unknown. 60 cents. S#1345c. Lenny Harris is pictured here with Mike Harley. *Illus. 226.*

8/3/89. St. Vincent, Quantity unknown. 60 cents. S#1235i. Harris shares this stamp with Chris Gwynn and Billy Bean. *Illus. 217.*

Hart, Edward

Eddie James Hart was born April 24, 1948, in Martinez, California. He was a prominent track and field athlete. He attended Pittsburgh High School and the University of California, Berkeley. His career was filled with triumphs and disappointments. He never finished prominently at the AAU meets. At the 1972 Summer Olympics, he failed to arrive on the start in time to compete for the second round. At the same games, he ran the anchor leg on the relay team that set a new world record. Although Hart retired in 1972, he made a comeback in 1978 and was ranked again among the top U.S. sprinters.

1973. Umm-al-Qiwain. Quantity unknown. 5 riyals. See Larry Black for more information.

Hastie, William

William Henry Hastie was born on November 17, 1904, in Knoxville, Tennessee. He was an educator, administrator, politician, newspaper columnist, government official, judge, governor of the Virgin Islands, and lawyer.

Hastie started his formal education in the Knoxville, Tennessee, public school system and completed his elementary and high school education in Washington, D.C. He was a formidable athlete as well as student. By the time he was twenty-eight years old, he had served as staff editor of the *Harvard Law Review*, received his law degree, and earned his Doctorate of Juridical Science degree. He held two appointed positions in the United States government, first as assistant solicitor in the United States Department of the Interior and then as a civilian aide to the secretary of war.

Hastie wrote the constitution for the Virgin Islands while with the Department of the Interior. This earned him the title of "Founding Father of the Virgin Islands." Later he became the first African American to be appointed to the federal bench as judge of the district court for the Virgin Islands. He was eventually made the first African American governor of the Virgin Islands.

In his service to the secretary of war, Hastie is given credit for the total desegregation of the United States military. Hastie held membership to several associations that were established for the benefits of blacks everywhere. For his many trials and tribulations in the fight against Jim Crowism in the military, William Henry Hastie was the recipient of the National Association for the Advancement of Colored People's Spingarn Award, the Charles Hamilton Hurston Medallion of Merit, and the National Newspaper Publishers Association Award.

After a brilliant career, he was laid to rest on April 14, 1976, in Morristown, Pennsylvania, at seventy-one years of age.

7/27/82. Grenada. Quantity unknown. 5 dollars. S#1110. (Perforated souvenir sheet.) This perforated souvenir sheet commemorates the 100th anniversary of the birth of Franklin D. Roosevelt. The stamp shows Hastie shaking hands with FDR and notes that Hastie was the first black judicial appointee. *Illus. 227.*

Hawkins, Coleman

Coleman Hawkins was born in Saint Joseph, Missouri, in 1904. A jazz musician, Hawkins is recognized as one of the influential figures in the development of the bebop style of 1922. Because of his stylistic full-bodied sound of music, he is also considered the father of the jazz tenor saxophone. In his early teens, Hawkins played professionally with renowned jazz ensembles such as the Hounds of Mamie Smith (1921) and the Fletcher Henderson Orchestra (1923). By the 1930s Coleman Hawkins had established himself as a leading jazz musician and performer. He toured Europe for five years (1934–1939) and returned to the United States. Upon his return, he recorded his first album *Body and Soul* (1939).

A solo musician for the rest of his career, Hawkins played faithfully and fervently until his death in 1969.

9/16/95. United States. Quantity unknown. 32 cents. S#2983. From the Legends of American Music series. *Illus. 228.*

Hayes, Bob

Athlete Bob (Robert Lee) Hayes was born on December 20, 1942, in Jacksonville, Florida. His professional career expanded into the sports arena of both track and field as well as football, where he excelled in both making and breaking several records. At the National AAU Championships he represented Florida A&M University and set a record for the 100 yard relay in 9.1 seconds. He was the first person to complete the indoor 60-yard dash relay in 6.6 seconds. During both the 1963 and 1963 track seasons, Bob Hayes remained undefeated in every event in which he participated. In 1964 he was unanimously elected as the greatest 100-meter sprinter of all time.

Because of Bob Hayes's unorthodox rolling and lumbering style of strength, he was able to become a professional football star. He played for ten years with the Dallas Cowboys and spent the last year of his football career with the San Francisco 49ers. Along with achieving a Super Bowl ring, he set several records in most yards receiving, averages per catches, most touchdowns, and highest punt return averages.

Bob Hayes died in September 2002. Many believe he should be in the Hall of Fame.

3/5/58. Honduras. Quantity unknown. 1 lempira. S#C435. Hard to find issue. Only a poor copy is shown here. *Illus. 229.*

Haywood, Spencer

Spencer Haywood was born April 22, 1949, in Silver City, Mississippi. He was an American basketball player. He was a two-time all-star forward center from 1969 through 1983 with six NBA teams. He was also a member of the United States Olympic team in 1968.

Spencer Haywood attended the University of Detroit. He played the positions of center and forward. After his college playing years, he joined the Denver Rockets of the ABA in 1969 and began his career. During his first year with the Denver Rockets, he was rookie of the year and MVP. He also made first team ABA.

Haywood later joined the Seattle SuperSonics and became one of the great forwards in the NBA. He made the first team for three years in a row and was named to the second team the following two years.

Haywood was traded to the New York Knicks in 1975 and played four seasons with them. He finished his career in 1983 with 14,592 career points and 7,038 rebounds.

227

228   229

230

1969. Ajman. Quantity unknown. 15 riyals. (Perforated souvenir sheet.) This perforated souvenir issue shows the 1968 U.S. Olympic basketball team. It includes the following black athletes who went on to have outstanding professional basketball careers: Spencer Haywood (second from left), Charlie Scott (third from right), and "Jo Jo" White (second from right). This team was the winner of the Olympic gold medal. Please note also that this same stamp was printed in Manama to recognize these players. The Manama stamp is not shown here. It is exactly like the Ajman stamp except that it bears the name of Manama. *Illus. 230.*

Henderson, Rickey

Rickey Henley Henderson was born December 25, 1958, in Chicago, Illinois. He is an American baseball player. He plays the positions of left field and designated hitter. He was drafted by the Oakland Athletics in the fourth round of the 1976 draft as a free agent. He is still among the best at working the strike zone and getting on base. He is also known for his base stealing skills. He has shown that he is an excellent player.

9/2/91. Congo. Quantity unknown. 200 francs. S#932. (Perforated souvenir sheet.) Other athletes who are recognized on this souvenir sheet are David Justice, Will Clark, Sandy Alomar, Jr., and Nolan Ryan. *Illus. 231.*

11/2/87. Grenada. Quantity unknown. 1 dollar. S#1552b. (Perforated souvenir sheet.) See Eric Davis, S#1552b, for more information.

Henderson, Stephen

A stamp is said to exist on twentieth-century author Stephen Henderson, but no information on such a stamp is available.

Henderson, Thomas

A stamp is said to exist on Thomas Henderson, an African American who played pro football in the Super Bowl, but no information on such a stamp is available.

Hendrix, Jimi

Jimi Hendrix was an American rock guitarist, singer and songwriter. Hendrix was born James Marshall Hendrix in Seattle, Washington, on November 27, 1942. Hendrix is considered one of the best guitarists in rock-and-roll music. He began his short career by touring with a number of rhythm and blues shows. In 1966 he moved to England and formed the Jimi Hendrix Experience. The trio included Hendrix, Mitch Mitchell, and Noel Redding. The group made its debut appearance in Paris and toured clubs on the European continent and England.

When he returned to the United States, Hendrix appeared at the Monterey Festival. He performed "Wild Thing," a performance that was documented in the film *Monterey Pop*. Hendrix's version of "The Star Spangled Banner," in which he plucked the guitar with his teeth, became legendary.

Jimi Hendrix died of complications from a drug overdose on September 18, 1970. He was only 27 years old and at the height of his fame. His best selling albums include *Are You Experienced* (1967), *Alis: Bold as Love* (1967), and *Electric Ladyland* (1968).

Even to this date there are many who worship the music of Jimi Hendrix. His albums continue to be best-sellers.

10/9/89. Grenada and the Grenadines. Quantity unknown. 25 cents. S#1116. Spells Hendrix's first name as "Jimmy." *Illus. 232.*

2/27/95. Tanzania. Quantity unknown. 2000 shillings. S#1311. (Souvenir sheet.) Celebrates Hendrix's appearance at the Woodstock Music Festival of 1969. *Illus. 233.*

12/1/95. The Gambia. Quantity unknown. 3 dalasis. S#1670d. This issue of Hendrix comes in a sheet of 8. *Illus. 234.*

1996. Liberia. Quantity unknown. 35 cents. S#1232h. (Not pictured.) This issue is done in recognition of the history of rock and roll. Other rock and roll stars recognized in this issue are Wilson Pickett (S#1232a); Bill Haley (S#1232b); Otis Redding (S#1232c); Fats Domino (S#1232d); Buddy Holly (S#1232e); Chubby Checker (S#1232f) and Marvin Gaye (S#1232g).

Henry, John

John Henry is one of the few figures of African American folklore who is known today by the general American population. John Henry represents not only the nineteenth-century struggle of the human spirit against the coming industrial era, but African American resistance to white labor domination. What isn't clear is how the legend represents actual events on the Chesapeake and Ohio Railroad in Summers County, West Virginia, in the 1870s.

The legend involves John Henry, an incredibly strong black steel driver, put in a contest against a steam drill intended to replace workers. According to the legend, John Henry wins by drilling more holes in granite than the machine can drill. The effort literally kills him.

This legend exists in many different musical versions. It is one of the most popular American folk songs and has been recorded hundreds of times, most often by African American blues singers. The first recording was by country music pioneer Fiddlin' John Carson in 1924. The first recording by black musicians was by the Francis and Sowell duo in 1927. Since then, Leadbelly, Brownie McGhee and Sonny Terry, Fred McDowell, Memphis Slim, Odetta, Mississippi John Hurt, Big Bill Broonzy, and Harry Belafonte have released versions.

7/11/96. United States. 113,000,000. 32 cents. S#3085. From the Folk Heroes issue. *Illus. 31.*

Henson, Josiah

Josiah Henson was born a slave near Port Tobacco, Maryland. He knew little about his father, who was taken from his family and sold. As a child Josiah was seized from his mother and also sold, but the two were somehow reunited.

In his early years Henson became a fervent Christian, and in 1828 the Methodist Episcopal Church ordained him as a preacher. By this time Henson had his own family and supervised operations on his master's plantation. Mounting evidence that he was to be sold away from his wife and children convinced him to escape. Following the North Star and carrying his two youngest children on his back, Henson arrived in Canada on 28 October 1830. In Canada he resumed preaching and acted as a leader of other escaped slaves. He co-founded a settlement and school for blacks near present day Dresden, Ontario. Hen-

231

232

233

234

235

236

237

238

239

son later became identified with the hero of the novel *Uncle Tom's Cabin*. He died in 1882.

Few Americans are familiar with Josiah Henson. The greater part his life was mostly spent in Canada, a non-slave country, where he helped many black Americans who escaped through the Underground Railroad to establish themselves in freedom.

Josiah Henson was the only African American recognized by the Canadian Postal System at the time this research was completed.

9/16/85. Canada. 20,000,000. 32 cents. S#997. Tony Kew, a Toronto artist, has based this stamp design on an authentic portrait of Josiah Henson combined with a symbolic rendering of the Underground Railroad, which transported him and his companions to freedom. *Illus. 235.*

Henson, Matthew

Matthew Alexander Henson was born in 1866 in Charles County, Maryland. He grew up in Washington, D.C., with his uncle. He worked in a restaurant and went to the North Street School for six years.

Henson was just thirteen years old when he began working as a cabin boy. He learned seamanship under a captain named Childs as he sailed through the Straits of Magellan. After six years with Captain Childs, he went to work in Boston, Massachusetts, as a stevedore. Henson then worked as a bellhop in Providence, Rhode Island, and as a coachman in New York City. When he returned to Washington, D.C., he was a much-traveled man.

Henson was recommended to be a valet to accompany Robert Peary on his trip to survey a canal route through Nicaragua. With his experiences and abilities to chart courses through jungles and his expert seamanship, Henson soon became more of a colleague than a valet.

The most notable excursion of the two occurred when Henson, Peary, and four Inuit made it to the North Pole on April 6, 1909. However, there are many distorted facts to this date as to who reached the North Pole first.

Matthew Henson died in March of 1955.

5/28/86. United States. Quantity 32,500,000. 22 cents. S#2223. Arctic Explorers issue. This stamp show Robert E. Peary and Matthew Henson. *Illus. 236.*

Hill, Ken

Ken Hill was born in Lynn, Massachusetts, on December 12, 1965. He has played for the Cardinals, Expos, Indians, Angels, White Sox and Devil Rays in the position of pitcher.

7/23/89. St. Vincent. Quantity unknown. 60 cents. S#1224f. *Illus. 237.*

Hines, Jim

Jim Hines is an American track and field athlete. Hines was born in Dumas, Arkansas, on September 10, 1946. He was the first person to break the ten-second barrier for the 100-meter relay.

Hines attended McClymonds High School in Oakland, California, and Texas Southern University. He was an avid runner during his high school years and his stay at Texas Southern. Coach Stan Wright of Texas Southern considered Jim Hines the best sprinter he ever coached.

Hines was the first athlete to better 10 seconds for 100 meters. At the 1968 Olympic Games in Mexico City, he won the Olympic crown by a full meter in an electrically timed 9.95 seconds, a world record until 1976.

After the 1968 summer Olympics and after setting various track and field records, Hines went into professional football. He had a brief career with the Miami Dolphins.

10/10/68. Fujeira. Quantity unknown. 15 dirhams. Minkus#177. (Overprint.) Hard to find. Jim Hines's name is overprinted on the front of this 1968 Olympic commemorative. *Illus. 238.*

1969. Manama. Quantity unknown. 1 dirhams. Minkus#229. Celebrates Hines's 1968 Olympic win. *Illus. 239.*

3/1/69. Ajman. Quantity unknown. 15 dirhams. Minkus#374. Celebrates Hines's 1968 Olympic win. *Illus. 240.*

Holiday, Billie

Billie Holiday was born Eleanor Fagan on April 7, 1915, in Baltimore, Maryland. She was brought up in a dysfunctional family and eventually raised by her grandmother after both of her parents left her. With barely an elementary education to her credit, Billie Holiday had experienced physical, sexual, and psychological abuse during her childhood and in her adult life. She moved to New York City at the age of thirteen and was reunited with her paternal mother. She changed her name during this time and began singing jazz.

Holiday's trademark was the white gardenia worn in her hair during performances. Her nickname, "Lady Day," was given to her for her warm demeanor. She expressed her own unique style of singing by injecting passion into her song. The passion stemmed from abusiveness surrounding the men that she loved.

For twenty-six years, Holiday was on top of the music world nationally and internationally. She died in New York City on July 17, 1959, from lung congestion complicated by substance abuse. A film about her life, *Lady Sings the Blues*, was released in 1972. Billie Holiday has been recognized on international and U.S. stamps.

4/3/89. St. Vincent. Quantity unknown. 5 dollars. S#1151. (Souvenir sheet; not pictured.) See Count Basie S#1151.

2/12/92. The Gambia. Quantity unknown. 20 dalasis. S#1192. (Perforated souvenir sheet.) See W.C. Handy, S#1179, for more information on this Gambia issue on spiritual, blues, and jazz singers. *Illus. 242.*

9/17/94. United States. Quantity unknown. 29 cents. S#2256. From the Legends of American Music series. *Illus. 241.*

Holyfield, Evander

Evander Holyfield was boxing's heavyweight world champion. A stamp recognizing Holyfield is said to exist, but no information on such stamp is available.

Hopkins, Lightnin'

Lightnin' Hopkins was born Sam Hopkins on March 15, 1912, in Centerville, Texas. He was an American blues singer and guitarist. He originally was a farm worker who became acquainted with the blues through Blind Lemon Jefferson and his cousin Texas Alexander. He made his first recordings in Los Angeles in 1946 and performed in New York and Chicago before settling in Houston in the 1950s. Many of his earlier recordings were reissued on long playing discs. He began a series of albums that made him more known to the public. He performed in clubs and festivals and became one of the most frequently recorded blues singers of the postwar era. Among his finest recordings are "Penitentiary Blues" and "Bad Luck and Trouble." Lightnin' Hopkins died January 30, 1982, in Houston, Texas.

2/12/92. The Gambia. Quantity unknown. 75 bututs. S#1171. From the History of the Blues series. *Illus. 243.*

House, Son

Son House (formally named Eddie James, Jr.) was born on the Mississippi River Delta on a plantation between the towns of Lyon and Clarksdale (Riverton) on March 21, 1902. By the time he turned fifteen, he was giving sermons. By the age of twenty, he was pastor of a Baptist church near Lyon. He rambled from job to job, picking cotton, gathering tree moss, etc.,

240

241

242

243

244

245

246

because he could never commit to a career in the church.

By 1926, House was considering going back to the church. After seeing local bluesmen like Willie Wilson play bottleneck guitar, however, House went out and bought himself a battered guitar. He had become mesmerized with the music he had heard. Willie Wilson taught him how to tune by ear. Another player, James McCoy, gave him lessons. The rest he picked up on his own.

In 1928, House was sent to the state penal farm for shooting and killing a man at a house party near Clarksdale. Even though he pleaded self-defense, House was found guilty and served two years in jail. When he was released, he was ordered not to return to Clarksdale. For this reason, he headed north.

House signed with Columbia Records and resurrected his signature tunes in 1964. He performed at blues festivals and colleges and concerts that took him throughout Europe. Through all his success, he remained a soft-spoken man who depended on the bottle to calm his nerves. His deteriorating health forced him to retirement in 1976.

Son House move to Detroit to be with family and died in his sleep on October 19, 1988. With his passing went the last of the great original Mississippi Delta blues.

2/12/92. The Gambia. Quantity unknown. 20 butut. S#1178. From the History of the Blues series. *Illus. 244.*

Houston, Whitney

Whitney Houston was born on August 9, 1963. She grew up in East Orange, New Jersey. She made her singing debut at the age of eleven with the New Hope Baptist Church Choir. She later appeared as a backup singer on several recordings featuring her mother, Cissy Houston, and cousin, Dionne Warwick.

Even though Houston had success as a fashion model, she found it degrading. She quit modeling in order to seek a career in music. She sang backup for musicians such as Chaka Khan, Lou Rawls, and the Neville Brothers. Whitney had received several recording contract offers by the time she turned nineteen. She eventually signed with Arista Records. Her debut album, *Whitney Houston*, produced four hits: "Saving All My Love for You," "You Give Good Love," "How Will I Know," and "The Greatest Love of All." Her second LP, *Whitney*, also received rave reviews.

In 1982, she married singer Bobby Brown and made her acting debut in the film *The Bodyguard*. She continues to perform and has been recognized on several international stamps.

12/5/88. Grenada. Quantity unknown. 45 cents. S#1675. *Illus. 246.*

2/15/92. Tanzania. Quantity unknown. 75 shillings. S#811g. *Illus. 245.*

Hughes, James Langston

James Langston Hughes was born in Joplin, Missouri, on February 1, 1902. He was a poet, librettist, dramatist, newspaper columnist and lecturer. Hughes attended public school in Kansas and Illinois. He completed his secondary education at Central High School in Cleveland, Ohio. He enrolled at Columbia University in New York City at the request of his father. He left Columbia after one year to search for an understanding of people and the economy, which he felt would enhance his writing capabilities. He studied sociology and economics and received his undergraduate degree from Lincoln University in Lincoln, Pennsylvania. He was appointed poet in residence at Atlanta University in Atlanta, Georgia, and a special resource instructor with the University of Chicago in Chicago, Illinois.

During the early 1930s, Hughes lectured at all the African American colleges and universities located in the southern United States. Over the years, he refined his style of writing using humor and simple, direct English to convey with intensity his emotions about the living conditions of African Americans. He gained immense popularity among African Americans during the Great Depression years for his contribution of poems and other writings in magazines and periodicals.

During his lifetime, Langston Hughes published biographies and histories as well as poetry. He was one of America's most productive and honored writers. He was elected to numerous organizations and associations. A great genius with words by any measure, Lanston Hughes died in New York City on May 22, 1967, at the age of sixty-five.

9/25/69. Cameroon. Quantity unknown. 50 francs. S#C130. *Illus. 247.*

Hurston, Zora Neale

Zora Neale Hurston was a colorful novelist, anthropologist and folklorist. Zora was born in Eatonville, Florida, in 1891. Eatonville is considered the first city incorporated by African Americans. Zora attended Barnard College in New York with the famous scholar Franz Boas. Zora was the first African American to graduate from Barnard College. She conducted fieldwork all over the South in search of African American folklore. Her novel, *Their Eyes Were Watching God*, is recognized as one of her best publications.

Zora also taught for a short while at North Carolina Central University. She won the Guggenheim Fellowship to help her continue her writing career. One of her last major works was her autobiography, *Dust Tracks on a Road*. She was also most sensitive about the plight of African American women and women's rights in general.

Zora Neale Hurston died in 1960. If it

were not for the recognition of Zora Neale Hurston on a Ugandan stamp her significant contributions to African American culture and history would not have been brought to attention in this book.

4/6/98. Uganda. Quantity unknown. 300 shillings. S#1549b. (Not pictured.) This stamp features a colorful picture of Zora Neale Hurston wearing one of her fancy hats. The stamp pays tribute to Zora as a great American folklorist.

Hyman, Flo

A stamp is said to exist on Flo Hyman, a star volleyball player who led the United States to a silver medal at the 1984 Olympics, but no information on such a stamp is available.

Jackson, Bo

Bo Jackson was born Vincent Edward Jackson in Bessemer, Alabama. He is known for being a multitalented athlete. He excelled in baseball, football, and track and field. After graduating from high school, he turned down an offer to play baseball with the New York Yankees. Instead, he entered Auburn University and played football as a running back. He became Auburn's all-time leading rusher and won the Heisman Trophy as the nation's top college player.

Instead of signing on to play professional football, Jackson signed with the Kansas City Royals baseball team. Next, Jackson continued to surprise people by also signing a five-year football contract with the Los Angeles Raiders. He played baseball in the spring and summer and played football for the last half of the NFL season. He set a team record for the Raiders by rushing for 221 yards in a single game in 1987. In 1989 he was NFL Pro Bowl selection and the Most Valuable Player of baseball's all star game.

A hip injury ended Jackson's football career and threatened to end his baseball ca-

247

248

249

250

251

252 253

254 255

256 257

258 259

reer. He was eventually released by the Royals in 1990 and signed a contract with the Chicago White Sox. He underwent hip replacement surgery, which caused him to miss the 1992 season. The Royals didn't reissue his contract; therefore, Bo Jackson joined the California Angels before the 1994 season. Jackson was recognized on two international stamps before his retirement from the sports arenas of football and baseball.

9/2/91. Congo. Quantity unknown. 100 francs. S#930. (Perforated souvenir sheet.) Also shown in this souvenir stamp is a picture of Joe Montana, the great quarterback. Jackson is illustrated as both a football and baseball player. *Illus. 248.*

Jackson, Mahalia

Mahalia Jackson was born on October 26, 1911, in New Orleans, Louisiana. She rose to the title of "African American Mother of Gospel Music." She was a singer, actress, entrepreneur, author, philanthropist, diplomat and civil rights activist.

Mahalia Jackson had no more than an eighth grade education, and before she became a professional singer she worked odd jobs to make money. She was twenty years old when she began her professional singing career with the Johnson Gospel Singers of Chicago, Illinois. Although her life ambition was to become a nurse, she put it on hold when her singing became both popular and demanded. Her gospel single "Move on Up a Little Higher" sold over a million copies. This was a great accomplishment considering that she could not read sheet music and was told by her music teacher after one lesson that she could not sing.

By 1950 Mahalia Jackson had become a household name. She became so popular that wherever there was a gathering with national importance, she was always ex-

tended a special invitation to sing. She sang at President John F. Kennedy's inauguration. She also sang at the 1963 March on Washington, and at the 1968 funeral of Dr. Martin Luther King, Jr. She has been recognized on several national and international stamps.

3/14/75. Liberia. Quantity unknown. 3 cents. S#698. Recognizes International Women's Year (1975) and features a portrait of Jackson. *Illus. 249.*

2/12/92. The Gambia. Quantity unknown. 1.50 dalasis. S#1184. From the History of the Blues Series honoring American blues, jazz, and spiritual singers. See W. C. Handy, S#1179 for more information on this issue. *Illus. 250.*

7/15/98. United States. Quantity unknown. 32 cents. S#3216. *Illus. 251.*

Jackson, Michael

"Never Can Say Good-by," a song that was most popular during the early 1970s, continues to inspire the memory of Michael Joseph Jackson singing lead with his brothers—then known as the Jackson Five. At that time no one ever imagined the Jackson Five would break up, and that young Michael would go on his own and become one of the greatest rock stars and businessmen of the 1970s, 1980s and 1990s.

Michael was one of ten children born to Joseph and Katherine Corse Jackson in Gary, Indiana, on August 19, 1958. His brothers and sisters are Sigmund Esco (Jackie), Toriano Adaryl (Tito), Jermaine Lajaune, Marlon David, Steven Randall (Randy), Maureen, Latoya, Janet, and Rebbie.

Michael began his career when he was only five years of age and became universally known as a member of the "Jackson Five." After he became a solo act his style of music consisted of a distinct rhythm and dance beat featuring soul, rhythm and blues, and rock and roll. His dancing capabilities are what most distinguish him from other noted entertainers, and earned him the recognition as African America's and the world's number one exciting performer.

Michael's acting skills in *The Wiz*, his rock videos and his commercials for Pepsi-cola made his talent quite obvious. Michael's album *Thriller* is still the all-time number one and largest selling album ever recorded.

Michael Joseph Jackson has made the world recognize him for his great skills in the world of entertainment. And he has been recognized the world over on postage stamps for the contributions he has made to the world of music.

1985. British Virgin Islands. Quantity unknown. 1 dollar. See following stamp below. These stamps, if found, could be much more than the above estimated cost, or less. These stamps are multicolored, and very similar to those done by St. Vincent beginning with S#894 (see below). Only poor copies are shown here. *Illus. 252.*

1985. British Virgin Islands. Quantity unknown. 1 dollar. These 1985 issues of Michael Jackson were printed, but were never issued. The stamps shown here are copies of copies. According to Ernest Austin's *Black American Stamp Album*, British law prevented the release of these issues because no living person other than members of the royal family may appear on a British or British dependency stamp. St. Vincent later issued similar stamps. You will recognize these issues as you peruse the stamps issued in Jackson's honor by St. Vincent. These original issues were multicolored. These stamps are said to have been destroyed by the British government. *Illus. 253.*

12/2/85. St. Vincent. Quantity unknown. 60 cents. S#894. From a set of 8 stamps (S#894-901). *Illus. 254.*

12/2/85, St. Vincent. Quantity Unknown. 60 cents. S#895. *Illus. 255.*

12/2/85. St. Vincent. Quantity unknown. 1 dollar. S#896. *Illus. 256.*

12/2/85. St. Vincent. Quantity unknown. 1 dollar. S#897. *Illus. 257.*

12/2/85. St. Vincent. Quantity unknown. 2 dollars. S#898. *Illus. 258.*

12/2/85. St. Vincent. Quantity unknown. 2 dollars. S#899. *Illus. 259.*

12/2/85. St. Vincent. Quantity unknown. 5 dollars. S#900. *Illus. 260.*

12/2/85. St. Vincent. Quantity unknown. 5 dollars. S#901. *Illus. 261.*

12/2/85. St. Vincent. Quantity unknown. 45 cents. S#902. (Perforated souvenir sheet.) Sheet of 4 includes 2 each. *Illus. 262.*

12/2/85. St. Vincent. Quantity unknown. 90 cents. S#902a. (Perforated souvenir sheet.) Sheet of 4 includes 2 each of S#896 and 897. *Illus. 263.*

12/2/85. St. Vincent. Quantity unknown. 1 dollar and 50 cents. S#902b. (Perforated souvenir sheet.) Sheet of 4 includes 2 each of S#898 and 899. *Illus. 264.*

12/2/85. St. Vincent. Quantity unknown. 4 dollars. S#902c. (Perforated souvenir sheet.) Sheet of 4 includes 2 each of S#900 and 901. *Illus. 265.*

11/12/86. Guinea. Quantity unknown. 500 francs. S#1015. *Illus. 267.*

1990. St. Vincent. Quantity unknown. 2 dollars. *Illus. 269.*

3/30/90. Tanzania. Quantity unknown. 350 francs. S#589. (Perforated souvenir sheet.) *Illus. 266.*

11/19/92. Grenada. Quantity unknown. 90 cents. S#2156d. (Not pictured.) From an issue honoring gold record award winners. See Chuck Berry, S#2158a, for more comments.

1995. Burkina Faso. Quantity unknown. 150 francs. (Not pictured.)

12/1/95. Tanzania. Quantity unknown. 250 shillings. S#1414i. Souvenir sheet of 9, Scott Numbers 1414a-i. *Illus. 268.*

Jackson, Reggie

Reginald Martinez "Reggie" Jackson was born on May 18, 1946, in Wyncote, Pennsylvania. He played the position of outfielder on several American League baseball teams. He was the league MVP in 1973 and the leading home run hitter in 1973, 1980, and 1982. He developed the nickname "Mr. October" because of his outstanding batting performances in playoff and World Series games. He joined the Oakland Athletics after briefly playing in the minor leagues. He gained recognition as power hitter in 1969.

He was traded to the Baltimore Orioles in 1976. He signed with the New York Yankees as a free agent the following year. His biggest successes came with the Yankees. He led the team to three East division championships, two American League pennants, and two World Series championships. He retired after the 1987 season and was inducted into the Baseball Hall of Fame in 1993.

8/29/72. Manama. Quantity unknown. 3 dirhams. Minkus#961. (Not pictured.) This is a three-dimensional stamp that features two different portraits. Turn it toward the light one way and it shows Reggie Jackson; turn it another way and it shows Steve Carlton. A most rare and unusual stamp.

11/28/88. Grenada. Quantity unknown. 30 cents. S#1668c. From the "U.S. Baseball Series 1." *Illus. 270.*

11/17/89. St. Vincent. Quantity unknown. 30 cents. S#1275c. From the "U.S. Baseball Series 2." *Illus. 272.*

10/4/93. St. Vincent. Quantity unknown. 2 dollars. S#1965. Notes Jackson's election to the Hall of Fame. *Illus. 271.*

3/15/96. Nicaragua. Quantity unknown. 10 cordobas. S#2169. (Perforated souvenir sheet.) Perforated souvenir sheet in honor of Jackson's induction into the Baseball Hall of Fame. Reads (in Spanish), "Nicaragua 20th century great baseball players." *Illus. 273.*

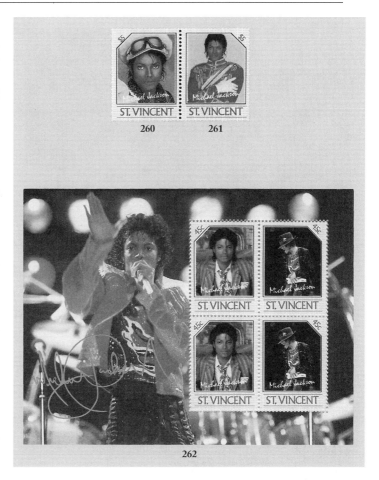

260   261

262

Jazz

Jazz: Where and when did it begin? There are many stories behind jazz and its beginnings. Many believe that it started in the fields where African American slaves worked under the scorching sun and endured harsh treatment from overseers and slave masters. To make the day move faster, and to create a more comfortable atmosphere, they entertained themselves with a mixture of improvised sounds. Many of these sounds and phrases led to spirituals, the blues, rock, pop, and even country music, and a combination of them all created the jazz sound. Jazz combines elements of ragtime, marching band music, and blues. What made it different from earlier styles of American music was its extensive use of improvisation.

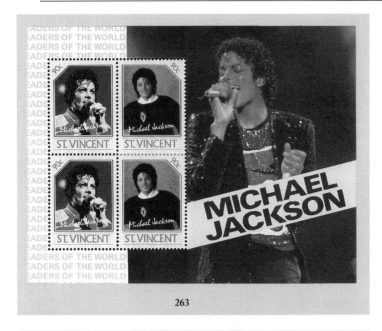

263

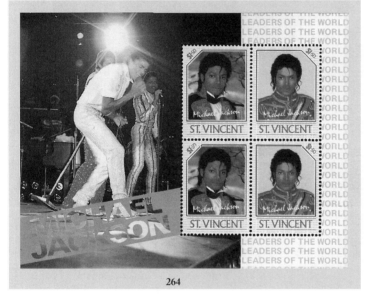

264

to great early clarinetists Johnny Dodds, Jimmy Noone and Sidney Bechet. One of the first great cornetist's, Joe "King" Oliver, along with his leading student and future star, Louis Armstrong, and others such as Jelly Roll Morton were from New Orleans.

Jazz began to gain wider notice as recordings were made in the Windy City of Chicago and sold throughout America. New York City also contributed to the development of jazz. The first piano style to be incorporated into jazz was stride, which developed from ragtime and was popular in New York.

Millions today in America and internationally love jazz music. Jazz musicians have been recognized on foreign stamps for years. In 1998, America finally paid tribute on a stamp to the country's great jazz heritage.

1998. United States. Quantity unknown. 32 cents. S#3184k. "Jazz flourishes" — part of a tribute to the twentieth-century. *Illus. 274.*

Jemison, Mae C.

Mae C. Jemison was the first African American woman astronaut. She was born in 1956. She holds an M.D. from Cornell Medical School (1981) and worked as a staff physician for the Peace Corps for two and a half years in Sierra Leone (West Africa). In 1992, she became the first African American woman in space.

2/21/95. Azerbaijan. Quantity unknown. 100

Two things about jazz we know for sure: 1) Jazz was born in America, and 2) it is one of the few cultures of America which came from the roots of American society. Jazz is the first indigenous American style to affect music in the rest of the world.

The music called jazz was born sometime around 1895 in New Orleans. The city of New Orleans features prominently in the early development of jazz. It was home manat. S#468a. (Not pictured.) A colorful portrait of Mae Jemison.

Jenkins, Charles Lamont

Charles Lamont Jenkins is an American track and field athlete. He surprised people in many ways. He was an unexpected winner of the gold medal at the 1956 Summer Olympics. He became a track and field coach at Villanova University in 1961 and eventually became head coach there. After earning a doctorate in education, Charlie Jenkins worked for the State Department.

265

10/20/58. Dominican Republic. Quantity unknown. 2 centavos. S#Cl06. This issue commemorates Jenkins' success in the Melbourne Olympics. It was also an overprint (+ 2 cents) to celebrate the International Geophysical Year, 1957–58. *Illus. 275.*

Jenkins, Ferguson

Ferguson Jenkins is an American professional baseball player. He was respected as one of the best pitchers during the mid sixties. With all of his talent, however, he was never able to pitch in a World Series game.

Ferguson Jenkins was born in Chatham, Ontario, Canada. His family on his mother's side had moved to Canada from the United States via the Underground Railroad to escape slavery. His father was from Barbados.

After his high school graduation, Jenkins signed with the Phillies, who called him up for the 1965 season. In 1966 the Phillies "packaged" Jenkins with Adolfo Phillips and John Herrnstein and traded them to the Chicago Cubs for Bob Buhl and Larry Jackson. Jenkins did well with the Cubs. In the 1967 All-Star game he pitched three innings, striking out six and allowing only one run. Over the next decade he would play for other teams, including the Texas Rangers and the Boston Red Sox.

Jenkins retired just short of his fortieth birthday with a career record of 284–226. Inducted into the Hall of Fame in 1991, he presently lives in Oklahoma.

1/23/97. St. Vincent and the Grenadines. Quantity unknown. 1 dollar. S#2380n. The stamp features a colorful portrait of Ferguson Jenkins. See Hank Aaron, S#2380g, for more information on the stamp.

Jenkins, Monte

A stamp is said to honor professional basketball player Monte Jenkins, but no information on such a stamp is available.

Johnson, Earvin A. "Magic"

Basketball star Magic Johnson was born Earvin Johnson in Lansing, Michigan, in 1959. He acquired the nickname "Magic" after playing impressively well in a college game at Michigan State University. He led the same team to the National Collegiate Athletic Association finals in 1979.

Johnson left Michigan State after his

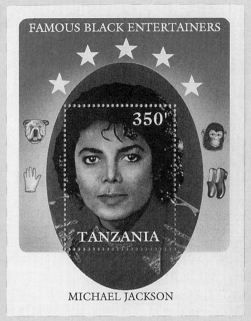

266

267

268

269

270

271

272

sophomore year to become a professional basketball player with the Los Angeles Lakers. He helped to lead the Lakers to five NBA championships. In 1980, he became the first rookie to be named Most Valuable Player of the NBA finals. He achieved the MVP title on two other occasions.

In 1991, Johnson announced that he had tested positive for the AIDS virus and that he was retiring from professional basketball. He became a national spokesman in the fight against AIDS. He attempted to come out of retirement for a brief two-year stint, but controversy surrounded his return and he retired again.

Johnson was a member of the United States basketball team that won the gold medal at the 1992 Summer Olympics in Barcelona, Spain. Magic served on the President's Council on AIDS. Today, he is an entrepreneur specializing in the theater business and other ventures.

1992. São Tomé and Principe. Quantity unknown. 60 dobra. (Souvenir sheet; not pictured.) This is a color snapshot of Magic Johnson and Michael Jordan during the 1992 Olympics in Barcelona.

12/22/92. St. Vincent. Quantity unknown. 2 dollars. S#1744b. Celebrates Olympic gold medal winners— specifically the United States basketball team of 1992. *Illus. 276.*

8/24/95. St. Vincent. Quantity unknown. 5 dollars. S#2202. (Souvenir sheet; not pictured.) Commemorates the 1996 summer Olympics. Done in litho.

Johnson, Jack

John Arthur "Jack" Johnson was born in 1878 in Galveston, Texas. A professional boxer, he became the first African American heavyweight champion of America. He began boxing in 1899 and fought his last bout in 1927.

Some of Johnson's famous victories came with controversy. He won a disputed world championship heavyweight title from the Canadian boxer Tommy Burns in 1908 in Sydney, Australia. In 1910 he knocked out the former heavyweight champion, American boxer Jim Jeffries, to retain the title. Johnson's lifestyle and his refusal to be subservient to white Americans caused him many problems. He was seen as a flamboyant and "uppity" black man for his time. The movie *The Great White Hope*, starring James Earl Jones, depicted Jack Johnson as a proud black man married to a white woman in the late 1800s.

Jack Johnson lost the title to the American boxer Jess Willard in Havana, Cuba, in 1915. He was knocked out in the 26th round. Jack Johnson died in 1946, but his name lives on. He has been recognized on international stamps, but not yet on an U.S. stamp.

7/15/93. Tanzania. Quantity unknown. 400 shillings. S#1079h. From a Black Athletes issue, 8 stamps per sheet. *Illus. 279.*

Johnson, James P.

What was it that made jazz composer and pianist James P. Johnson stand out from such great musical artists as Eubie Blake, Scott Joplin and others during the pioneering period of blues, jazz, and ragtime? It was a piano style known as stride. Earl Hines, Fats Waller, and others played the stride well, but it was James P. Johnson who was the master and became known as the father of stride. The stride was a combination of jazz, blues, pop, and ragtime.

Johnson was born in New Brunswick, New Jersey, on February 1, 1894. He made up his mind at an early age that he wanted to become a pianist. Great players surrounded him. Johnson admired the styles of these and copied many of their playing styles. At the age of fourteen James P. and his family moved to New York, where he met an even greater variety of musicians. Even though while he was in New Jersey he had heard country set and square dances, church hymns, marches, stomps, blues,

273

274

275

276   277

278   279

pop, folk songs, and ballads, nothing excited him more than what he was now listening to in New York City.

Around 1922 Johnson was good enough to play professionally in bars and movie houses for parties, where the fees were usually paid in food and drink. Johnson wanted badly to become a first-class act, and he was acquiring impressive standards. His first professional job was at a local sporting house, playing for two hours straight. By taking lessons, he had improved his technique and execution. Johnson soon became recognized as one of the best piano players on the East Coast. During his lifetime he made more than 400 recordings and wrote approximately 230 popular tunes. One of his greatest was "If I Could Be with You, One Hour Tonight." His recording of "Carolina Shout," in 1921, is considered the first jazz piano solo on record. Johnson also backed up Ida Cox, Ethel Waters, and Bessie Smith, all popular singers during his time.

According to *The New Grove Dictionary of Music and Musicians*, "James P. Johnson from 1928 until illness incapacitated him composed large scale works, of which few are performed, because the execution requires a rare amalgam of classical and jazz techniques."

James P. Johnson died in New York City on November 17, 1955, and was recently (1995) recognized on a U.S. postage stamp.

9/16/95. United States. Quantity unknown. 32 cents. S#2985. From the Legends of American Music series. *Illus. 277.*

Johnson, James Weldon

James Weldon Johnson was a poet, novelist, songwriter, editor, historian, civil rights leader, human rights advocate, lawyer, lyricist, administrator, journalist, lecturer, educator, politician, and diplomat. He was born in 1871, the middle child of James Johnson (a Baptist minister) and Helen (Dillette) Johnson (a school-teacher). Johnson was married to Grace Nail; they had no children.

Johnson received his primary education in Jacksonville, Florida, and since there was no high school for African Americans during that time, he completed his secondary education and graduated from Atlanta University in Atlanta, Georgia. He was valedictorian and an outstanding baseball player for the school. He studied English and drama at Columbia University in New York City. He also received honorary degrees from Atlanta University, Howard University, and Talladega College.

Johnson is most noted for his poetry, novels and music. His writing and musical talents were passed down from his parents; his father played the guitar and his mother taught him and his brother, J. Rosamond Johnson, to play the piano. James, with the assistance of his brother, is credited with writing "Lift Every Voice and Sing," today recognized as the "black national anthem." James Weldon Johnson died in 1938.

2/2/88. United States. 97,300,000. 22 cents. S#2371. From the Black Heritage series. *Illus. 278.*

Johnson, Pete

A stamp honoring Pete Johnson, an African American professional football player who was a Super Bowl star, is said to exist, but no information on such a stamp is available.

Johnson, Rafer

Rafer Johnson was born August 18, 1936, in Hillsboro, Texas. He was a tremendous track and field athlete. He excelled in the decathlon. He won the silver medal in the decathlon at the 1956 Summer Olympics and the gold medal at the 1960 Summer Olympics. His career led to his winning of the James E. Sullivan Award. He also had the honor of lighting the Olympic Flame at the 1984 Summer Olympics in Los Angeles, California. He is now the president of the Special Olympics for the state of California.

1972. Paraguay. Quantity unknown. 18.15 guaranies. Issued for the 1972 Munich Olympics. Celebrates Johnson's 1960 win in Rome. *Illus. 282.*

5/25/72. Equatorial Guinea. Quantity unknown. 5 pesetas guineanas. Minkus#622. Issued for the Munich 1972 Olympics, this stamp celebrates Johnson's 1960 decathlon win in Rome. *Illus. 280.*

1975. Nicaragua. Quantity unknown. 25 córdobas. Celebrates Johnson as one of the decathlon winners. *Illus. 281.*

7/2/84. Liberia. Quantity unknown. 4 cents. S#1000. Issued for the 1984 Olympics in Los Angeles. Celebrates Johnson's 1960 win. *Illus. 283.*

8/6/84. Burundi. Quantity unknown. 30 francs. S#626. Issued in honor of the 1984 Summer Olympics in Los Angeles. Celebrates Johnson's 1960 win. *Illus. 284.*

Johnson, Robert

Many musicians and blues fans regard Robert Johnson as the greatest, most important blues musician ever — even though he died very young, leaving only a handful of recorded songs.

Johnson was born on May 8, 1911, in Hazlehurst, Mississippi. Robert Johnson's early years of life were filled with pain and turmoil. His father, Noah Johnson, was not the man his mother, Julia Dodds, was married to. His mother left her husband and moved to Memphis with Robert and his little sister. Later, Robert moved into the home of his biological father and took his father's surname.

Johnson's first instrument was the harmonica; later he took up the guitar. Heavily influenced by the great country-bluesmen Charley Patton, Son House, and Willie Brown, he made the Mississippi Delta blues style his own. He traveled extensively in both North and South, from the Delta to Chicago and New York and back again, playing at juke joints and even on the street. Johnson's greatest songs, such as "Come On in My Kitchen," and

"Me and the Devil Blues," are widely played today.

Robert Johnson is said to have been poisoned by a jealous man who thought Robert wanted his woman. Robert died at a very young age from alcohol mixed with poison. It was sad that such a thing could happen to such a young man with so much talent. Even with a short life, Robert left a treasure of music to the world.

9/17/94. United States. 19,988,800. 29 cents. S#2857. From the Legends of American Music series. *Illus. 285.*

Jones, Cobi

A stamp is said to exist that recognizes Cobi Jones, an African American soccer player, but no information on such a stamp is available.

Jones, Ed "Too Tall"

A stamp is said to exist on Ed "Too Tall" Jones, an African American professional football player and Super Bowl star, but no information on such a stamp is available.

Jones, James Earl

Actor James Earl Jones was born in Tate County, Mississippi, on January 17, 1931. His grandparents raised him on a farm near Jackson, Michigan. Jones's desire to become an actor didn't become evident until late in his life. Originally he was a premedical student at the University of Michigan and did military service with the army's Cold Weather Mountain Training command in Colorado.

Jones later moved to New York and studied acting at the American Theater Wing. He made his off-Broadway debut in *Wedding in Japan* (1957). His other plays and on and off-Broadway portrayals include *Sunrise at Campobello* (1958), *The Cool World* (1960), *The Blacks* (1961), *and The Blood Knot* (1964). His acting career really took wing when he appeared in the Broadway smash hit entitled *The Great*

African Americans of Liberia (examples)

Harriet Tubman
Black Heritage USA 13c

Martin Luther King Jr.
Black Heritage USA 15c

Benjamin Banneker
Black Heritage USA 15c

Whitney Moore Young
Black Heritage USA 15c

Jackie Robinson
Black Heritage USA 20c

Scott Joplin
Black Heritage USA 20c

Carter G. Woodson
Black Heritage USA 20c

Mary McLeod Bethune
Black Heritage USA 22

Sojourner Truth 22
Black Heritage USA

Jean Baptiste Pointe Du Sable 22
Black Heritage USA

James Weldon Johnson 22
Lift ev'ry voice and sing
Black Heritage USA

A. Philip Randolph 25
Black Heritage USA

Ida B. Wells
25
Black Heritage USA

Jan E. Matzeliger
Shoe Lasting Machine No.274,207 Patented March 20,1883
29
Black Heritage USA

W.E.B. Du Bois 29
Black Heritage USA

Percy Lavon Julian 29
Black Heritage USA

BLACK HERITAGE
USA 29
DR. ALLISON DAVIS

BLACK HERITAGE
USA 32
BESSIE COLEMAN

BLACK HERITAGE
USA 32 Biologist
Ernest E. Just

BLACK HERITAGE
32 USA
Benjamin O. Davis, Sr.

BLACK HERITAGE
32 USA
Madam C. J. Walker

BLACK HERITAGE
USA 33
MALCOLM X

The Black Heritage Series

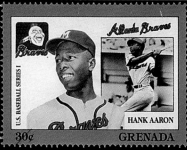

C1

C2

C3

C4

C5

C6

C7

C8

C9

C10

C11

C12

C13

C14

C15

C16

C17

C18

C19

C20

C21

C22

C23

C24

C25

C26

C27

C28

C29

C30

C31

C32

C33

C34

C35

C36

C37

C38

C39

C40

C41

C42

C43

C44

C45

C46

C47

C48

C49

C50

C51

C52

C53

C54

C55

C56

C57

C58

C59

C60

SAMMY DAVIS JR.
TANZANIA
C61

TANZANIA 75/-
SAMMY DAVIS, JR.
C62

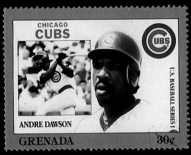
C63

HARRISON W. DILLARD - USA
1948 100 metres
C64

C65

Frederick Douglass
C66

C67

ST. VINCENT
OLYMPIC GOLD MEDAL WINNERS
Clyde Drexler
DREAM TEAM
Barcelona '92
C68

C69

C70

C71

Paul Laurence Dunbar
American poet
10 cents U.S. postage
C72

C73

C74

C75

C76

C77

C78

C79

C80

C81

C82

C83

C84

C85

C86

C87

C88

C89

C90

C91

C92

C93

C94

C95

C96

C97

C98

C99

C100

C101

C102

C103

C104

C105

C106

C107

C108

C109

C110

C111

C112

C113

C114

C115

C116

C117

C118

C119

C120

C121

C122

C123

C124

C125

C126

C127

C128

C129

C130

C131

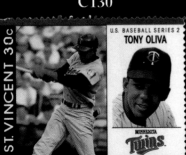

C132

C133

C134

C135

C136

C137

C138

C139

C140

C141

C142

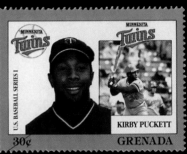

C143

C144

C145

C146

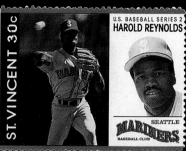

U.S. BASEBALL SERIES 2
HAROLD REYNOLDS

ST. VINCENT 30c

SEATTLE
MARINERS
BASEBALL CLUB

C147

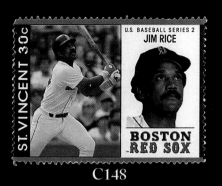

U.S. BASEBALL SERIES 2
JIM RICE

ST. VINCENT 30c

BOSTON
RED SOX

C148

25c

LIONEL RITCHIE

GRENADA

C149

TANZANIA 75/-

LIONEL RITCHIE

C150

REPUBLIC LIBERIA

POSTAGE ONE CENT

C151

LIBERIA
JOSEPH J. ROBERTS
PRESIDENT
OF LIBERIA
1848-1856
1872-1876
1c POSTAGE

C152

LIBERIA
JOSEPH J. ROBERTS
PRESIDENT
OF LIBERIA
1848-1856
1872-1876
1c POSTAGE

C153

LIBERIA
POSTAGE
10 CENTS 10
ROBERTSPORT

C154

1c JOSEPH J. ROBERTS

LIBERIA

C155

SESQUICENTENNIAL · 1961
5c POSTAGE

JOSEPH J. ROBERTS
FIRST PRESIDENT
OF LIBERIA
1848

LIBERIA

C156

SESQUICENTENNIAL 1961
10c POSTAGE

EXECUTIVE MANSION - PAST AND PRESENT

LIBERIA
JOSEPH J.
ROBERTS
FATHER OF THE NATION

C157

LIBERIA
25c AIRMAIL

PROVIDENCE ISLAND

"I BELIEVE THAT THE ALMIGHTY INTENDS
THROUGH THE INSTRUMENTALITY OF
THESE COLONIES TO RESTORE TO
AFRICA HER LONG-LOST GLORY"

SESQUICENTENNIAL YEAR · 1961

C158

AMERICAN INDEPENDENCE
BICENTENNIAL YEAR 1976
GEORGE
WASHINGTON
JOSEPH J. ROBERTS

AMERICAN REVOLUTION BICENTENNIAL
1776-1976

$1.00 POSTAGE
LIBERIA

PRESIDENT GERALD FORD
PRESIDENT
WILLIAM R. TOLBERT JR.

C159

FÜR FRIEDEN
GEGEN RASSISMUS
ЗА МИР
ПРОТИВ РАСИЗМА
FOR PEACE
AGAINST RACISM
20 DDR
PAUL ROBESON 1898-1976
1983

C160

C161

C162

C163

C164

C165

C166

C167

C168

C169

C170

C171

C172

C173

280

281

282

283

284

285

286

287

288

289

290

White Hope, which depicted the life of the first black heavyweight champion, Jack Johnson. For that performance he received the 1969 Tony Award for the best dramatic actor in a Broadway play and Drama Desk Award for one of the best performances of the 1968-1969 New York season. He also received a Tony Award for his performance in August Wilson's Pulitzer Prize–winning play *Fences* in 1987.

Jones is also a presence in film and television. Among his other performances, he portrayed Alex Haley in *Roots: The Next Generation* (1979) and is the dark menacing voice of Darth Vader from the *Star Wars* movie series.

James Earl Jones was elected to the Board of Governors of the Academy of Motion Picture Arts and Sciences in 1976. He was presented with the Mayor's Award of Honor for Arts and Culture in the state of New York in 1979. He received an honorary doctorate of humane letters from the University of Michigan in 1971 and the New York Man of the Year Award in 1976. Jones was inducted into the Theater Hall of Fame in 1985.

3/25/93. The Gambia. Quantity unknown. 20 cedis. S#1349c. (Not pictured.) This multicolored stamp was one of a series issued to recognize American movies and their stars.

Joplin, Scott

Scott Joplin is credited with changing America's musical tastes in the late nineteenth century from a quiet, tame style to a new kind of popular music: ragtime. Because of his own compositions, style of playing and sound, he earned the title "Father of Ragtime Music."

Joplin's father and mother were both musicians and singers. This not only created a strong family bond, but it also encouraged Joplin's ability to make music. At the age of twelve, he studied piano and learned to read music. At the age of twenty, he developed a desire to be a professional musician, despite the fact that racial differences made it very hard for an African American to establish himself as a musician. After several years of traveling through the country and playing music, he settled in St. Louis, Missouri, at the age of 30. It was around this time that he composed the piano rags from which he is best known today, including "Maple Leaf Rag" and "The Entertainer."

Scott Joplin died on April 1, 1917, at the age of 48. Many Americans had not heard of ragtime music until Robert Redford starred in the popular movie *The Sting* in the early '70s. The score for this movie used Joplin's musical compositions. After a little over a half-century, Scott Joplin was awarded the Pulitzer Prize posthumously in 1976 for his ragtime opera *Treemonisha*. (published in 1911).

6/9/83. United States. 115,200,000. 20 cents. S#2044. From the Black Heritage series. *Illus. 286.*

2/15/1992. Tanzania. Quantity unknown. 75 shillings. S#811a. *Illus. 287.*

Jordan, June

A stamp is said to exist on the twentieth century author June Jordan, but no information on such a stamp is available.

Jordan, Michael

Michael Jordan is recognized to as one of the greatest basketball players who ever lived. Jordan was born in Brooklyn, New York, and raised in Wilmington, North Carolina. He attended the University of North Carolina and as a freshman scored the point that won the University of North Carolina its 1982 National Collegiate Athletic Association (NCAA) championship game. He was selected college player of the year for the 1983-1984 season.

Michael Jordan left the University of North Carolina in 1984 to play professional basketball with the Chicago Bulls of the NBA (National Basketball Association). He completed his first season with the Bulls (1984–1985) as one of the top scoring players in the league, with an average of 28.2 points per game. That same year Jordan was named rookie of the year and made the first of his eight All-Star game appearances.

Jordan ended the 1986–1987 season as the second player, after Wilt Chamberlain, to score more than 3000 points in a single season. He led the NBA in scoring for seven consecutive seasons (1987–1993), matching Chamberlain's record, and averaged more than 30 points per game in each season. He became the Chicago Bulls' all-time leader in scoring, with 21,541 points. His NBA scoring records include highest career scoring average (32.3 points per game) and the highest scoring average for an NBA championship series (41 points per game in the 1993 NBA final playoff series). He led the Chicago Bulls to their first NBA championship title in 1991. With Jordan as key leader of the Bulls' team, they won again in 1992 and 1993. In addition to his three Most Valuable Player (MVP) awards—1988, 1991 and 1992—Jordan won the All-Star game MVP award.

Jordan decided that he had lost the desire to continue playing professional basketball and announced his retirement prior to the 1993-1994 season. In 1994 he again found himself in a professional sport: baseball, a game he had played in high school, when he dreamed of being a professional baseball player. He signed with the Chicago White Sox's minor league team. Jordan stayed in the minor league for one season, then returned to basketball and the Chicago Bulls in 1995. Jordan changed his jersey from the famous 23 number to 45, and later back to number 23. Jordan led the Chicago bulls to three more NBA championships (1995, 1996, 1997), and added another three MVP's to his record.

In January of 1999 Michael Jordan again announced his retirement to the world. Today he is not only known as the greatest basketball player, but considered a shrewd businessman. He endorses many products and is involved in several businesses. The world has found him worthy of recognition on postage stamps for his contribution to world basketball.

1992. São Tomé and Príncipe. Quantity unknown. 60 dobras. (Souvenir sheet; not pictured.) This is a color snapshot of Michael Jordan and Magic Johnson during the 1992 Olympics in Barcelona.

3/6/92. The Gambia. Quantity unknown. 12 dalasis. S#1203. (Not pictured.) This stamp features a colorful U.S. map and reads, "Michael Jordan, Basketball, USA 1984." It comes in a souvenir sheet (Numbers 1197–1204) of 8 stamps.

12/17/1992. St. Vincent. Quantity unknown. 2 dollars. S#1745a. Part of an issue honoring the U.S. Olympic basketball "Dream Team," Barcelona Olympics, 1992. *Illus. 288.*

7/15/93. Tanzania. Quantity unknown. 40 shillings. S#1079b. From an issue in recognition of black athletes. 8 per sheet. *Illus. 289.*

12/1/95. Nicaragua. Quantity unknown. 5 córdobas. S#2120a. (Souvenir sheet; not pictured.) Souvenir sheet of 6 stamps honoring the 1996 Summer Olympics in Atlanta.

4/17/96. St. Vincent. Quantity unknown. 2 dollars. S#2268Ab. (Not pictured.) This stamp is done in litho. It also comes in a sheet of 17, 16 #b, 1 #c.

4/17/96. St. Vincent. Quantity unknown. 30 dollars. S#2268D. (Not pictured.) This stamp is done in litho and embossed with gold. It features a portrait of Michael Jordan.

Joyner, Al

Al Joyner is an American track and field athlete. He won the 1984 Olympic triple jump (hop, step, and jump) gold medal. Al Frederick Joyner was born January 19, 1960, in East St. Louis, Illinois. His life story in sports began at Arkansas State University. There he became a member of the Bud Light Track America Club. Al reached his peak in

1983 when he placed second at the NCAA meet and third at the TAC meet. He took eighth place at the world championships that same year and set a personal record of 56 feet, 2¾ inches in 1983, a performance that earned him the ranking of tenth in the world. He went on to win the Modesto Relays on May 11, 1984, and finished third at the UCLA/Pepsi meet the next day. Although a decided underdog going into the 1984 Olympics, he took the gold medal.

Al Joyner is also a national-class high hurdler with a best time of 13.51 seconds, recorded in Zurich in 1985.

In October 1987 Joyner married sprinter and Olympic champion Florence Griffith, one of the superstars of the 1988 Summer Olympics. He became his wife's coach in 1988 after she stopped training with Bob Kersee.

10/8/84. Niger. Quantity unknown. 300 francs. S#341. From an issue honoring 1984 Olympic winners. *Illus. 290.*

Joyner, Florence Griffith

Florence Griffith Joyner died in her sleep at 6:30 A.M. on September 21, 1998. She was 38 years old. That death should come so early to a world-class athlete was a shock to many.

Delorez Florence Griffith was born in 1959 in Los Angeles, California, and educated at the University of California at Los Angeles. In 1987 she married Olympic athlete Al Joyner.

Florence won three gold medals in the 1988 Summer Olympic Games in Seoul, South Korea, winning in the 100 and 200 meter dashes and the 400-meter relay. She came close to winning four gold medals when the American team came in second place in the 1,600-meter relay.

"Flojo," as she was often called, still holds world records in the 100 and 200 meter dashes. She also set the 100 meter mark of 10.49 seconds at the Olympic trial quarterfinal in Indianapolis in 1988, and since then, no woman has broken 10.60. At the Seoul games, Flojo won the gold at 10.54. She was also voted the Associated Press Female Athlete of the Year in 1988. Florence also won the Sullivan Award as the nation's top amateur athlete.

Long before her death, Flojo was recognized internationally on postage stamps from around the world for her outstanding performances in track and field events.

2/15/88. Mongolia. Quantity unknown. 60 mongo. S#1682. *Illus. 291.*

2/15/89. Grenada. Quantity unknown. 2 dollars. S#2015. (Not pictured.) Recognition of 1988 Olympic athletes. This stamp is also issued in a souvenir sheet of 6 stamps.

2/15/89. Guyana. Quantity unknown. 2 dollars. S#2014. (Not pictured.)

7/15/93. Tanzania. Quantity unknown. 150 shillings. S#1079f. *Illus. 292.*

Joyner-Kersee, Jackie

Jackie Joyner-Kersee was born in East St. Louis, Illinois, as Jacqueline Joyner. She is known as a great track and field athlete. She attended the University of California in Los Angeles. Jackie won her first of four consecutive national pentathlon championships at age fourteen. Jackie was also an excellent basketball player at the University of California. She married her coach, Bob Kersee. He encouraged her to train for multiple event contests.

Jackie and her brother, Al Joyner, in 1983 represented the United States at the world championships in Helsinki, Finland. She and her brother also competed in the 1984 Summer Olympic Games in Los Angeles. There she won the silver medal in the heptathlon — a two-day event in which athletes compete in 100-meter hurdles, high jump, shot put, and 200-meter race on the first day and in the long jump, javelin, and 800-meter race on the second day.

Joyner-Kersee continued her success in 1987 at the indoor and outdoor track and field championship in the United States, at

291

292

293

294

295

296

297

298

299

300

301

302

the Pan-American Games in Indianapolis, Indiana, and at the world championships in Rome. She also won the gold medals in the long jump and heptathlon at the 1988 Olympics in Seoul, South Korea. She won the gold medal and set world, Olympic, and American records in the events. She also won the gold medal and set the Olympic record in the long jump at Seoul, with a leap of 24 ft 3½ in (7.3m).

Joyner-Kersee again won the heptathlon and came in third in the long jump in the 1992 Olympics in Barcelona, Spain. She then overcame illness to capture the 1993 heptathlon gold medal at the world championships in Stuttgart, Germany. She has been the recipient of many athletic awards, and earned a reputation as the world's best all around female athlete and the greatest heptathlete of time.

1988. Grenada Quantity unknown. 10 cents. S#1685. From an issue honoring 1988 Olympic winners. *Illus. 294.*

1992. Uganda. Quantity unknown. 20 shillings. Commemorates the 1992 Barcelona Olympics. Photo of Joyner-Kersee in the heptathlon *Illus. 293.*

Julian, Percy Lavon

Russell Adams, in his book *Great Negroes Past and Present* describes Dr. Percy Lavon Julian as "perhaps the most famous living Negro scientist during his time." He went on to state that just as George Washington Carver demonstrated what could be done with the ordinary peanut, Dr. Julian found important new uses for the soybean, which was until his time just another bean. From the soybean Julian extracted an ingredient to relieve inflammatory arthritis.

The ingredient was a steroid, a chemical compound occurring naturally in organic substances. Steroids are widely used today as medications for many conditions. Arthritis has been treated with steroids since the mid-twentieth century. Before Dr. Julian's research with soybeans these steroids were extracted from the bile of animals at a cost of several hundred dollars a gram. Substituting a steroid from the oil of the soybean made it less costly.

Dr. Julian graduated from De Paul University in 1920. He spent several years teaching at Fisk and Howard universities and West Virginia State College. He also attended Harvard and completed his doctorate at the University of Vienna. He taught at De Paul and later became director of research and manager of fine chemicals at the Glidden Company and formed his own company, which was devoted mainly to the production of steroids.

Percy Julian was a millionaire by 1969. His company merged with Smith, Kline and Beecham. Smith, Kline and Beecham at that time paid Dr. Julian several millions of dollars for his steroid research. SmithKline and Beecham Corporation is still a very productive large pharmaceutical company.

Dr. Percy Julian was born in 1899, and before his death in 1975, he found a way to mass produce the drug physostigmine, used to treat glaucoma, and perfected the mass production of sex hormones which led the way to birth control pills.

1/29/93. United States. 105,000,000. 29 cents. S#2746. From the Black Heritage series. *Illus. 295.*

Just, Ernest E.

Dr. Just was a modest man. He was a great biologist who made vital contributions to the understanding of egg fertilization and the study of the cell. Ernest E. Just was a native of South Carolina born in 1893 in Charleston. Just attended Dartmouth College on a scholarship. He graduated magna cum laude and Phi Beta Kappa.

It is hard to overestimate the importance of Just's contributions to biological science. Dr. Charles Drew, himself an outstanding researcher in blood plasma preservation, described Dr. Just as a "biologist of unusual skill and the greatest of our original thinkers in the field." He was seen as producing new concepts of cell life and metabolism that would assure him a permanent place in the history of science.

Dr. Just wrote two major books and more than sixty scientific papers in his field. He was for many years Howard University's outstanding professor in the biological sciences and received many awards and grants for his research. Scientists from America and abroad sought him out for his knowledge on cells.

Dr. Just died in 1941. He was recognized on a United States stamp in 1996 for his contributions in the field of natural science.

2/1/96. United States. 92,000,000. 32 cents. S#3058. From the Black Heritage series. *Illus. 296.*

Justice, David

Professional baseball player David Justice was born on November 4, 1966, in Cincinnati, Ohio. He attended Covington Latin High School in Kentucky and Thomas More College in Kentucky. The Atlanta Braves in the fourth round free agent status drafted David on June 3, 1985. During his time with the Braves, Justice had many injuries and was on Atlanta's disabled list from June 27 to August 20, 1991. He continued with injuries and remained on the disabled list through 1997. David was traded in 1997 to the Cleveland Indians for Kenny Lofton.

David holds a major league single season record for fewest errors by outfielders who led league in errors. He was named N.L. (National League) Rookie Player of the year by the *Sporting News* in 1990 and named to the N.L. Silver Slugger team in 1993. He continues to garner many honors.

David Justice has been traded to several different teams in the past several years. He is now (June 2001) with the New York Yankees as their designated hitter.

9/2/91. Congo. Quantity unknown. 200 francs. S#932. (Souvenir sheet.) See Rickey Henderson, S#932 (page 102). David Justice is at left standing at the plate waiting for a pitch.

King, Martin Luther, Jr.

Ten years before his death by an assassin's bullet, Martin Luther King, Jr., was described by Dr. Benjamin E. Mays of Morehouse College in the following words: "You are mature beyond your years, wiser at twenty-nine than most men at sixty, more courageous in a righteous struggle than most men can ever be, living a faith that most men preach about and never experience…. Your name has become a symbol of courage and hope for oppressed people everywhere."

Martin Luther King, Jr., was one of three children born to the Reverend and Mrs. M.L. King, Sr., on January 15, 1929, in Atlanta, Georgia. He was married to Coretta Scott; they were the parents of four children.

Martin Luther King, Jr., attended Booker T. Washington High School in Atlanta and at the age of fifteen was accepted at Morehouse College, also in Atlanta. At Morehouse he completed studies for his undergraduate degree. Dr. Benjamin E. Mays, president of Morehouse, influenced him to become a minister. With Dr. Mays' encouragement King entered Crozer Theological Seminary in Chester, Pennsylvania. While there he was elected president of the student government and recognized as a scholar. He continued to pursue his studies in the ministry and earned his doctor of philosophy degree from Boston University.

While the pastor of Dexter Avenue Baptist Church in Montgomery, Alabama, King was chosen by the African American community as spokesperson and motivator behind the Montgomery bus boycott. He went on to lead many protests aimed at winning civil rights for African Americans. Adopting Mohandas (Mahatma) Gandhi's strategy of nonviolent protest, King and the civil rights movement made great progress in America, and significant legislation was passed to assure the rights of African Americans and other minorities in American society.

Dr. Martin Luther King, Jr., the "father of the African American social revolution" and Nobel Peace Price winner, made a difference in world peace and helped to change the segregated system in America. For his contributions, the United States and more than 85 other countries have recognized Dr. King on more than 150 postage stamps.

Issue date unknown. Dominica. (Perforated souvenir sheet.) Quantity unknown. 5 dollars. Perforated souvenir sheet honoring the "40th anniversary of human rights." Shows King, Mahatma Gandhi, Albert Einstein, and Eleanor Roosevelt. *Illus. 323.*

Issue date unknown. Guinea-Bissau. Quantity unknown. 5 pesos. S#7701. Stamp honoring the United States bicentennial. Only a copy is shown here. *Illus. 339.*

Issue date unknown. Guyana. Quantity unknown. 600 dollars. (Gold foil; not pictured.) This gold foil stamp is rather rare. It is also identified by a number on the back. The following individuals are found on the stamp: left to right—back row, King, John F. Kennedy, Lincoln; front row, Franklin D. Roosevelt and Winston Churchill. A duplicate of this stamp was also issued in silver foil. *Illus. 340.*

Issue date unknown. Guyana. Quantity unknown. 100 dollars. *Illus. 341.*

1968. Congo. Quantity unknown. 60 francs. (Perforated souvenir sheet.) This souvenir sheet includes portraits of John F. and Robert Kennedy as well as King. *Illus. 314.*

1968. United States. Quantity unknown. 25 cents. (See color section.) This was the first stamp issued in the United States of America recognizing Martin Luther King, Jr. It was issued by the Independent Postal System (IPS) of America. In fourteen years of research the author has seen this actual stamp only once. Others do exist somewhere, but they are difficult to find. *Illus. C118.*

1968. Manama. Quantity unknown. 60 dirhams. Minkus#104. (Imperforate). This unique stamp is a large circle (2½ inches in diameter) and is done in gold foil. It is a difficult stamp to find. There are three overprints of this stamp recognizing the following: "APOLLO 13 1970," "UNITED NATIONS 1945–1970," and "APOLLO 14 1970." *Illus. 363.*

1968. Mutawakelite Kingdom of Yemen. Quantity unknown. 18 buqsha. Same artwork as Michell#588, but in an imperforate version. In honor of "world racial peace." *Illus. 402.*

1968. Yemen Arab Republic. Quantity unknown. 16 riyals. (Souvenir sheet.) This stamp comes in 24-karat gold in a specially designed booklet issued by the Yemen Arab Republic. A most rare stamp. *Illus. 403.*

1968. Mutawakelite Kingdom of Yemen. Quantity unknown. 2 buqsha. This is an imperforate stamp. It is also issued in a perforated version, Michel#542. *Illus. 390.*

1968. Mutawakelite Kingdom of Yemen. Quantity unknown. 4 buqsha. This is an imperforate stamp. It is also available in a perforated version, Michel#546. *Illus. 391.*

1968. Mutawakelite Kingdom of Yemen. Quantity unknown. 6 buqsha. This is an imperforate stamp. It is also available in a perforated version, Michel#550, and on a souvenir sheet, (see below). *Illus. 392.*

1968. Mutawakelite Kingdom of Yemen. Quantity unknown. Each stamp valued at 6 buqsha. (Imperforate souvenir sheet.) This imperforate souvenir sheet includes King with two popes. *Illus. 393.*

1968. Mutawakelite Kingdom of Yemen. Quantity unknown. 10 buqsha. (Perforated souvenir sheet). In honor of "world racial peace." King shown with Abraham Lincoln and John F. Kennedy. This perforated souvenir sheet is trimmed in gold and white. *Illus. 394.*

1968. Mutawakelite Kingdom of Yemen. Quantity unknown. 10 buqsha. Michel#587 (Perf). *Illus. 395.*

1968. Mutawakelite Kingdom of Yemen. Quantity unknown. 10 buqsha. Imperforate. An imperforate version of Michel#587 (see above). *Illus. 396.*

1968. Mutawakelite Kingdom of Yemen. Quantity unknown. 20 buqsha. (Imperforate souvenir sheet). In honor of "world racial peace." This imperforate souvenir sheet shows King

303

304

305

306

307

308

309

holding a little girl with his left arm; his right hand is placed on the shoulder of a little boy. *Illus. 397.*

1968. Mutawakelite Kingdom of Yemen. Quantity unknown. 24 buqsha. (Perforated overprint.) *Illus. 398.*

1968. Mutawakelite Kingdom of Yemen. Quantity unknown. 24 buqsha. (Imperforate overprint.) *Illus. 399.*

1968. Mutawakelite Kingdom of Yemen. Quantity unknown. Two stamps, with face values of 10 buqsha (on left) and 20 buqshas (on right). (Imperforate souvenir sheet). *Illus. 400.*

1/4/68. Mauritania. Quantity unknown. Face value unknown. S#C78a. (Souvenir sheet; not pictured.)

1/10/68. Yemen Arab Republic. Quantity unknown. 12 buqsha. Minkus#607. See Minkus#659 below. *Illus. 388.*

1/10/68. Yemen Arab Republic. Quantity unknown. 16 buqsha. Minkus#659. Minkus#653, 607, and 659 were also issued in souvenir sheets under Minkus#660A and 662. *Illus. 389.*

2/1/68. Togo. Quantity unknown. 15 francs. S#665. (See color section.) Issued in honor of the International Year of Human Rights. This stamp can be found in litho ink, the most rare. The original stamp is designed in litho to print the stamps. *Illus. C107.*

2/1/68. Togo. Quantity unknown. 30 francs. See S#665 above. *Illus. C108.*

2/1/68. Togo. Quantity unknown. 90 francs. S#668. (See color section.) See S#665 above. S#665, 667 and 668 were issued a souvenir sheet under S#C103a. *Illus. C109.*

3/30/68. St. Kitts–Nevis–Anguilla. Quantity unknown. 50 cents. S#190. *Illus. 383.*

5/25/68. Ras al-Khaima. Quantity unknown. 2 riyals. Michel#157. In recognition of the International Human Rights Year. *Illus. 370.*

6/8/68. Mexico. Quantity unknown. 80 cents. S#c339. According to Ernest Austin's *Black American Stamp Album*, this was the first legitimate stamp issued in memory of Martin Luther King, Jr.—two months after his assassination. *Illus. 367.*

6/17/68. Dahomey. Quantity unknown. 30 francs. S#C71. (Perforate.) Recognition of King as Nobel Peace Prize Winner for 1964. Features

a quote from King—"We must meet hate with creative love"—in French, English, and German. S#C72 and C73 were also issued in imperfs. Please note the two imperfs that follow C72 and C73. *Illus. 317.*

6/17/68. Dahomey. Quantity unknown. 55 francs. S#C72. (Perforated). Recognizes King's 1964 Peace Prize win. Photograph of King receiving prize. Also issued as an imperf. (See below.) *Illus. 318.*

6/17/68. Dahomey. Quantity unknown. 100 francs. S#C73. (Perforate). Recognizes King's 1964 Peace Prize win. Also issued as an imperf. (See below.) *Illus. 319.*

6/17/68. Dahomey. Quantity unknown. 55 francs. S#C72. (Imperforate.) This is same as S#C72 except that it is an imperf. *Illus. 320.*

6/17/68. Dahomey. Quantity unknown. 100 francs. S#C73. (Imperforate.) This is the same as S#C73 except that it is an imperf. *Illus. 321.*

7/4/68. St. Lucia. Quantity unknown. 25 cents. S#235. *Illus. 382.*

7/4/68. St. Lucia. Quantity unknown. 35 cents. S#236. *Illus. 384.*

7/10/68. Yemen Arab Republic. Quantity unknown. 50 buqsha. Michel#750. (Overprint; not pictured.) This stamp is done in gold foil and it is also an overprint. This is a difficult stamp to find.

7/11/68. Liberia. Quantity unknown. 15 cents. S#480. Unusual artwork shows King's coffin in his funeral cortege, below the words "Free at last, free at last...." *Illus. 349.*

7/11/68. Liberia. Quantity unknown. 25 cents. S#481. *Illus. 350.*

7/11/68. Liberia. Quantity unknown. 35 cents. S#482. *Illus. 351.*

7/11/68. Liberia. Quantity unknown. 55 cents. S#480. (Perforated souvenir sheet.) The perforated stamp on the center of this souvenir sheet shows King and J.F. Kennedy shaking hands in recognition of King's winning of the Nobel Peace Prize in 1964. This souvenir sheet was issued in memory of King and bears the words "In Memoriam 1968." *Illus. 352.*

7/22/68. Mali. Quantity unknown. 100 francs. S#59. Recognizes King as Nobel Peace Prize winner. *Illus. 353.*

7/25/68. Manama. Quantity unknown. 1 riyal. (Perforated.) *Illus. 357.*

310

311

312

313

314

315

316

317

318

7/25/68. Manama. Quantity unknown. 2 riyals. (Perforated.) *Illus. 358.*

7/25/68. Manama. Quantity unknown. 2 riyals. (Perforated.) See Minkus#245. *Illus. 359.*

7/25/68. Manama. Quantity unknown. 2 riyals. (Perforated). A white man and black man shaking hands symbolizing brotherhood. Top left corner reads "In memory of Martin Luther King." *Illus. 360.*

7/25/68. Manama. Quantity unknown. 2 riyals. *Illus. 361.*

7/25/68. Manama. Quantity unknown. 1 riyal. Minkus#95. (Perforated.) (Not pictured.)

7/25/68. Manama. Quantity unknown. 1 riyal. Minkus#95. (Perforated). *Illus. 356.*

7/25/68. Manama. Quantity unknown. 5 riyals. Minkus#99. (Imperforate souvenir sheet.) *Illus. 362.*

7/25/68. Ajman. Quantity unknown. 1 riyal. Minkus#242. Portrait of King. Inscription at the top left reads, "In Memory of Martin Luther King." Ajman released a series of portraits of American leaders, all bearing this inscription. This stamp also bears the words "Human Rights." *Illus. 298.*

7/25/68. Ajman. Quantity unknown. 1 riyal. Portrait of Abraham Lincoln. Inscription in upper left corner of this stamp: "In memory of Martin Luther King." *Illus. 299.*

7/25/68. Ajman. Quantity unknown. 1 riyal. Portrait of John F. Kennedy. Inscription in upper left corner: "In memory of Martin Luther King." *Illus. 300.*

7/25/68. Ajman. Quantity unknown. 2 riyals. Vietnam Soldier carrying a wounded solider. Inscription at top left: "In Memory of Martin Luther King." *Illus. 301.*

7/25/68. Ajman. Quantity unknown. 2riyals. Minkus#245. Pictured left to right: Abraham Lincoln, Dr. Martin Luther King, Jr., and John F. Kennedy. Inscription, upper left: "Human Rights In Memory of Martin Luther King." *Illus. 302.*

7/25/68. Ajman. Quantity unknown. 5 riyals. Minkus#246. (Imperforate souvenir sheet.) Dr. Martin Luther King, Jr. (Mikus#242), and John F. Kennedy on a souvenir sheet. *Illus. 303.*

8/8/68. Sharjah. Quantity unknown. 1 riyal. Minkus#355. (Perforated souvenir sheet.) Hard to find stamp. Minkus #355–Minkus#357 are perforated versions of Minkus#146–Minkus #148. See Minkus#146 (Khor Fakkon). *Illus. 376.*

8/8/68. Sharjah. Quantity unknown. 35 riyals. Minkus#356. (Perforated.) Hard to find stamp. See Minkus#355 (perf) above. *Illus. 377.*

8/8/68. Sharjah. Quantity unknown. 60 riyals. S#357. (Perforated.) Hard stamp to find. See Minkus#355 (perf) above. *Illus. 378.*

8/15/68. Congo. S#C70. Quantity unknown. 50 francs. In recognition of King's nonviolent philosophy. *Illus. 311.*

8/26/68. St. Vincent. Quantity unknown. 5 cents. S#259. (See color section.) *Illus. c102.*

8/26/68. St. Vincent. Quantity unknown. 25 cents. S#260. (See color section.) *Illus. c103.*

9/23/68. Samoa I Sisifo (Western Samoa). Quantity unknown. 7 sene. S#298. *Illus. 372.*

9/23/68. Samoa I Sisifo (Western Samoa). Quantity unknown. 20 sene. S#299. *Illus. 373.*

9/26/68. St. Vincent. Quantity unknown. 35 cents. S#261. (See color section.) *Illus. C104.*

9/28/68. Rwanda. Quantity unknown. 100 francs. S#255. (Perforated souvenir sheet.) The words below the stamp on this perforated souvenir sheet are a quote from King, translated into French. In English the quote is, "A man who would not die for something is not capable of living." *Illus. 371.*

9/30/68. Mutawakelite Kingdom of Yemen. Quantity unknown. 18 buqsha. Michel#588. In honor of "world racial peace." *Illus. 401.*

10/4/68. Niger. Quantity unknown. 100 francs. S#C95. *Illus. 365.*

10/4/68. Niger. Quantity unknown. Face value unknown. S#C97a (Souvenir sheet; not pictured.)

10/15/68. Virgin Islands. Quantity unknown. 4 cents. S#192. (See color section.) *Illus. C121.*

10/15/68. Virgin Islands. Quantity unknown. 25 cents. S#193. (See color section.) *Illus. C122.*

11/4/68. Mauritania. Quantity unknown. 50 francs. S#C77. *Illus. 364.*

11/28/68. Panama. Quantity unknown. 0.40 balboas. Minkus#1133. (Perforated souvenir sheet.) Portraits of three "leaders of human rights": King, John F. Kennedy, and Robert Kennedy. *Illus. 369.*

319   320   321

322

323

324

325   326   327

12/1/68. Turks and Caicos Islands. Quantity unknown. 1/6 dollar. S#178. (See color section.) *Illus. C113.*

12/1/68. Turks and Caicos Islands. Quantity unknown. 2 dollars. S#179. (See color section.) *Illus. C114.*

12/1/68. Turks and Caicos Islands. Quantity

unknown. 8 dollars. S#180. (See color section.) *Illus. C115.*

12/2/68. Montserrat. Quantity unknown. 1 dollar. S#207. In recognition of the International Human Rights Year, 1968. *Illus. 366.*

12/5/68. Cameroon. Quantity unknown. 30 francs. S#111. *Illus. 308.*

329

328

330

331

332

12/5/68. Cameroon. Quantity unknown. 70 francs. S#C115. *Illus. 309.*

12/16/68. Guinea. Quantity unknown. 75 francs. S#520. *Illus. 337.*

12/16/68. Guinea. Quantity unknown. 100 francs. S#Cl80. *Illus. 338.*

12/21/68. Paraguay. Quantity unknown. 30 centimos. Minkus#1618. Hard to find stamp. Recognizes King as a Nobel Prize winner. *Illus. 315.*

1969. Khor Fakkan. Quantity unknown. 1 riyal. Minkus#146. (Imperforate; overprint.) The original issue is from Sharjah (ash–Sharigah), of which Khor Fakkan is an enclave. The overprint reads, "Khor Fakkan." This is a hard to find stamp. *Illus. 346.*

1969. Khor Fakkan. Quantity unknown. 35 riyals. Minkus#147. (Imperforate; overprint.) See Minkus#146. *Illus. 347.*

1969. Khor Fakkan. Quantity unknown. 60 riyals. Minkus#148. (Imperforate; overprint.) See Minkus#146. *Illus. 348.*

1/10/69. Yemen Arab Republic. Quantity unknown. 1 buqsha. Minkus#651.

1/10/69. Yemen Arab Republic. Quantity unknown. 4 buqsha. Minkus #653. See Minkus#659.

1/15/69. Gabon. Quantity unknown. 100 francs. S#C81. *Illus. 329.*

1/25/69. India. Quantity unknown. 20 naya paise. S#486. *Illus. 345.*

3/7/69. Ghana. Quantity unknown. 12½ new pence. S#349. *Illus. 330.*

3/7/69. Ghana. Quantity unknown. 20 new pence. S#350. *Illus. 331.*

3/7/69. Ghana. Quantity unknown. S#351a. See comments. (Imperforate souvenir sheet.) This imperforate souvenir sheet was issued to honor the International Human Rights Year, 1968. Four stamps are pictured, including the King stamps S#349 (12 1/2 new pence) and S#350 (20 new pence). The other two stamps feature a portrait of Ghananian nationalist J.B. Danquah (face values 4 new pence and 40 new pence). *Illus. 332.*

4/1/69. Venezuela. Quantity unknown. 1 bolivar. S#934. (See color section.) *Illus. C119.*

5/20/69. Chad. Quantity unknown. 50 francs. S#C54. (Perforated.) In recognition of Dr. King's nonviolent philosophy. *Illus. 310.*

6/5/69. Fujeira. Quantity unknown. 50 dirhams. Minkus#304. (Perforated.) *Illus. 325.*

6/5/69. Fujeira. Quantity unknown. 50 dirhams. Minkus#311. (Perforated; overprint.) This is Minkus#304 with an overprint reading, "International Human Rights Year." Difficult stamp to find. *Illus. 326.*

6/5/69. Fujeira. Quantity unknown. 50 dirhams. Minkus#304. (Imperforate). This is an imperf of S#304. *Illus. 327.*

6/8/69. Grenada. Quantity unknown. 25 cents. S#321. Honoring the International Human Rights Year, 1968. *Illus. 333.*

9/1/69. Togo. Quantity unknown. 30 francs. S#683. (Overprint; see color section.) This is an overprint in memory of Dwight D. Eisenhower. Note the overprint of Eisenhower's head above the King portrait. *Illus. C110.*

9/1/69. Togo. Quantity unknown. 90 francs. S#685. (Overprint; see color section.) See S#683. *Illus. C111.*

9/1/69. Togo. Quantity unknown. 15 francs. S#C111. (Overprint; see color section). See S#683. These overprints (S#683, 685, and C111) were also issued in a souvenir sheet (S#C111a). *Illus. C112.*

1970. Congo. Quantity unknown. 10 francs. Only a poor copy is shown here. *Illus. 312.*

1970. Fujeira/Congo. Quantity unknown. 60 francs. (Imperforate souvenir sheet.) Imperforate souvenir sheet includes King, John F. Kennedy and Robert Kennedy. Please note there is a face value of 12 riyals in Fujeira monetary value. *Illus. 328.*

1/1/70. Ecuador. Quantity unknown. 4 sucres. S#787. Shows King, J. F. Kennedy and R. Kennedy standing in a graveyard. This is a hard to find stamp. *Illus. 324.*

1/2/70. Haiti. Quantity unknown. 10 centimes. S#633. Recognizes King as Nobel Peace Prize winner. *Illus. 342.*

1/12/70. Haiti. Quantity unknown. 20 centimes. S#634. Recognizes King as Nobel Peace Prize winner. *Illus. 343.*

1/12/70. Haiti. Quantity unknown. 25 cents. S#635. (Not pictured.) Same artwork as S#633.

1/12/70. Haiti. Quantity unknown. 50 cents. S#C351. (Not pictured.) Same artwork as S#633.

333

334

335

336

337

338

339

340

341

342

343

344

1/12/70. Haiti. Quantity unknown. 1 gourde. S#C352. Recognizes King as Nobel Peace Prize Winner. *Illus. 344.*

1/12/70. Haiti. Quantity unknown. 1.50 gourde. S#C353. (Not pictured.) Same artwork as S#633.

1971. Guinea. Quantity unknown. 300 francs. S#C14. (Silver foil.) (Not pictured.) This stamp is silver foil, embossed with images of John F. and Robert Kennedy facing King. Not easy to find.

1972. Guinea. Quantity unknown. 1500 francs. S#C14a. (Gold foil.) (Not pictured.) Same artwork as S#C14, but in gold foil. Not an easy to find issue.

12/15/73. Upper Volta. Quantity unknown. 250 francs. S#C310. (Perforated souvenir sheet; see color section.) *Illus. C117.*

1977. Cameroon. Quantity unknown. 400 francs. Minkus#350. (Not pictured.)

7/4/77. Mali. Quantity unknown. 700 francs. S#C310. Recognizes King in the "fight against racism" ("lutte contre le racisme") and as a Nobel Peace Prize winner. *Illus. 354.*

6/27/78. Senegal. Quantity unknown. 150 francs. S#488. The same stamp featured on the souvenir sheet S#489b. *Illus. 375.*

6/27/78. Senegal. Quantity unknown. 200 francs. S#489b (Perforated souvenir sheet.) This perforated souvenir sheet features Mahatma Gandhi and Martin Luther King, "apostles of nonviolence." *Illus. 374.*

7/28/78. Benin. Quantity unknown. 300 francs. S#406. In recognition of the 10th anniversary of King's assassination. Only a poor copy is shown here. *Illus. 304.*

1/13/79. United States. 963,370,000. 15 cents. S#1771. (See color section.) This was the first legitimate United States stamp honoring King. It was part of the Black Heritage series in 1979. *Illus. C120.*

2/28/79. St. Lucia. Quantity unknown. 2 dollars. S#464. Shows Pope Paul VI receiving King in the Vatican, Sept. 18, 1964. *Illus. 380.*

10/23/80. St. Lucia. Quantity unknown. 50 cents. S#527. From in issue recognizing Nobel Prize winners. *Illus. 381.*

12/22/80. Turks and Caicos Islands. Quantity unknown. 20 cents. S#457. (See color section.) *Illus. C116.*

4/4/83. Mali. Quantity unknown. 800 francs. S#496. This is a most unique and rare stamp. Very hard to find. *Illus. 355.*

5/18/83. Djibouti. Quantity unknown. 150 francs. S#C181. (Perforate.) This same stamp comes in the face value of 250 francs. *Illus. 322.*

11/18/85. Sierra Leone. Quantity unknown. 12 leones. S#744. (Perforated souvenir sheet.) This perforated souvenir sheet honors the fortieth anniversary of the United Nations. *Illus. 379.*

4/28/86. Niger. Quantity unknown. 500 francs. S#366. *Illus. 368.*

6/27/86. Cuba. Quantity unknown. 20 cents. S#2873. Only a copy of this stamp is shown here. This is a difficult stamp to find, mostly because of longstanding United States economic sanctions against Cuba. *Illus. 316.*

9/15/86. Grenada. Quantity unknown. 4 dollars. S#1405. Honoring the International Year of Peace. *Illus. 334.*

11/26/86. Sweden. Quantity unknown. 2.90 Kronor. S#1621. (See color section.) This King stamp comes in a booklet. Five personalities are recognized in this booklet issue. They are Martin Luther King, Jr., Bertha Sutiner, Carl Ossiet Zky, Albert Luthuli and Mother Teresa. Sweden is one of the few Western countries that paid tribute to King on a stamp. This is the only stamp issued in Dr. King's honor by a European country. *Illus. C106.*

1/15/87. São Tomé and Príncipe. Quantity unknown. 16 dobras. S#799. In recognition of the International Year of Peace. This hard-to-find stamp features King surrounded by the outline of a dove drawn by Pablo Picasso. Other stamps in this issue feature Mahatma Gandhi, The Red Cross, the International Peace Year, the UN, UNESCO, the Olympic emblem, the Nobel Peace Prize medal, and Albert Luthuli. *Illus. 385.*

1988. Quantity unknown. 35 cents. St. Vincent. S#1164. (See color section.) Recognition of the 25th anniversary of two 1963 events: the March on Washington and the launch of Telstar II. *Illus. C105.*

7/11/88. Benin. Quantity unknown. 200 francs. S#649. In recognition of the twentieth anniversary of King's death. *Illus. 305.*

11/22/88. Burkina Faso. Quantity unknown. 235 francs. S#863. Twentieth anniversary of the assassination of King. *Illus. 307.*

345

346

347

348

349

350

351

352

353   354   355   356

357   358   359

360   361

1990? Congo. Quantity unknown. 75 francs. In recognition of King's 1964 Nobel Peace Prize. Pictures King and Gandhi. *Illus. 313.*

1992. Guyana. Quantity unknown. 7 dollars and 65 cents. (Not pictured.) This stamp depicts multicolored orchids overprinted in black with "Martin Luther King 1929–1968." This stamp and the similar (see below) are not easy to come by.

1992. Guyana. Quantity unknown. 7 dollars and 65 cents. (Not pictured.) This stamp depicts multicolored orchids overprinted in red with "Martin Luther King 1929–1968." See above for further comments.

6/24/93. Benin. Quantity unknown. 190 francs. S#696. In recognition of twenty-fifth anniversary of King' s assassination. *Illus. 306.*

1995. Congo. Quantity unknown. 205 francs. S#C414. (Not pictured.) Portrait of King.

10/2/95. St. Vincent and The Grenadines. Quantity unknown. 1 dollar. S#2219g. (Not pictured.) Portrait of King.

1996. Central African Republic. Quantity unknown. 300 francs. S#1108. (Not pictured.) This stamp features a woman running. Dr. Martin Luther King's memorial is pictured in the lower left side of the stamp.

1996. Central African Republic. Quantity unknown. 175 francs. S#1145b. (Not pictured.) Portrait of King.

3/1/96. Grenada. Quantity unknown. 1 dollar. S#2821a. (Not pictured.) Portrait of King.

8/96. St. Vincent and the Grenadines. Quantity unknown. 1 dollar. S#2346h. (Not pictured.) Features portraits from left to right of Dr. Martin Luther King, Jr., John F. Kennedy, and Bobby Kennedy.

1997. Chad. Quantity unknown. 150 francs. S#730. (Not pictured.) Portrait of King and a bird.

1997. Niger. Quantity unknown. 400 francs. S#949b. (Not pictured.) Portrait of King, with both hands together.

1997. Niger. Quantity unknown. 400 francs. S#9496c. (Not pictured.) From an issue in recognition of famous people. Others recognized in this souvenir issue are President Bill Clinton and President John F. Kennedy. This stamp can also be bought in a sheet of four.

3/15/98. Albania. Quantity unknown. 150 leke. S#2584c. (Not pictured.) Portrait of King.

10/4/98. Kyrgyzstan. Quantity unknown. 10 cents. S#119c. (Not pictured.) Portrait of King.

1999. Angola. Quantity unknown. 200,000 Kwanzaas. (Not pictured.) Portrait of King.

1999. Angola. Quantity unknown. 750,000.00 Kwanzaas. (Not pictured.) Portrait of King.

1999. Niger. Quantity unknown. 2000 francs. Portrait of King.

1999. Angola. Quantity unknown. 500,000 Kwanzas. (Not pictured.) Features a portrait of Dr. King in the upper right of the stamp (trimmed in solid red) and a portrait of President John F. Kennedy in the lower right of the stamp.

1999. Turkmenistan. Quantity unknown.

120.00 Turkmen manata. (Not pictured.) This multicolored stamp depicts Dr. King speaking to a large audience.

5/7/99. Somalia. Quantity unknown. 6,000 shillings. Portrait of King. (Not pictured.)

5/26/99. United States Quantity unknown. 33 cents. S#3188a. (Not pictured.) From the Celebrate the Century series (1960s), recognizes the March on Washington with a portrait of King, showing the Washington Monument in the background and the words "I have a dream" along one side. This is the second stamp issued in honor of Dr. King by the United States Postal Service.

10/15/99. Laos. Quantity unknown. 5500 Kip. Portrait of King. (Not pictured.)

12/6/99. Belgium. Quantity unknown. 17 francs. S#1779f. (Not pictured.) Portrait of King.

Kingsdom, Roger

A stamp honoring Roger Kingsdom, an African American track and field athlete, is said to exist, but no information on such a stamp is available.

Knight, Gladys

Gladys Knight was born on May 28, 1944, in Atlanta, Georgia. Gladys achieved her greatest popularity in the music world during the 1960s and 1970s. She is considered one of the great soul singers of her time.

Gladys Knight was a performer from her childhood years. With her brother Merald and a couple of cousins, she formed a singing group, the Pips. They made the Top Ten in 1961 with the heavily do wop–influenced "Every Beat of My Heart," and recorded some fine pop soul sides for the Fury and Maxx labels in the early and middle '60s. During this period, the group recorded "Letter Full of Tears" and "Giving Up."

These songs made the Top 40, but Knight didn't hit her commercial stride until she moved to Motown in 1966. Steeped in the gospel tradition like so

362

363

364

365

366

367

368

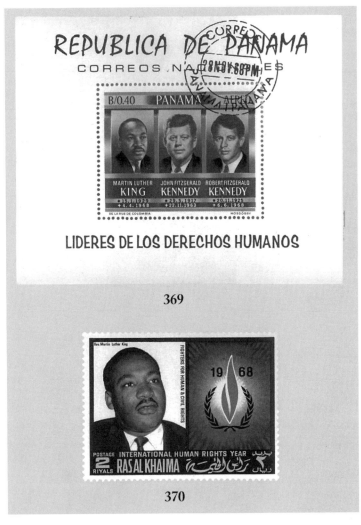

369

370

"Neither One of Us," 1973; then she and the Pips left Motown for Buddah. They were briefly superstars from 1973 to 1974, reeling off the smashes "Midnight Train to Georgia" (their only number one), "I've Got to Use My Imagination," and "Best Thing That Ever Happened to Me." This ranked as some of their best material, but Knight soon moved toward an easy listening, adult contemporary direction, one that she has maintained to this day.

Knight now performs separately from the Pips, who have retired. Though her days as a high-charting star ended after the mid–70s, she remains popular.

3/30/90. Tanzania. Quantity unknown. 100 shillings. S#584. *Illus. 405.*

Kwanzaa

Kwanzaa is a unique African American celebration with focus on the African American family. In 1966 Dr. Maulana Karenga, a California State University professor of African American History, felt that African Americans needed more opportunities to focus on family and community. He believed that the racial unrest that led to violent confrontations like the 1965 Watts riots could be somewhat overcome if African-Americans would reconnect with their African heritage. Dr. Karenga sought to reinstill in the African-American community the principles that had allowed their ancestors to endure slavery, oppression and racism. These princi-

many soul singers, Gladys Knight & the Pips developed into one of Motown's most dependable acts, although they never quite scaled the commercial or artistic heights of fellow stars on the label like the Supremes, Marvin Gaye, and the Temptations.

With Norman Whitfield providing the production and much of the songwriting, the Pips fit well into Motown's machine. With Motown they produced such songs as "Friendship Train" and the original version of "I Heard It Through the Grapevine," "It Should Have Been Me" and "The End of Our Road," and smooth ballads like "If I Were Your Woman."

Knight had her biggest Motown hit with

371

372

373

RÉPUBLIQUE DU SÉNÉGAL

Apôtres de la non violence

374

375

376

377

378

379

380

381

382

383

384

385

ples, as defined by Dr. Karenga, were unity, self-determination, collective work and responsibility, cooperative economics, purpose, creativity, and faith.

The seven-day celebration of Kwanzaa begins on December 26. The growing popularity of Kwanzaa is evidenced by the fact that the United States' 1997 holiday stamp issues included a Kwanzaa stamp.

10/22/97. United States. Quantity unknown. 32 cents. S#3175. Holiday issue. *Illus. 297.*

Ledbetter, Huddie William

Huddie William Ledbetter, professionally known as Leadbelly, was born in Mooringsport, Louisiana, on January 21, 1885. (Many dispute the latter date of his birth and argue that it was January 29, 1889). He was a folk singer, guitarist, and composer. The singer of mostly so-called work blues, he composed such songs as "Rock Island Line" and "Good Night Irene." Leadbelly's music is deeply rooted in early African American tradition and recognized as a significant contribution to jazz, folk, and popular music.

As a young man Ledbetter got himself into a lot of trouble. He quit school and worked on the family farm. By 1908, Ledbetter had fathered two children with Margaret Coleman, but he married Aletta Henderson and settled in Harrison, Texas, where he worked on farms and became a song leader in the local Baptist church.

Ledbetter was jailed and sentenced to a chain gang for possession of a weapon in 1915. He escaped from prison and went under the false name of Walter Boyd for several years. Later, however, Ledbetter shot and killed a man in a bar fight and was sentenced up to thirty years for murder and assault with intent to kill. He served time at Shaw State Farm Prison in Hunterville, Texas, from 1918 to 1925, when he was released by the governor. He returned to Louisiana and to his musical

performances but was again imprisoned for attempted murder in 1930.

While serving this sentence he was discovered by folklorists John and Alan Lomax, who launched a campaign for his release on parole. He was released in 1934 and recorded and performed for several years. He died in 1949.

A movie was made 1976 on Leadbelly's life story. He has also been recognized on postage stamps internationally.

2/12/92. Grenada. Quantity unknown. 60 cents. S#1107. This stamp recognizes the 100th anniversary of the birth of Franklin D. Roosevelt. In the background, Leadbelly is shown giving a WPA concert. *Illus. 406.*

2/12/92. The Gambia. Quantity unknown. 7 dalasis. S#1188. *Illus. 410.*

6/26/98. United States. Quantity unknown. 32 cents. S#3212. *Illus. 407.*

Leland, George Thomas (Mickey)

George Thomas (Mickey) Leland was a United States representative from Houston, Texas. Mickey Leland was born November 27, 1944, in Lubbock, Texas, and grew up in Houston. Mickey attended Texas Southern University in Houston and graduated in 1970 with a BS degree in pharmacy. As a student Leland was active in civil rights and other movements on campus. He also served as an instructor of clinical pharmacy at Texas Southern.

Leland first ran for public office in 1972. He won the election as a representative to the Texas State legislature.

Leland became involved with party politics as a member of the Democratic National Committee from 1976 to 1985. He served as a delegate to the Texas Constitutional Convention in 1974.

Barbara Jordan's surprise decision not to seek reelection to her U.S. congressional

386   387

388

389

390

391   392

seat in 1978 offered Mickey Leland an opportunity to move from the Texas legislature. After winning a plurality in the Democratic primary of 1978, Leland won the runoff and the election and in November succeeded Jordan as representative from the Eighteenth District of Texas.

In his first term in Congress Leland received a valuable seat on the Interstate and Foreign Commerce (later Energy and Commerce) Committee, where he served throughout his term. He also served on the Post Office and Civil Service Committee and was chairman of the Subcommittee on Postal Operations and Services. Leland served on the Committee on the District of Columbia in the Ninety-sixth through ninety-ninth congresses.

Leland was instrumental in establishing the Select Committee on Hunger in 1984 and served as chairman through the remainder of his term. In addition to his regular committee responsibilities, Leland was chairman of the Congressional Black Caucus for the Ninety-ninth Congress. During his tenure he successfully urged passage of stronger sanctions against the South African government.

In the summer of 1989, Leland, as he often had before, traveled to Ethiopia to visit a United Nations refugee camp. On August 7, 1989, a plane carrying Leland, congressional staff members, State Department officials, and Ethiopian escorts crashed in a mountainous region near Gambela, Ethiopia, killing all on board. Leland's death was a great loss to the United States Congress, and to those who depended on him internationally for the

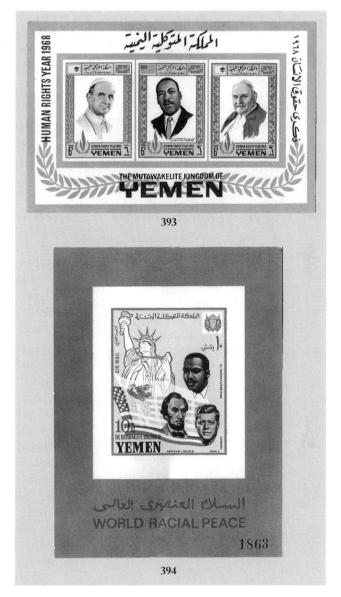

393

394

humanitarian services he had dedicated himself to over the years.

2/29/91. Niger. Quantity unknown. 300 francs. S#815. *Illus. 408.*

3/29/91. Niger. Quantity unknown. 500 francs. S#816. *Illus. 409.*

Leonard, Jeffrey

Jeffrey Leonard was born on September 22, 1955, in Philadelphia, Pennsylvania. Jeffrey Leonard is an American Major

League baseball player. He considers his hometown to be Foster City, California. He was an outfielder for the Milwaukee Brewers. Early career batting average: .253; home runs: 5; and RBIs 37. Later career average: batting .230; home runs 5; and RBIs 27.

11/28/88. Grenada. Quantity unknown. 30 cents. S#1672d. *Illus. 411.*

Leonard, Sugar Ray

Boxer Sugar Ray Leonard was born on May 17, 1956, in Wilmington, North Carolina, and now considers his home Potomac, Maryland. When Sugar Ray made it to the 1976 Olympic Games, he had already made a name for himself. He was a three-time Golden Gloves champion, two-time AAU champion and 1975 Pan-American Games gold medalist. He turned to professional boxing after he won the 1976 Olympic gold medal, and in 1979 he won his first world title (WBC welterweight), which he lost in 1980 to Roberto Duran in Montreal, Canada. He subsequently regained the title from Duran the same year. He then won the WBA junior middleweight championship in 1981 and went on to win the WBA version of the welterweight crown by defeating Thomas Hearns, earning one of the largest amounts of money paid to a boxer.

Leonard's career was interrupted in 1982 by a detached retina, which was surgically repaired. He returned in 1987 to defeat Marvin Hagler for the WBC middleweight title. In 1988 he won the WBC super middleweight and light heavyweight titles.

Leonard served as a television commentator for a brief time, analyzing boxing events. In the nineties Ray Leonard had a difficult time in his life when he struggled with cocaine addiction. He appeared on several television shows expressing his concerns about drug use to others.

9/18/95. Tanzania. Quantity unknown. 200 shillings. S#1359i. (Not pictured.) This stamp can be bought in a sheet of 9 stamps representing athletes.

Lewis, Carl

Carl Lewis is a popular American track and field star who was famous during the 1980s and early 1990s.

Frederick Carlton Lewis was born in Birmingham, Alabama, on July 1, 1961. In the 1984 Summer Olympics he won the same four gold medals in Los Angeles, California, that Jesse Owens won in the 1936 Olympics (100m, 200m, long jump, 4 × 100-m replay). He repeated in the 100m and long jump and won a silver medal at 200m; he also won two 1992 Olympic gold medals for the long jump and 4 × 100-m relay. Carl set the 100-m world record of 9.86 seconds in 1991. Carl also received the Sullivan Award as the finest U.S. amateur athlete.

Carl Lewis's career as an American track and field athlete has been an impressive one. He is the winner of nine Olympic medals, eight of them gold. He was considered the fastest person for track and field events during the 1980s. He also ranked first in the world in both the 100-meter race and the long jump, and second in the 200 meters.

Issue date unknown. Paraguay. Quantity unknown. 10 guaranies. Celebrating the 1988 Olympic Games in Seoul, Carl Lewis's name is in the upper right corner of this stamp. *Illus. 418.*

Issue date unknown. Republic Togolaise. Quantity unknown. 500F. S#522. (Overprint.) The original stamp was issued to commemorate Bob Beamon's 1968 win in the Mexico City Olympics. Beamon is pictured leaping over a hurdle. The overprint on the stamp reads (in French), "Carl Lewis United States gold medal." Only a poor quality copy of the stamp is shown here. *Illus. 420.*

8/8/84. Niger. Quantity unknown. 80 francs. S#C338. *Illus. 412.*

8/24/84. Cook Islands. Quantity unknown. 1 dollar and 20 cents. S#828. (Overprint.) This stamp honoring the Los Angeles games is overprinted with the words, "Four Gold Medals Carl Lewis USA." *Illus. 413.*

12/15/84. Côte d'Ivoire. Quantity unknown. 150 francs. S#C87. Commemorating Lewis's 100 and 200m wins in the Olympic Games in Los Angeles, 1984. *Illus. 415.*

12/27/84. Guinea-Bissau. Quantity unknown. 6 pesos. S#611. Commemorating the Los Angeles Olympics in 1984. *Illus. 414.*

3/18/85. Guinea. Quantity unknown. 30 sylis. S#924. (Perforated souvenir sheet; not pictured.) Commemorates the Olympic Games in Los Angeles, 1984. Also listed in this souvenir are Kirk Baptiste, Ron Brown, Sam Graddy, and Calvin Smith.

1/30/89. Uganda. Quantity unknown. 300 shillings. S#654. (Overprint.) This stamp celebrating the 1988 Olympics in Seoul is overprinted with the words "Long jump Carl Lewis USA." The face value of the original stamp (without overprint) was 45 shillings. *Illus. 416.*

2/15/89. Grenada. Quantity unknown. 2 dollars. S#2016. (Not pictured.) See Florence Griffith Joyner (S#2015) for more comments.

4/28/89. Sierra Leone. Quantity unknown. 30 leones. S#1030. Commemorates Carl Lewis's win in the men's 100m. *Illus. 417.*

1992. Maldives. Quantity unknown. 2 rufiyaa. Celebrating the 1988 Olympic Games in Seoul and Lewis's 100m win. *Illus. 419.*

1992? The Gambia. Quantity unknown. 50 bututs. Photograph of the 100m race in Barcelona, 1992. *Illus. 421.*

1992. Uganda. Quantity unknown. 40 shillings. Photograph of Lewis in the long jump, Barcelona 1992. *Illus. 422.*

1992. Sierra Leone. Quantity unknown. 20 leones. Photograph of Lewis in the 100m race in Barcelona, 1992. *Illus. 424.*

7/10/92. Palau. Quantity unknown. 50 cents. S#307. (Perforated souvenir sheet.) "Palau salutes the Olympian Innovators" of Barcelona 1992. Six miniature sheets (S#304–309) were issued. *Illus. 423.*

5/2/95. Ghana. Quantity unknown. 500 cedis. S#1797. (Not pictured.) From a set of 4 (S#1797–1800).

395   396

397

Lewis, Steve and Deloach

A stamp is said to exist honoring Steve and Deloach Lewis, African American track and field athletes, but no information on such a stamp is available.

Lipscomb, Mance

Mance Lipscomb, guitarist and songster, was born to Charles and Jane Lipscomb on April 9, 1895, in the Brazos bottoms near Navasota, Texas. He lived most of his life as a tenant farmer in Navasota. Mance represented one of the final chapters in the nineteenth century songster tradition, which predated the development of the

398

399

400

401

402

nineteenth century blues. Lipscomb himself insisted that he was a songster, not a guitarist or "blues singer," since he played "all kinds of music." His eclectic repertoire has been reported to contain 350 pieces spanning two centuries.

Lipscomb had a full family of musicians. His father was a fiddler, his uncle played the banjo, and his brothers were guitarists. This gave Mance an early start as a musician. His mother bought him his first guitar when he was eleven. Thereafter he was accompanying his father, and later he began working solo at local suppers and Saturday night dances. He had contact with such early recording artists as Blind Lemon Jefferson and Blind Willie Johnson and country star James Charles (Jimmie) Rodgers. Mance did no recordings until his "discovery" by whites during the folk-song revival of the 1960s.

Between 1905 and 1956 he lived in an atmosphere of exploitation, farming as a tenant for a number of landlords in and around Grimes County. He was taped at his first session in 1960 but released the tape anonymously (Arhoolie LP 1017, Texas Blues, Volume 2), presumably to protect the singer. He returned to Navasota and was finally able to buy some land and build a house of his own. He made numerous recordings and appeared at such festivals as the Berkeley Folk Festival of 1961, where he played before a crowd of more than 40,000. Despite his popularity he remained a poor man for the rest of his life.

After 1974, declining health confined him to a nursing home and hospitals. He died in Grimes Memorial Hospital, Navasota, on January 30, 1976, and was buried at West Haven Cemetery.

The country of Gambia recognized Lipscomb and others who had made contributions to blues and jazz on a stamp in 1992.

2/12/92. The Gambia. Quantity unknown. 1.25 dalasis. S#1183. Comes in a set of 12 stamps (S#1178–1189) celebrating the "History of the Blues." See W. C. Handy (S#1179) for a listing of the other musicians in this issue. *Illus. 425.*

Locke, Alain Leroy

It has been said that the Rhodes Scholarship is to the world of academic preparation what the Nobel Prize is to the world of international achievement. In addition to intellectual ability, the Rhodes Scholarship is given on the basis of moral character on the recipient's potential for significant achievement in later life. Alain Le Roy Locke was the first African American recipient of this most prestigious graduate scholarship since its creation by Cecil Rhodes in 1899, and he more than satisfied the criteria for all three categories.

Alain Le Roy Locke was born September 13, 1886, in Philadelphia, Pennsylvania, to Pliny and Mary Hawkins Locke (both schoolteachers). He was an only child, and Locke remained a bachelor for his entire life.

Locke attended Central High School in Philadelphia, Pennsylvania. He received his Bachelor of Arts and doctoral degrees from Harvard University. He was an honor student at Harvard. Locke studied British Literature at Oxford University in London, England. He also did additional graduate study at the University of Berlin in Berlin, Germany.

Dr. Locke was a member of the faculty at Howard University in Washington, D.C., for over four decades, serving as professor and chairperson of the philosophy department. He was professor at Fisk University in Nashville, Tennessee, inter–American exchange professor in Haiti, and a visiting professor at the University of Wisconsin in Madison and the New School for Social Research in New York City, New York.

Although noted for his academic and educational endeavors, Dr. Locke is most recognized for his role in spearheading the "Harlem Renaissance" movement during

403

404

405

406

407

408

409

410

411

412

413

414

415

the 1920s. Dr. Locke almost singlehandedly was responsible for the growth and diverse literary and artistic activities that occurred during that era. This wave of experience brought inspiration and pride to the rich African American cultural heritage.

Locke edited, contributed to and wrote literary works dealing with race relations such as *The New Negro: An Interpretation* (anthology); *Four Negro Poets*; *Plays of Negro Life: A Source-Book of Native American Drama*; *The Negro in America* (bibliography); *The Negro and His Music*; *Negro Art Past and Present*; and many more, to build the pride of the African American cultural heritage.

Locke died at age 67 on June 9, 1954, in New York City.

4/10/71. Senegal. Quantity unknown. 60 francs. S#C97. *Illus. 426.*

Louis, Joe

Joe Louis, professionally known as the "Brown Bomber," was born Joseph Louis Barrow near Lafayette, Alabama, on May 13, 1914. Louis won his first professional fight with a knockout in 1934. Repeated victories followed until he suffered his first professional loss, to the former world champion Max Schmeling, a German boxer. Despite this loss, he went on to win his first professional heavyweight championship of the world in June of 1937, defeating the American boxer James Jack Braddock by a knockout.

Louis and Schmeling had a rematch in 1938. Louis won this fight in the first round. After this fight Joe became something of a wartime hero, giving inspirational speeches to help recruit African American soldiers for World War II.

Louis retired in 1949 after successfully defending his title 25 times. He returned to the ring in 1950, but in this comeback attempt he lost to Ezzard Charles. In 1951, the American heavyweight contender

Rocky Marciano knocked Louis out. After this bout Joe retired permanently.

Joe Louis died in 1981. He was elected to the Boxing Hall of Fame in 1994, and has been recognized on U.S. and international stamps.

2/7/89. Tanzania. Quantity unknown. 350 shillings. S#496. (Perforated souvenir sheet.) This is a hard to find souvenir sheet. *Illus. 427.*

7/14/93. United States. 100,000,000. 29 cents. S#2266. *Illus. 428.*

Makeba, Miriam

Miriam Zenski Makeba was born in Johannesburg, South Africa, in 1932. Later in life she came to America, where she has made great contributions to American music culture. She has been significant in popularizing African music in the West, and she is a leading figure in the campaign against apartheid in South Africa.

Makeba began singing at home and in church choirs and eventually was invited to join a local touring band. She became a regional musical figure, and Coca-Cola even used her picture on billboard advertising that was aimed at Africans. In 1957, Makeba had a cameo singing part in a semi-documentary antiapartheid film, *Come Back, Africa.* She attended the Venice Film Festival and also went to London, where she met Harry Belafonte — the leading black American entertainer at the time — who became her mentor and sponsor.

When she went to the United States with Belafonte, Makeba became an immediate star performer. Belafonte introduced her as "the most revolutionary new talent to appear in any medium in the past decade." Her concerts sold out, and her albums achieved immense sales. She made her nightclub debut at the Village Vanguard, a popular club in New York's Greenwich Village. Her visits to Africa were triumphs— she sang at the liberation ceremonies for

416

417

418

419

420

421

422

424

423

425

426

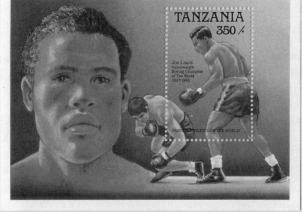

427

428

429

430

431

432

433

434

Côte d'Ivoire, Tanzania, and Kenya and at the inauguration of the Organization of African Unity.

Makeba's professional career was accompanied and disrupted by upheavals in her personal life. She was forced to become an exile from South Africa when, after attempting to go home to visit her mother in 1960, the government canceled her passport and banned her music. In 1962 she had her first bout with cervical cancer. That same year saw the breakup of her marriage to musician Hugh Masekela. In 1968 she married the radical African American activist Stokely Carmichael which had disastrous effects on her professional career. Her recording contract and concerts were canceled, and for 17 years she suspended touring. The FBI followed the couple constantly until they fled to Guinea, where they became honorary citizens. The marriage dissolved in 1978. In 1985 she lost her only child, Bongi, who died in childbirth.

Makeba's career was revitalized in 1987 when she took part in Paul Simon's Graceland tour. In 1990 she finally was able to return to South Africa. One of the positive things that happened to her during this period was becoming the protégé of President Sékou Toure, who appointed her to represent Guinea at the United Nations.

Makeba's repertoire is eclectic. She has sung Hebrew songs. Her best-known single recordings have been popularized versions of African music, the most dramatic being her trademark "Click Song." Sung in Xhosa, which uses a series of clicking sounds, it plays on words in a style more commercially clever than musically memorable. It is, however, her renditions of traditional African songs that are most enduring. With these songs she retains some of the township Kwela sound, a South African type of jazz marked by the use of instruments such as penny whistles and sticks. She returned to this music in her

album *Sangoma* (1988), dedicated to her mother, who was a sangoma, or traditional spirit medium.

3/30/90. Tanzania. Quantity unknown. 9 shillings. S#580. From a "Tribute to Black Entertainers" sheet of 9. *Illus. 430.*

2/15/92. Tanzania. Quantity unknown. 75 shillings. S#811e. From a "Tribute to Black Entertainers" (1992) sheet of 9. *Illus. 431.*

Malone, Karl

Karl Malone is a popular basketball player. He was born in Summerfield, Louisiana, on July 24, 1963. He attended Louisiana Tech University. He presently lives in Salt Lake City, Utah, and plays with the Utah Jazz. Malone was named to the All-NBA first Team in 1989, 1990, and 1991.

Karl "the Mailman" Malone knows how to deliver great basketball. He led the league in defensive rebounding with 731, and led the Jazz in rebounding with 11.8 a game — good for fourth in the league. His speed, strength, power, and agility produce solid gold results, which is what the U.S. needed for the 1992 Olympic game. Malone has played in quite a few national championships, though he has yet to win one. If there is one thing "the Mailman" wants to deliver, it is a world championship for his team.

He is recognized on an international stamp with the other "Dream Team" members of 1992.

12/22/92. St. Vincent. Quantity unknown. 2 dollars. S#1744e. From an issue recognizing members of the 1992 Olympic "Dream Team." *Illus. 429.*

Martin, Roberta

A unique event in 1931 led to a major change in American music. The change was the birth of modern gospel, as it is now known. That year gospel pioneers Thomas A. Dorsey and Theodore R. Frye appointed Roberta Martin as their accompanist for a newly formed youth gospel choir at Ebenezer Baptist Church in Chicago.

Roberta's role in this new gospel music cannot be taken lightly. She became at once composer, arranger, publisher, soloist, inspirational group leader, and recruiter. Her contributions grew out of the accomplishments of her predecessors, mainly Dorsey and Frye, and a chain of composers, singers, and worshippers stretching back to the eighteenth century African American heritage.

Roberta Evelyn Martin was born in Helena, Arkansas, on February 12, 1907. Her family moved to Cairo, Illinois, when she was eight and then to Chicago when she was ten. There she graduated from Wendell Phillips High School. During her schooling at Wendell Phillips High, Roberta took piano lessons under the direction of Mildred B. Jones. This was not new to Roberta; she had been taking lessons since the age of six under her aunt, and playing for Sunday school and various choirs.

She continued her musical studies at Northwestern University, with the ambition of preparing for a career as a concert pianist. At first her gospel music did not venture far from the traditional, but with the shared experience of Fry and Dorsey she was on her way. A quick learner, she modified the then prevalent style, and her leadership as a composer and singer began to spread the "good news" of her gospel ministry. She also innovated, improvised and added her own flavor.

Roberta Martin married James Austin in 1947 and they had one son, Leonard Austin. Gospel musicians, singers and supporters throughout the country particularly admired her, especially in her hometown of Chicago.

Roberta Martin passed away in Chicago on January 18, 1969. Following her death, at perhaps the largest funeral in Chicago's history, an estimated 50,000 persons visited Mount Pisgah Baptist Church to pay homage to this great lady of gospel music.

6/26/98. United States. Quantity unknown. 32 cents. S#3217. *Illus. 432.*

Mathis, Johnny

Johnny Mathis is described by many as one of the most exciting and smooth singing artists of his time.

John Royce Mathis was born in Gilmer, Texas, on September 30, 1935, and he was raised in San Francisco, California. It is not well known that Mathis's early interest was in sports. He was in fact offered a trial with the 1956 Olympic field and track team, but chose to pursue a recording contract with Columbia records instead.

It was at San Francisco State College that Mathis gained recognition as an outstanding high jumper. It was also there that he began singing in a jazz sextet. During the mid fifties Johnny Mathis sang in nightclubs in San Francisco and New York, where his smooth, mellow style led to his recording of "Wonderful, Wonderful" (1956). This was a great hit for Johnny. Nineteen-fifty-seven was also a very good year. He recorded more million-selling records such as "Chances Are" and "It's Not for Me to Say."

His album *Johnny Mathis's Greatest Hits* sold more than two million copies during 1957-58. He appeared in two films, *Lizzie* and *A Certain Smile.*

Mathis is also considered one of the great crossover singers during the '50s and '60s. He was extremely popular with white and black audiences. During the '60s and '70s he toured widely, and recorded prolifically — hits such as "Too Much, Too Little, Too Late" and "Friends in Love" (with Dionne Warwick, 1982). Mathis has maintained his popularity into the new millennium with numerous successful recordings, concert tours, radio and television appearances.

11/19/92. Grenada. Quantity unknown. 90 cents. S#2156e. (Not pictured.) Celebrates Mathis as a gold record award winner. See Chuck Berry (S#2158a) for more comments.

Matthews, Vincent

Vincent Matthews is an American track athlete (sprinter). He was born in Queens, New York, on December 16, 1947. Matthews attended Johnson C. Smith University and there developed his skills for becoming a great track star. He took the silver medal in the 1967 Pan Am Games 400 meters in 45.11 and won the NAIA 440 yard for Johnson C. Smith during that same year. Matthews was also successful in winning the AAU in 45.0 in the 1968 U.S. Preliminary Olympic trials meet at South Lake Tahoe by running his 44.4. He won gold medals in the 1968 and 1972 Olympics for 4 × 400m relay and 400m run.

1972. Ras Al Khaima. Quantity unknown. 1.75 riyals. Commemorating the Olympic Games in Munich, 1972. Only a poor copy of the stamp is shown here. *Illus. 433.*

Matzeliger, Jan E.

Jan Ernest Matzeliger came to Lynn, Massachusetts, in 1876. Jan was born to a Dutch father and Surinamese mother in his native Dutch Guyana. There are no records of his getting married or having children. When he arrived in Lynn, Matzeliger was destitute and friendless. He had been a sailor for two years.

Hundreds of inventors had at this time invested thousands of dollars to develop a machine that could manufacture a complete shoe. Inventors such as Thompson, McKay and Copeland (the top shoe makers during this period) had developed crude shoe making machines, but could not perfect the final problem of shaping the upper leather and attaching the leather to the bottom of the shoe. This created a problem, and they could only manufacture about forty pairs of shoes per day.

Matzeliger was most competent with machinery. When he heard of the problem, he set out to challenge it. He also had heard that many believed the problem could not be resolved. In secret he started to experiment with a model made out of crude and scrap iron. He worked for ten years steadily and patiently with no encouragement.

Jan tried to join several community churches in Lynn but was denied membership. Many who heard about his machine laughed and rumored that he could not do it.

In 1882 Matzeliger felt that he had resolved the impossible and submitted his patent. The diagram he submitted for his patent in Washington, D.C., was so complicated that the Patent Office dispatched a man from Washington to Lynn to see the actual model. On March 20, 1883, Patent Number 274,207 was granted to Jan E. Matzeliger.

Matzeliger died of tuberculosis in 1889. In 1991 he was recognized on a U.S. postage stamp in the Black Heritage Series for his significant contribution to the American shoe industry.

9/15/91. United States. 149,000,000. 29 cents. S#2567. From the Black Heritage series. *Illus. 438–9.*

Mays, Willie

Willie Howard Mays (the "Say Hey Kid") was born in 1931 in Westfield, Alabama. His father, William Howard Mays, Sr., and his aunt, Sarah Mays, raised him. Willie is married to Marghuerite Chapman. They have one adopted son, Michael.

Everyone knows that Willie was one of the first African Americans to play professional baseball with a non–Negro league professional ballclub. Mays was the National League Rookie of the Year in 1951, MVP in 1954 and 1965, batting champion in 1954, and leading home run hitter in 1955, 1962, and 1965. He is the third leading all-time home run hitter.

Willie's father, who played baseball in the Negro League, trained and taught Willie. Willie played one year in the Negro League for the Birmingham Black Barons of Birmingham, Alabama. In 1951, at the age of 19, he began playing center field for the National League New York Giants (later the San Francisco Giants). He played for the Giants until 1972, when he was traded to the New York Mets.

Over the twenty-two years Willie Mays played in the Major League, he hit 600 home runs; amassed a career batting average of .302; won the Major League's batting championship in 1954; and led the league in home runs four times. He has been named, at various times, Player of the Year, Baseball Player of the Decade, and Male Athlete of the Year. He was elected to the Baseball Hall of Fame in 1979.

After serving as a coach with the New York Mets, he officially retired from baseball in 1973.

8/29/72. Ras Al Khaima. Quantity unknown. 70 dirhams. Minkus#548. Willie Mays and Futoshi Nakanishi are shown on this hard-to-find stamp. *Illus. 434.*

11/28/88. Grenada. Quantity unknown. 30 cents. S#1664g. *Illus. 435.*

7/23/89. St. Vincent. Quantity unknown. 60 cents. S#1226c. Rookie of the Year 1951 recognition. *Illus. 436.*

7/23/89. St. Vincent. Quantity unknown. 2 dollars. S#1212. Celebrates Mays's election to the Hall of Fame, 1979. *Illus. 437.*

McCovey, Willie

Willie Lee McCovey is an American baseball player. He was born in 1938 in Mobile, Alabama. He was an infielder who began his Major League baseball career with the San Francisco Giants in 1959. McCovey was the National League Rookie of the Year in 1959, MVP in 1969, and leading home run hitter in 1968 and 1969.

8/29/72. Manama. Quantity unknown. 25

dirhams. Minkus#965. (Not pictured.) This unusual 3D stamp shows two different pictures, depending on the way the light hits it. One view shows Willie McCovey; the other shows Tom Sayvor. A difficult stamp to find.

McDaniel, Mildred Louise

Mildred Louise McDaniel was an American track and field athlete. She won the 1956 Olympic high jump (WR) gold medal. Evidence indicates that Mildred L. McDaniel was the second African American woman to be recognized on a stamp anywhere in the world (1960 by the Dominican Republic).

Mildred McDaniel was born on November 4, 1933, in Atlanta, Georgia. Mildred was educated at Tuskegee Institute, Tuskegee, Alabama. She won the AAU outdoor high jump in 1953 and the outdoor and indoor titles in 1955 and 1956. McDaniel achieved the ultimate in track and field, winning an Olympic gold with a new world record performance. She also beat the future world record holder, Iolanda Balas of Romania. McDaniel later won the high jump at the 1959 Pan Am Games.

9/14/60. Dominican Republic. Quantity unknown. 3 centavos. S#527. Not easy to find. This is a perforated stamp. It is also available in an imperforate version. *Illus. 441.*

9/14/60. Dominican Republic. Quantity unknown. 3 centavos +2 centavos overprint surcharge. S#527. (Overprint.) Not easy to find. The overprint reads (in Spanish), "XV Anniversary of UNESCO." *Illus. 440.*

9/14/60. Dominican Republic. Quantity unknown. 3 centavos. S#527. Not easy to find. This is an imperforate stamp with the same artwork as S#527. *Illus. 442.*

McGee, Willie

American baseball player Willie Dean McGee was born November 2, 1958, in San Francisco, California. He attended Harry Ellis High School in Richmond, California, and Diablo Valley College in California. He

435   436   437

438-9

440

441   442

was selected by the New York Yankees organization in the secondary phase of the free-agent draft on January 11, 1977. McGee spent much of his time on the disabled list. Traded by the Yankees to the St. Louis Cardinals for P. Bob Sykes on October 21, 1981, he was later traded to both the Oakland Athletics and the Boston Red Sox before returning to the Cardinals in 1995.

McGee holds the modern National League single-season record for highest batting average by switch-hitter (100 or more games)—.353 (1985). He's a three-time Golden Glove Award winner and led his league in batting average in 1985 and 1990, and he has been honored with many other awards in the sporting arena of baseball.

Willie's off-season activities are well known. He participates in the Police Activities League and has donated items to celebrity auctions in the St. Louis area. He provides much of his time to the community during his off season.

11/30/89. St. Vincent. Quantity unknown. 30 cents. S#1270b. From the "U.S. Baseball Series 2." *Illus. 443.*

McGriff, Fred

Fred "the Crime Dog" McGriff was born October 31, 1963, in Tampa, Florida. McGriff is a graduate of Jefferson High School in Tampa. It was high school where he earned All-League honors in baseball. Fred was offered a scholarship at the University of Georgia, Athens, but he made the decision to sign with the Yankees after he was chosen on the ninth round. Later he moved to the Atlanta Braves. In 1997 he was traded from the Braves to Tampa Bay in an expansion-draft trade. Fans wondered whether McGriff would still have the hitting power that he had with the Atlanta Braves, which had made him a top slugger. That year he hit .353 in April.

In 2000, McGriff hit his 400th home run and collected his 2000th hit. He is one of three players (Fred, Frank Robinson and Mark McGwire) to hit at least 200 home runs in each league.

11/30/89. St. Vincent. Quantity unknown. 30 cents. S#1273i. From the "U.S. Baseball Series 2," in a sheet of 9. *Illus. 444.*

McGuire, Edith Marie

Edith McGuire is an American female track and field athlete. She won the 1964 Olympic 200m for the gold medal, and the 100m run and 4×100m relay silver medal.

Edith Marie McGuire was born in Atlanta, Georgia, on June 3, 1944. She graduated with honors and as best all-around student from her high school. She received awards in basketball and track as well as a scholarship to Tennessee State University. McGuire graduated from Tennessee State in 1966.

McGuire was considered best at shorter sprints and the long jump, until she won her Olympic title at 200 meters. She won the 100 meters and long jump at both the AAU indoor and outdoor meets in 1963. She established herself as a sprinter by winning the 100 meter run in São Paulo, Brazil, setting a Pan Am record of 11.5 seconds and equaling Wilma Rudolph's record in the 100m. McGuire established six records in 1964: 70 yard dash (world), 100 meter run (American), 100 meter run (senior champion in California), 200 meter run (Olympic tryouts and Olympics), and 220 yard dash (American outdoor record). McGuire specialized in the longer sprint to good effect in the Olympic year and was undefeated in major races over 200 meters throughout the season.

McGuire won the AAU 200 in 1964 prior to her Olympic victory and defended her title at 220 yards in 1965. She won the AAU 220 yards in 1965 and 1966. McGuire participated in over 50 meets during her 7 years of national and international competition. She held world, Olympic, Canadian, AAU American, and AAU champion records in the 200 meter run and 220 yard dash. McGuire has a place on six AAU All-American women's track and field teams.

After her professional track and field career Edith McGuire taught school and worked with underprivileged children in a federal programs in Detroit.

9/24/68. Grenada. Quantity unknown. 1 Cent. S#280. Celebates McGuire's 200m win in the

443

444

445

446

447

448

449

1968 Olympics. A hard-to-find stamp. Blue background on left; blue ink for drawing on right. *Illus. 445.*

9/24/68. Grenada. Quantity unknown. 10 cents. S#283. Same art as S#280 above, but in orange, instead of blue. *Illus. 446.*

1/1/69. Grenada. Quantity unknown. 5 cents. S#310. (Overprint.) Same art as S#280, overprinted with "Visit Carifta Expo '69 April 5–30." *Illus. 447.*

1/1/69. Grenada. Quantity unknown. 35 cents. S#313. (Overprint.) Same art as S#283, but overprinted with "Visit Carifta Expo '69 April 5–30." *Illus. 448.*

McNair, Ronald

Ronald E. McNair was born in Lake City, South Carolina, in 1950. He was the second African American (after Guion Bluford) to be a part of the American space team. He was an astronaut and physicist with a Ph.D. from the Massachusetts Institute of Technology. McNair was an expert in laser physics.

Ronald E. McNair was killed on his second mission into space when the space shuttle *Challenger* exploded shortly after take-off on January 28, 1986. Other crew members of that tragic space flight are also recognized on the stamps that include Ronald E. McNair.

1986. Hungary. Quantity unknown. 20 forint. S#2971 (Perforated souvenir sheet.) The following are recognized: Francis R. Scobee, Michael J. Smith, Judith Resnik, Ronald E. McNair, Ellison S. Onizuka, Gregory B. Jarvis and Christa McAuliffe. Not an easy stamp to find. *Illus. 449.*

7/1/86. Guinea. Quantity unknown. 600 francs. S#C169. (Perforated souvenir sheet.) Features both names and pictures of the crew. *Illus. 450.*

7/1/86. Guinea. Quantity unknown. 100 francs. S#C167. List as names of crew members. *Illus. 452.*

10/14/86. Mauritania. Quantity unknown. 100 ouguiya. S#613. (Perforated souvenir sheet.) Features names and pictures of crew. *Illus. 451.*

10/14/86. Mauritania. Quantity unknown. 32 ouguiya. S#612. *Illus. 453.*

10/14/86. Central African Republic. Quantity unknown. 300 francs. S#821. Not easy to find. *Illus. 454.*

11/2/87. Uganda. Quantity unknown. 150 shillings. S#568. (Perforated souvenir sheet.) Features names and pictures of crew members. *Illus. 456.*

8/4/94. Grenada and the Grenadines. Quantity unknown. 1 dollar and 10 cents. S#1600f. (Not pictured.) Features a portrait of McNair with the space shuttle on the far left.

11/19/96. Central African Republic. Quantity unknown. 500 francs. S#823. Features names and pictures of crew. *Illus. 455.*

McPhatter, Clyde

Clyde McPhatter was born on November 15, 1933, in Durham, North Carolina. McPhatter started his singing career as lead tenor with the Drifters and stayed with them from 1953 to 1956. He began his solo career in 1956 and popularized a number of hit songs such as "Stagger Lee." McPhatter died on January 13, 1972, in New York City. He was most recently recognized in an American postage stamp that paid tribute to a number of African Americans who made significant contributions in blues, jazz, and pop music in America and the world over.

6/16/93. United States. 14,000,000. 29 cents. S#2726. *Illus. 457.*

7/26/93. Gambia. Quantity unknown. Face value unknown. S#1395g. (Not pictured.) This stamp issue was in recognition of entertainers. Others recognized were Buddy Holly, Otis Redding, Bill Haley, Dinah Washington, Esther Williams, musical instruments, Ritchie Valens, Elvis Presley, Madonna, and Marilyn Monroe.

Metcalfe, Ralph Harold

Ralph Harold Metcalfe was born on May 30, 1910, in Atlanta, Georgia. Metcalfe is considered one of the most sensational African Americans in track history. During 1934–35 he was called "the world's fastest human." He started his track career in high school. In 1932, as a student at Marquette

450

451

452

453

454

University, he won both metric sprints in the NCAA in 10.2 and 20.3. Metcalfe also won both sprints in the AAU. The latter are only a few of the track events Metcalfe won during his career in track. He made the Olympic team behind Jesse Owens in the 100 but failed in the 200. He also ran second to Owens in the 200 meters at the 1936 Games in Berlin. He finally won his gold medal in the 400 meter relay. Metcalfe tied the world 100 meter record of 10.3 seconds 10 times and broke it once.

After his superb career in track he became a coach and political science instructor, then a city councilman of Chicago, and finlly a member of the U.S. House of Representatives. Metcalfe became well known in Chicago politics. He served under Mayor Daley while serving on the City Council of Chicago for many years. Metcalfe was also elected to the Board of Directors of the U.S. Olympic Committee in 1969. As an elected congressman from Illinois first District, he served until his death on October 10, 1978, in Chicago.

11/14/89. Turks and Caicos Islands. Quantity unknown. 50 cents. S#778a. This stamp commemorates the 200th anniversary of George Washington's inauguration; prominently features a portrait of Herbert Hoover with the years of his presidency (1929–33); and includes portraits of Ralph Metcalfe (with his name erroneously printed as "Metcalf" beside his picture) and an unidentified figure skater. *Illus. 458.*

Milburn, Rodney, Jr.

Rodney Milburn, Jr., was born on May 18, 1950, in Opelousas, Louisiana. Rody, as he is called, attended Southern University in Baton Rouge, Louisiana, and was a member in the International Track Club. He held the world record in the 120 yard high hurdles and in 1971 was name World Athlete of the Year by *Track and Field News*. During his freshman year in college

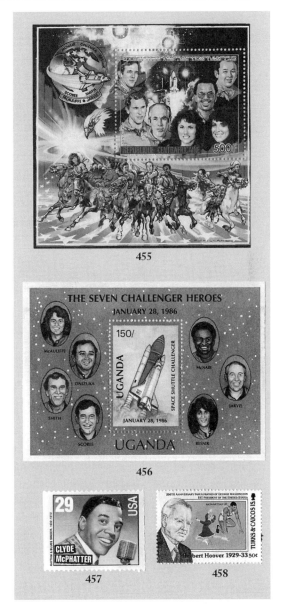

455

456

457   458

he won the NAIA championship in the 120 yard hurdles and the gold medal at the 1971 Pan Am Games in 13.4.

Milburn won many track events in the NCAA and AAC. He went through 28 races unbeaten. In the Olympics in Munich, Germany, in 1972, he won the gold in 13.2, equaling the world record for the 110 meter event. He also competed professionally 1973–74. Milburn also had a short unsuccessful professional football career.

1972. Umm-al-Qiwain. Quantity unknown. 5 riyals. *Illus. 459.*

1972. Chad. Quantity unknown. 250 francs. Only a poor copy of this hard-to-find stamp is shown here. *Illus. 460.*

1972. Upper Volta. Quantity unknown. 90 francs. Only a poor copy of this hard-to-find stamp is shown here. *Illus. 461.*

1972. Ajman. Quantity unknown. 1 riyal. *Illus. 462.*

1972. Haiti. Quantity unknown. 25 centimes. S#662D. *Illus. 463.*

10/16/72. Mauritania. Quantity unknown. 75 francs. S#126. (Overprint.) *Illus. 464.*

Miller, Cheryl

A stamp is said to exist honoring the great women's basketball player Cheryl Miller, but no information on such a stamp is available.

Mingus, Charles

Charles Mingus was born in Nogales, Arizona, in 1922. A unique American Jazz musician, he is credited with establishing the double bass as a melodic rather than rhythmic instrument. Charlie played with such great musicians as Louis Armstrong and saxophonist Charlie Parker. Mingus was also an excellent pianist and played several other musical instruments as well. As leader of his band Mingus also experimented with group improvisation which added to the strength of his innovations as a jazz musician. His autobiography, *Beneath the Underdog*, was published in 1971.

Charlie Mingus died in 1979.

9/16/95. United States. Quantity unknown. 32 cents. S#2989. Legends of American Music series. *Illus. 466.*

Mitchell, Kevin

Kevin Mitchell was born in San Diego, California, on January 13, 1962. His hometown is also San Diego, California. As a pitcher for the San Diego Giants, over the years Kevin has maintained the following

record: Walk ratio 4.5; strikeout ratio 5.1; and opposing batters average .252.

11/30/89. St. Vincent. Quantity unknown. 30 cents. S#1267d. See Tony Gwynn, S#1225 (souvenir sheet) for further recognition of Kevin Mitchell. His name is recognized on this stamp also. *Illus. 467.*

Monk, Thelonious

Thelonious Sphere Monk was born in Rocky Mount, North Carolina, in 1920. Monk is considered a unique jazz American pianist and composer. Monk played and worked with musical giants such as saxophonist Charlie Parker and trumpet player Dizzy Gillespie during the 1940s. He is given credit as being one of the innovators in the creation and execution of bebop style jazz.

Monk's signature was his unorthodox "homemade" piano technique. Because of this style in the presentation of his jazz compositions his following was small until the 1950s. When jazz lovers began to catch on to the depth and complexity of his music, he was recognized, and thereafter established himself as a popular jazz musician and composer. Many of his works have become jazz classics such as *'Round Midnight, Criss Cross, Epistrophy, Well, You Needn't,* and *Blue Monk.* Thelonious Sphere Monk was recognized on his first American stamp in 1995.

9/16/95. United States. Quantity unknown. 32 cents. S#2990. *Illus. 465.*

Moore, Archie

A stamp is said to exist honoring Archie Moore, the great African American boxer, but no information on such a stamp is available.

Morgan, Garrett A.

Garrett Morgan was a black man born in Kentucky or Tennessee in 1875. As is often the case for people of color at that time, historical records are incomplete, so different resource books give different information.

In 1901, Garrett Morgan created his first invention: a safe belt-cover for sewing machines. At that time, sewing machine belts were in the open and dangerous to people's hands.

Garrett Morgan continued to invent equipment to make people's lives safer. In 1914, he invented a breathing helmet for rescuers who were entering areas filled with smoke or gas. Two years later he demonstrated the importance of this in rescuing trapped workers in a smoke filled tunnel under Lake Erie. For that he received a gold medal from the city of Cleveland. People were impressed, and at first, his invention sold rapidly. Then it became known that a black man invented the helmet. People were so prejudiced that even though the helmet saved lives, they wouldn't use it.

Garrett Morgan continued to invent more safety items. In 1923 he invented the automatic traffic light. The stamp that follows is an indirect way of recognizing Morgan for his contributions (valuable inventions). Today we take a traffic signal for granted. Yet, when he introduced the idea, traffic lights did not seem valuable to people. Morgan couldn't sell his idea. Finally, years later, General Electric bought his idea and paid him $40,000 for it. That sounds like quite a lot

459

460

461

462

463

464

465

466

467

of money, but it doesn't sound as much when you realize that in 1981 a single traffic light cost $2,500.00.

Garrett A. Morgan died in 1963.

9/3/65. United States. Quantity 114,000,000. 5 cents. S#1272. This stamp reminds the public that the nation can "stop traffic accidents" with "enforcement, education, engineering." Pictured is a traffic signal — the invention of Garrett Morgan. *Illus. 468.*

Morgan, Joe

Joe Morgan was born Joseph Leonard on September 19, 1943, in Bonham, Texas. Joe became an American professional baseball player. He started with the National League in 1963 as a second baseman. Joe Morgan was National League Most Valuable Player for 1975 and 1976. He was considered the National League's most complete player during his peak.

11/30/89. St. Vincent. Quantity unknown. 30 cents. S#1270a. From the "U.S. Baseball Series 2." *Illus. 469.*

Morrison, Toni

Novelist Toni Morrison was named the winner of the 1993 Nobel Prize in Literature. She was the first African American to receive this highest of all literary honors. She was also awarded the Pulitzer Prize for fiction for her book *Beloved* on March 31, 1988.

Born Chloe Anthony Wofford in 1931, Morrison attended Howard University in Washington, D.C., where she received her B.S. in 1953. She went on to Cornell to complete her masters in English. Working as an editor at Random House, she sought out young black authors, encouraging them to publish materials on black history and other subject matter.

Both of Morrison's first two novels *The Bluest Eye* and *Sula*, were critically acclaimed. After the publication of her third novel, *Tar Baby*, Morrison began teaching at the State University of New York at Albany, where she wrote *Dreaming Emmett*, a play about Emmett Till, the 14-year-old black boy who was murdered in 1954 because he whistled at a white woman.

Perhaps Morrison's best known work is her Pulitzer Prize–winning novel, *Beloved*, based on the true story of a slave who killed her own daughter rather than see her live as a slave. Morrison has also written numerous essays and the novel *Jazz*.

11/25/93. Sweden. Quantity unknown. 6 Kronor. S#2040. (Not pictured.) There are two stamps in Morrison's honor, both commemorating her winning the Nobel Prize for Literature. The second stamp is identified S#2041. Neither of these stamps is pictured. Both feature a portrait of Morrison.

Morton, Jelly Roll

Jelly Roll Morton was a Creole who was born Ferdinand LaMenthe in New Orleans, apparently on October 20, 1890, though it is rumored that Morton shifted his birth date around as it suited him. His father was also a Creole who made his living as a carpenter.

Jelly Roll Morton became interested in music at an early age. As a child he would beat on pots and pans. He learned to play the guitar and then the piano. He studied music under a number of teachers; however, Morton didn't stick close to sight-reading or adhere to the general standards of music, nor did he acquire a first-rate piano technique. Nevertheless, by the time he became a teenager, he was able to handle rags, quadrilles, and popular tunes of his time. With these skills he was able to get work at cabarets and brothels of the Storyville sporting district. He was popular with the madams and their prostitutes. Because of his social life his grandmother had thrown him out of her house. His father had abandoned him, and his mother was dead.

Jelly Roll Morton at the age of seventeen had composed his first blues song, "New Orleans Blues." This became a favorite among the city bands, as did his later compositions, "King Porter Stomp" and "Jelly Roll Blues."

Jelly Roll Morton worked as the house pianist at the Red Apple Club in Harlem, New York City, and recorded with white trumpeter Wingy Manone. In the '30s, Morton's health begin to decline. His investments in a cosmetics company that

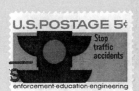

468

469

470

471

472

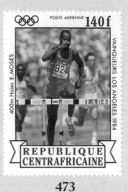

473

474

475

went bad didn't help matters. To add insult to injury, the record industry had virtually collapsed.

In 1935 Morton moved to Washington, D.C., and played a two-year engagement at the Jungle Club. He worked as a nightclub manager in 1937. In 1938 Morton recorded eight hours of music and anecdotal reminiscences for John Lomax at the Library of Congress. He moved back to New York in 1938 and organized a music publishing company.

Morton, who died in Los Angeles on July 10, 1941, is greatly responsible for creating jazz's balance between composition and improvisation.

In 1963, Morton was elected by the critics into the DownBeat Hall of Fame. Recognition was also granted to him on an American issue in 1995, Legends of American Music series.

9/16/95. United States. Quantity unknown. 32 cents. S#2986. From the Legends of American Music series. *Illus. 470.*

Moseby, Lloyd

Lloyd Moseby was born on November 5, 1959, in Portland, Arizona. He considers his hometown Loomis, California. In 1983, playing for the Toronto Blue Jays, he became the first Blue Jay to score 100 runs in a season. He became the Blue Jays' first base coach in 1998.

11/28/88. Grenada. Quantity unknown. 30 cents. S#1670g. From the "U.S. Baseball Series 1." *Illus. 471.*

Moses, Edwin

Edwin Moses was the winner of the 1983 Sullivan Award. This award makes a clear statement that Moses is America's finest amateur athlete.

Edwin Corley Moses was born in Dayton, Ohio, August 31, 1955. He is best known for his 400m hurdler in track his-

tory. He won the gold medal in that event at the 1976 Olympics in Montreal with a time of 47.64 seconds, breaking John Akii-Bua's 4-year-old world record. He lowered the record three more times—to 47.45 (1977), 47.13 (1980), and 47.02 (1983)—before winning another gold medal at the 1984 Games in Los Angeles. Moses earned only a bronze at the 1988 Olympic Games in Seoul, but his domination of a single event remains unchallenged in track history—from 1977 to 1987. He was undefeated in 107 consecutive meets. Over an eight year span, Moses won 122 consecutive races in various Olympic events.

11/27/84. Guinea-Bissau. Quantity unknown. 40 pesos. S#617. (Not pictured.) Celebrates Moses's win in the Olympic Games, Los Angeles, 1984.

12/3/84. Ghana. Quantity unknown. 3 cedis. S#948. (Overprint.) Celebrates Moses's win in the 1984 Olympic Games, Los Angeles. *Illus. 474.*

7/7/85. Central African Republic. Quantity unknown. 140 francs. S#304. Celebrates Moses's win in the Olympic Games, Los Angeles, 1984. *Illus. 473.*

7/25/85. Sierra Leone. Quantity unknown. 4 leones. S#700. Celebrates Moses's win in the Olympic Games, Los Angeles, 1984. *Illus. 472.*

8/85. Uganda. Quantity unknown. 1200 Shillings. S#462. (Perforated souvenir sheet.) *Illus. 475.*

Murphy, Eddie

Edward Regan Murphy was born April 3, 1961, in Brooklyn, New York, the son of a New York policeman. He began performing stand-up comedy by age 15, and today he is widely known as an actor and comedian. Eddie Murphy's films have grossed more than one billion dollars in worldwide sales, making him one of the most celebrated and powerful of contemporary African American entertainers.

Murphy was known by many who saw

him featured on *Saturday Night Live*, a TV satiric comedy that became one of the most watched programs during the 1980s. He made his first appearance on that show in January 1984, having passed six auditions to get there. Once he became a permanent member of the *SNL* cast, his popularity grew quickly, and he easily made the transition to the silver screen. In December 1982, Murphy made his film debut in the action comedy *48 Hours.* Other big films followed, including *Trading Places, Beverly Hills Cop* (written and directed by Murphy), and many others.

Murphy's success has been great. He owns his own production studio. He has helped many African Americans go in Hollywood where they have not gone before. Eddie has made himself one of the most likable popular performers, appealing to urban and rural Americans alike.

3/30/90. Tanzania. Quantity unknown. 150 shillings. S#585. (See color section.) From a series in recognition of American entertainers. *Illus. C125.*

6/20/91. Lesotho. Quantity unknown. 4 maloti. S#824. Murphy is pictured with Arsenio Hall in the movie *Coming to America.* An illustration of this stamp is found with the listing for Arsenio Hall.

1997. Niger. Quantity unknown. 300 francs. S#951a. (Not pictured.) This issue was in honor of "Stars of American Cinema." Others recognized in this issue are Elizabeth Taylor (S#9516), Bruce Willis (S#951c), James Dean (S#951d), Clint Eastwood (S#951e), Elvis Presley (S#951f), Michelle Pfeiffer (S#951g), Marilyn Monroe (S#951h), and Robert Redford (S#951i). This issue comes in a sheet of 9 stamps.

Murray, Eddie Clarence

Eddie Clarence Murray was born on February 24, 1956, in Los Angels, California. Eddie is an American League baseball player who started with the Baltimore Orioles. Eddie's career highlights: Oriole's-time HR leader ... missed a month of '86

with hamstring injury ... had 3 HR and 9 RBI in 1 game 8/26/85 vs. Angels ... 2nd in AL in RBI in '85 ... set Oriole record by hitting safely in 22 straight games in '84 ... runner-up for AL MVP honors in 1983 (.306, 33 Hr, 111 RBI), culminating season with 2 HR in final World Series game vs. Phillies ... 7-time All Star. He led the American League in 1977 in home runs and in RBIs in 1981.

8/31/89. St. Vincent. Quantity unknown. 60 cents. S#1234g. (See color section.) *Illus. C123.*

9/24/90. St. Vincent. Quantity unknown. 60 cents. S#1344c. (See color section.) *Illus. C124.*

Newport, Matilda

There is little available information on Matilda Newport in America. However, it is a known fact that she was born in the state of Georgia. Newport was one of the many black slaves during the early and middle 1800s who returned to Africa (Liberia) under the Monroe Administration rather then remain in America as slaves.

All the stamps issued in her honor depict her lighting the cannon to protect her new country of Liberia during the civil war that the immigrants fought with the natives of Liberia. These stamps were issued to celebrate Newport's 125th anniversary in defense of Monrovia (capitol of Liberia), December 1, 1822. According to Ernest Austin she was a widow from Georgia, considered an Americo-Liberian heroine because, on December 1, 1822, she fired a cannon which frightened and dispersed the native tribesmen, who were about to overrun the ex-slaves. Maltilda Newport was the first African American woman to be recognized on a stamp. Liberia recognized her on a stamp in 1947.

12/1/47. Liberia. Quantity unknown. 1 cent. S#301. (See color section.) *Illus. C126.*

12/1/47. Liberia. Quantity unknown. 3 cents. S#302. (See color section.) *Illus. C127.*

12/1/47. Liberia. Quantity unknown. 5 cents. S#303. (See color section.) *Illus. C128.*

12/1/47. Liberia. Quantity unknown. 10 cents. S#304. (See color section.) *Illus. C129.*

12/1/47. Liberia. Quantity unknown. 25 cents. S#C57. (See color section.) *Illus. C130*

3/14/75. Liberia. Quantity unknown. 25 cents. S#701. (See color section.) Commemorates the International Women's Year (1975). *Illus. C131.*

Norman, Jessye

Singer Jessye Norman is a native of Augusta, Georgia. She was born in 1945, the daughter of Silas and Jane Norman, who worked hard to make a good life for their five children. The focus of the family was in the church and at school. The family attended Mount Calvary Baptist Church.

The church is where Jessye Norman began to focus on her music. She sang and played the piano. It was there in church that Norman's powerful voice was discovered. She won numerous contests and awards for her musical talents. Norman strongly believes that when she first heard an opera, it took total charge and gave her inspiration. She just could not get enough of it. Norman was also inspired by Marian Anderson, Leontyne Price, and Nat King Cole. In addition, she had the encouragement of her family, and with that, Jessye Norman was on her way to a successful career.

Norman attended Howard University on a scholarship to study piano and voice. She also sang with the university choir. She graduated in 1967 with honors and continued her music career at the University of Michigan, earning a master's degree. She now sings opera around the world. She is considered one of the world's greatest versatile singers. Norman has not forgotten her hometown, and she visits to do concerts.

11/5/97. St. Vincent and the Grenadines. Quantity unknown. 1 dollar and 10 cents. S#2509h.

(Not pictured.) Color portrait of Jessye Norman.

Olajuwan, Hakeem

A stamp is said to exist recognizing Hakeem Olajuwan, a professional basketball player, but no information on such a stamp is available.

Oliva, Tony

Tony Oliva was born in 1940 in the village of Pinar del Río, Cuba, approximately seventy-five miles from the city of Havana. He grew up on the Oliva Plantation in Entronque de Herradora, one of five sons of Pedro Oliva and his wife. Señor Oliva was a backcountry Cuban plantation worker who spent time with his sons. He provided a homemade diamond on the plantation for Tony to develop his baseball skills. Tony practiced relentlessly with his father, and the hard work paid off when a Minnesota Twins scout spotted Tony in 1960 while he was playing in Havana. He was offered a minor league tryout, but he needed a passport, something difficult for a Cuban citizen to obtain. He used his brother's passport to make his way to the tryouts in America.

After a three-day tryout, the Twins released Oliva. He was offered to Houston, Charlotte, and Belmont, but all three clubs turned him down. He ended up with a charity offer to play for Wytheville, Virginia, a Twins Class D team in the Appalachian Rookie League.

After an excellent first year of organized baseball at Wytheville, Oliva went on to Charlotte in 1962, Dallas–Fort Worth in 1963, and the Puerto Rico Winter League, which landed him a starting spot with the Minnesota Twins in the spring of 1964.

Tony became the first player ever to lead the American League with his batting average in his rookie season. He led the league again in his second season and was also a key player in the Twins' successful battle for the 1965 American League pennant. In nine seasons of his fifteen year major league career, Tony Oliva had a batting average over .300. In five seasons, he led the American league in total number of hits.

Had Tony gone back to Cuba for any reason, he could not have returned to the United States. This was difficult for him, since he missed his family. And he never really learned to speak English well.

Oliva is still considered by many as having the greatest rookie year in baseball history.

7/30/89. St. Vincent. Quantity unknown. 30 cents. S#1274g. (See color section.) From the "U.S. Baseball Series 2." *Illus. C132.*

Oliver, Joseph (King)

Not many people, unless they are real jazz historians or lovers of jazz, know much about the "king," Joseph (King) Oliver. Many people recognize the name of Louis Armstrong. But it was cornet player Joseph (King) Oliver who provided Louis Armstrong with the basics of playing jazz.

According to the *African American Almanac* (1997) Oliver is "one of the founding fathers of jazz." Two of his influences were Buddy Bolden and Kid Ory. Oliver teamed with Ory to form what was to become the leading jazz band in New Orleans.

During the Storyville era, Oliver met Louis Armstrong and became something of an unofficial father to the boy, who called him "Papa Joe." Oliver gave Armstrong his old horn and taught him what he had learned about music over the years.

When the speakeasies of Storyville closed, Oliver left for Chicago. In 1922 he was doing well enough to bring Armstrong from New Orleans to play in his Creole Jazz Band as second cornetist. A 1923 series of recordings of the Creole Jazz Band brought attention to Chicago as a hotbed of jazz.

Sadly, however, within just a few short years Oliver's music had fallen out of fashion. He moved to New York and in the early 1930s made an unsuccessful tour of the South before finally settling in Savannah, Georgia, where he worked in a pool room until his death in 1938. The "king" received his first recognition on a stamp in 1998, sixty years after his death.

2/2/98. St. Vincent. Quantity unknown. 1 dollar. S#2525a. (Not pictured.) In recognition of jazz musicians King Oliver and Louis Armstrong for their contribution to jazz. The stamp was issued in a souvenir sheet of 4. It features King Oliver's portrait.

O'Neal, Shaquille

A stamp is said to exist honoring Shaquille O'Neal, an African American basketball player, but no information on such a stamp is available.

Owens, Jesse

James Cleveland Owens, a significant African American role model during the mid–1930s, was considered by many as "the world's swiftest human" for a quarter of a century. This track star was born the seventh of eight children to sharecroppers Henry and Emma Owens on September 12, 1913, in Danville, Alabama.

While Owens was attending grade school in Cleveland, Ohio, his teacher mistook his nickname "J.C." as Jesse, and he was called by that name ever after. It was also while in grade school that James Cleveland Owens's athletic ability was discovered and he began receiving formal instructions in running and jumping. Before that time his father had assisted him with his desire to be a runner.

During his years at East Technical High School in Cleveland, Ohio, he became nationally and internationally known when he tied, broke, and set world records in running and jumping events.

He became even more world renowned

while attending Ohio State University in Columbus, Ohio, as a student-athlete. His fame grew with his appearance in the 1936 Olympic Games in Berlin, Germany, where he represented the United States of America as the captain of the Olympic Team and received a total of four gold medals for his successful participation in the 100m dash (10.3 seconds), 200m dash (20.7 seconds), broad jump (with a leap of 26 ft. 5⅜ inches—a new world record), and 400m relay (39.8 seconds). Adolf Hitler, leader of Germany at the time, only increased Owens's fame and stature when he refused to shake Owens's hand because he was black.

President Dwight D. Eisenhower in 1956 appointed James Cleveland Owens ambassador of sports for the United States of America. Owens died in 1980 at the age of 67.

Issue date unknown. Mahra State. Quantity unknown. 25 fils. Hard to find. This stamp is also available in an overprint with the words "Gold Medal." Celebrates Owen's 1936 Olympic wins. *Illus. 477.*

1/24/57. Dominican Republic. Quantity unknown. 2 centavos. S#475. (Perforated; see color section). From an issue representing Olympic winners and flags. *Illus. C133.*

2/8/57 (Engraved and lithographed). Dominican Republic. Quantity unknown. 2 centavos + 2 centavos overprint surcharge. S#B2. (Perforated overprint; see color section.) Designed with a lithographed surtax to aid Hungarian refugees. *Illus. C134.*

9/10/59 (Engraved and lithographed). Dominican Republic. Quantity unknown. 2 centavos +2 centavos overprint surcharge. S#B27. (Imperforate overprint.) Type of 1957 surcharged in red. Issued for the Third Pan American Games in Chicago. *Illus. 476.*

1968. Rwanda. Quantity unknown. 20 cents. Portrait of Owens on a stamp celebrating the 1968 Olympics in Mexico City. *Illus. 478.*

1968. Rwanda. Quantity unknown. 60 cents. Portrait of Owens on a stamp celebrating the 1968 Olympics. *Illus. 479.*

11/10/68. Sharah. Quantity unknown. 35 dirhams. Minkus#386. From an issue celebrating Olympic winners. This is a difficult to find stamp. Only a poor quality copy is shown. There is also an overprint of this stamp which is not pictured or listed here. *Illus. 480.*

3/25/69. Mongolia. Quantity unknown. 10 mongo. S#516. Recognition of Jesse Owens's wins in Berlin, 1936. *Illus. 481.*

1971. Manama. Quantity unknown. 50 dirhams. Minkus#609. Difficult to find stamp. From an issue celebrating "Great Olympic Champions." *Illus. 482.*

5/25/72. Equatorial Guinea. Quantity unknown. 1 peseta guineana. (Imperforate). Issued to honor the 1972 Olympics in Munich. Outer border silver, inner border green. Owens's name is misspelled "Ovens." *Illus. 483.*

5/25/72. Equatorial Guinea. Quantity unknown. 1 peseta guineana. Minkus#619 (Perforated.) Same artwork as the imperforate version (see above), but with a gold outer border and red inner boarder. Owens's name misspelled "Ovens." *Illus. 484.*

7/21/84. Liberia. Quantity unknown. 3 cents. S#999. 1984 Olympics stamp celebrates Jesse Owens's 1936 medals. *Illus. 487.*

7/24/84. Togo. Quantity unknown. 500 francs. S#C521. (Overprint.) Overprint reads (in French), "Kirk Baptiste United States Silver Medal." *Illus. 486.*

7/27/84. Togo. Quantity unknown. 500 francs. S#C495. "Olympic winners" commemorative. Hard to find stamp; only a poor copy is shown. Following is an overprint with Kirk Baptiste's name, S#496. *Illus. 485.*

8/16/84. Burundi. Quantity unknown. 10 francs. S#625. This stamp comes with a souvenir sheet, S#C287a, featuring other athletes. Issued for the 1984 Olympics. *Illus. 489.*

7/6/90. United States. 36,000,000. 25 cents. S#2496. Celebration of Jesse Owens in the Olympics of 1936. *Illus. 490.*

7/15/93. Tanzania. Quantity unknown. 200 shillings. S#1079g. *Illus. 488.*

7/25/94. St. Vincent. Quantity unknown. 75 cents. S#2103. (Not pictured.) In recognition of Jesse Owens's 1936 medals in the 100m and 200m.

8/1/96. Lesotho. Quantity unknown. 2 maloti.

476

477

478

479

480

481

483

482

484

485　　　　486

487

488

489　　　　490　　　　491

492

S#1044. (Not pictured.) From an issue recognizing past Olympic Medalists in honor of the 1996 Olympics in Barcelona.

1998. United States. Quantity unknown. 32 cents. S#3185j. In celebration of the American 20th century. Recognizes Owens's setting of 6 world records. *Illus. 491.*

2/9/98. Dominica. Quantity unknown. 1 dollar. S#2040a. (Not pictured.) This issue recognized famous 20th century athletes. Other famous athletes in the issue included Isaac Berger, Boris Becker, and Arthur Ashe. Two stamps are done on each athlete for a sheet of eight.

2/9/98. Dominica. Quantity unknown. 1 dollar. S#2040b. (Not pictured.) Depicts Owens jumping in the 1936 Summer Olympic Games in Berlin. See S#2040a (above) for further comments.

Paige, Satchel

Leroy Robert "Satchel" Paige was born in Mobile, Alabama, on July 7, 1906. Many baseball fans consider him the greatest pitcher ever. The great majority of his career was spent in the Negro Leagues, where he played for many teams, including the Birmingham Black Barons and the Kansas City Monarchs. During his exciting career Satchel also played (off the record) against top major-league white stars.

Satchel Paige was described as a consummate showman and control specialist. He often pitched two games a day in two different cities in the Negro Leagues. At the age of 42, he became the first black pitcher in the American League when he was signed (1948) to the Cleveland Indians by Bill Veeck, an owner with a reputation for attendance-building publicity stunts.

Paige became a national phenomenon. He played until 1953. After his retirement, he made a special appearance in 1965, pitching three innings for the Kansas City Athletics. Although he had only 28 major league wins, by some accounts Paige had pitched a total of 2,500 games during his career.

Leroy Robert "Satchel" Paige was inducted into the Baseball Hall of Fame in 1971. He lived to cherish his membership for more than ten years. He died on June 8, 1982.

1/23/97. St. Vincent and the Grenadines. Quantity unknown. 1 dollar. S#2380b. (Not pictured.) From a souvenir sheet honoring black baseball players. See Hank Aaron, S#2380g, for more information.

Paris, Bubba

A stamp is said to exist on "Bubba" Paris, an African American professional football player and Super Bowl star, but no information on such a stamp is presently available.

Parker, Charlie

Charles "Bird" Parker, Jr., was born in Kansas City, Kansas, on August 29, 1920. Parker was a superb alto saxophonist who helped influence the jazz movement known as bebop. Although he played in big bands, most notably in the band led by Ja MeShann, Parker was happiest in small jazz groups. In 1915, while he was playing in New York's 52nd Street jazz clubs, he and Dizzy Gillespie made the first definitive bebop records. Bebop's ragged, rhythmically erratic and harmonically extended style exerted enormous influence on jazz musicians, and Parker is now recognized as one of the jazz greats.

The movie *Bird* depicted the sad life story of Charlie Parker. Much of it centered around his life in France as he struggled as a musician and ruined himself with drugs and alcohol that brought an early end to his life at age of 35 on March 12, 1955.

Parker most definitely contributed to jazz, and deserves the recognition he has received on stamps in the USA and internationally.

8/5/84. Gabon. Quantity unknown. 125 francs. S#566. This is a difficult stamp to find. Only a poor copy is shown here. *Illus. 493.*

4/3/89. St. Vincent. Quantity unknown. 5 dollars. S#1150. (Perforated souvenir sheet.) Shows Parker playing his sax. Seated at the piano is Bud Powell. *Illus. 492.*

9/16/95. United States. Quantity unknown. 32 cents. S#2987. From the Legends of American Music series. *Illus. 494.*

10/12/98. The Gambia. Quantity unknown. 4 dalasis. S#2049h. (Not pictured.) This stamp shows a portrait of Charlie Parker and his dates of birth and death (1920–1955). See Louis Armstrong, S#2049e, for more comments on this issue.

Parks, Rosa

Most people recognize the name Rosa Parks when the words "civil rights" are mentioned. Today, most American school children know she was the black woman who refused to give up her seat on the back of the bus for a white person. Her action brought about the Montgomery bus boycott that ignited the civil rights movement and brought Martin Luther King, Jr., to national prominence.

Born Rosa Louise McCauley in Tuskegee, Alabama, on Febrary 4, 1913, at the age of two she moved to her grandparents' farm in Pine Level, Alabama, with her mother and younger brother, Sylvester. At age eleven she enrolled in an all girls' private school (Montgomery Industrial School for Girls), a school supported by liberal minded women from the North. This school was designed to help women take advantage of opportunities regardless of their circumstances.

Parks recognized those opportunities were few for African Americans, and she took advantage of the ones that were available. She attended Alabama State Teachers College, and settled in Montgomery, Alabama, with her husband, Raymond Parks. They both joined the local chapter of the NAACP (National Association for the Advancement of Colored People) and worked quietly to help improve conditions for African Americans.

Rosa Parks has been recognized and granted many awards for her role in Civil Rights in America. She is especially noted for that important date of December 1, 1955, when she refused to give up her seat to a white passenger. She was recognized in 1999 on an international stamp. Mrs. Parks still lives in Montgomery, and still occasionally speaks on Civil Rights issues.

3/15/99. Marshall Islands. Quantity unknown. 60 cents. S#702j. (Not pictured.) Depicts Rosa Parks, standing to the far left with four individuals standing behind her.

Patterson, Floyd

Floyd Patterson was an American professional boxer. He also was an Olympic gold medalist and the first to lose and then regain the heavyweight championship title.

Patterson was born in Waco, North Carolina, on January 4, 1935. His family moved to Brooklyn, New York, when Floyd was a boy. It was a very difficult time in Brooklyn for the young Patterson. He was sent to the Wiltwychk School, a school for emotionally disturbed children, where he learned to box. He then returned to New York City and entered the Golden Gloves competition, winning the national titles in 1951 and 1952 as a middleweight. At the 1952 Summer Olympics in Helsinki, Finland, he won all of his fights and the gold medal. After winning the Olympics he turned professional.

Patterson lost only one of the first 36 professional fights that he fought. He beat Archie Moore for the heavyweight title in 1956. Patterson became the youngest heavyweight champion and the first Olympic gold medalist to hold the title. He made four successful title defenses before losing to Sweden's Ingemar Johansson in 1959. Johansson knocked Patterson down seven times before the fight was stopped. A year later Patterson knocked out Johansson in the fifth round and became the first boxer to regain the heavyweight title.

493

494

495

496

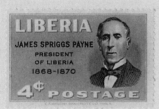

497

498

499

Patterson defended his title successfully until losing to Sonny Liston in 1962. Patterson continued to fight but never won another title. In his last fight, in 1972, Muhammad Ali knocked him out. Patterson later became a sport official in the state of New York.

4/26/67. Ajman. Quantity unknown. 1 riyal. Minkus#1144. This stamp was reproduced on an imperforate souvenir sheet (see below.) *Illus. 495.*

4/26/67. Ajman. Quantity unknown. 5 rivals. (Imperforate souvenir sheet.) *Illus. 496.*

Payne, James Spriggs

Not much is known about James Spriggs Payne. He was born in America in the state of Maryland or Virginia. He arrived in Liberia around the early or middle 1800s. Following Daniel Bashiel Warner, James Spriggs Payne became the fourth African American president of Liberia. He served as president of Liberia from 1876 through 1878.

1948–50. Liberia. Quantity unknown. 4 cents. S#316. *Illus. 497.*

1958–60. Liberia. Quantity unknown. 4 cents. S#437. *Illus. 498.*

Perry, Gerald

Gerald Perry was born in Savannah, Georgia, on October 30, 1960. He considers his hometown Lithonia, Georgia. Perry is a professional baseball player and plays first base for the Braves. Perry's overall professional baseball average before the All Star Break (1989): batting .337; home runs 5; RBI 42. After: batting .265; home runs 3; RBI's 32.

11/30/89. St. Vincent. Quantity unknown. 30 cents. S#1268i. From the "U.S. Baseball Series 2." *Illus. 499.*

Pickett, Ben

The story of Ben Pickett's stamp involves a most unusual mistake by the United States Postal Service. The mistake was discovered by one of Pickett's family members, who recognized that in trying to honor the legendary cowboy Bill Pickett as part of its tribute to Legends of the West, the Postal Service had used the portrait of Bill's brother, Ben Pickett. The Postal Service had to make a fast decision about how to handle the error. The mistake was a windfall for a few collectors who had bought the stamps previous to the discovery of the error. The value during this time had been estimated to be as much as $250,000 to $500,000 for those who had access to the error stamps. To bring things back to normal, the Postal Service decided to offer 150,000 of the error stamps to the public by using the lottery system. This action would decrease the cost of the rare collectible and allow the new stamp to be reissued with the real legend, Bill Pickett.

Apart from his inadvertent role in this case of mistaken identity, not much is known about Bill Pickett's brother.

10/18/94. (Reissued.) United States. 150,000 issued and sold randomly by lottery. 29 cents. S#2870g. (See color section.) This is the error issue with Ben Pickett. Note that this issue comes with a Souvenir Sheet titled "Legends of the West." See Bill Pickett, S#2869g, for more comments. *Illus. C135.*

Pickett, Bill

Bill Pickett was born in 1870 in Oklahoma to parents of African and Native American descent. He was the second oldest of thirteen children.

Not a great deal is known about Pickett's early life, except that he quit school after attending for about five years. He learned to ride and rope cattle early. Some say the skill that he parlayed into an art form was learned while he was young by holding down calves to be branded. Although some say he "invented" bulldogging and steer-wrestling, it is not a known fact that he did.

The agile Pickett was a smallish man,

only five feet and six inches tall, weighing about 145 pounds. He became a cowhand on the famous 101 Ranch around the turn of the century. The ranch consisted of some 10,000 acres and had 200 men working. A man named Zack Miller owned 101. It was Miller who described Pickett as "the greatest sweat and dirt cowhand that ever lived."

Two famous Hollywood actors, Will Rogers and Tom Mix, worked at the 101 Ranch. There are photographs showing Rogers, Mix, and Pickett in the same group.

From about 1901 through 1932, the rodeo was a popular western event. It brought together on a Saturday afternoon thousands of people who were used to cowboy routines, in cities like Cheyenne, Casper, and Kansas City. In many cases, "the Wonderful Bill Pickett" was the featured attraction. Pickett also played in big cities like Chicago, New York, London and Mexico City, as well as places in between. He also performed in England and had the pleasure of meeting King George V and Queen Mary.

One day while trying to please his boss by cutting out some horses, Pickett was badly hurt when a flying hoof caught him in the head. The force knocked him down. He was stomped and kicked by the horse. Eleven days after the incident, Bill Pickett died in the year 1932.

10/18/94. United States. 20,000,000. 29 cents. S#2869g. (See color section.) This is the reissued stamp (see Ben Pickett, S#2870g, above). Also note that these stamps come in souvenir sheets with 20 stamps recognizing the following Legends of the West: Buffalo Bill Cody, Jim Bridger, Annie Oakley, Native American culture, Chief Joseph, Bill Pickett, Bat Masterson, John C. Fremont, Wyatt Earp, Nellie Cashman, Charles Goodlight, Geronimo, Kit Carson, Wild Bill Hickok, western wildlife, Jim Beckwourth, Bill Tilghman, Sacagawea, and the Overland Mail. *Illus. C136.*

Pickett, Wilson

"Don't Let the Green Grass Fool You." Popularized by Wilson Pickett during the 1970s, this song still rings in the ears of those who recall the soulful and raw sounds of Pickett. No one could argue that Wilson Pickett was not one of the top soul singers of the 1960s.

Pickett was born in Prattville, Alabama, in 1941 and sang in gospel groups both before and after he moved to Detroit with his family at age 14. He was recruited by the Falcons, a local R&B group, in 1961. Pickett was with the Falcons for two years before he ventured out on his own. After recording some songs that were minor hits with Lloyd Price's Double-'L label, he signed with Atlantic Records. When Pickett initially met with little success, Jerry Wexler of Atlantic sent him to Memphis to work with producer and guitar player Steve Cropper at Stax Records.

In Memphis Wilson Pickett began to sing with one of the top back-up groups of all-time, Booker T and the MG's. A short time later, in 1965, he reached the pop charts with his successful crossover "In the Midnight Hour," which he co-wrote with Steve Cropper. Cropper and Eddie Floyd gave him his next hit song, "634-5789 [Soulsville USA]," and he was on his way, picking up the nickname "the Wicked Pickett" as he moved ahead.

Next up was a cover of "Land of 1000 Dances," which proved to be his most successful record on the pop charts (he continued to be huge on the R&B charts as well). He recorded songs in Memphis, in Muscle Shoals and in Miami. In 1967 his "Funky Broadway" went top ten.

The Wicked Pickett recorded many, many songs, among them "Mustang Sally" in 1966 and "Don't Let the Green Grass Fool You" as late as 1971. He was extremely popular on the R&B charts and had a great deal of success on the pop charts as well. Although he never had a #1 pop song, Wilson Pickett deserves the position he won in the Rock and Roll Hall of Fame in 1991.

1996. Liberia. Quantity unknown. 35 cents. S#1232a. (Not pictured.) Depicts Wilson Pickett singing. See Jimi Hendrix, S#1232h, for more comments about this issue.

Pippen, Scottie

Scottie Pippen is an American professional basketball player, a friend of Michael Jordan. Like Jordan, he was one of the top stars with the Chicago Bulls.

Scottie Pippen was born on September 25, 1965, in Hamburg, Arkansas. He attended the University of Central Arkansas. Pippen was drafted in the first-round, pick 5, by Seattle, and was traded to the Chicago Bulls on June 22, 1987. Scottie Pippen of the Chicago Bulls came into his own in the 1991 NBA world championship. He was a fair starter his rookie year. Pippen averaged 7.9 points, 3.8 rebounds, 1.1 steals, and .66 blocks, but went on to double all of these figures, plus triple his assists in only three seasons.

Pippen finished 14th in the league in scoring, led Chicago with seven assists per game and was second among the Bulls in rebounding, blocked shots and steals. At the end of the season, the accolades poured in for the Central Arkansas product. Pippen was selected for the NBA All-Defensive First Team and was named to the All-NBA Second Team.

Perhaps the most important and prestigious honor came when Pippen was chosen to represent the United States in the 1992 Olympic Games in Barcelona, Spain — along with the best the NBA had to offer. Pippen was also honored on a stamp for his play with the U.S. Olympic "Dream Team."

12/22/92. St. Vincent. Quantity unknown. 2 dollars. S#1744a. (See color section.) From an issue recognizing the 1992 Olympic "Dream Team." *Illus. C137.*

Poitier, Sidney

A stamp is said to exist on Sidney Poitier, a prominent American actor and director, but no information on such a stamp is presently available.

Poor, Salem

Salem Poor, a free black man of colonial America, was born in 1752 in Andover, Massachusetts. Poor enlisted in the Continental Army and is credited with killing British Lt. Colonel James Abercrombie at the Battle of Breed's Hill (Bunker Hill).

The April battles of Lexington and Concord in 1775 marked the end of the talking and the beginning of the fighting for American independence from Great Britain. The city of Boston and its environs were the focus of the spreading conflict between the settlers and the British Redcoats, and on June 17, 1775, the colonists and Redcoats squared at Bunker Hill. More than a score of blacks stood shoulder to shoulder with the white American rebels. Poor's valor and intrepidness at the Battle of Bunker Hill caused 14 officers, including Colonel William Prescott, to cite him with heroism and thus petition the General Court of Massachusetts:

"We declare that A Negro Man Called Salem Poor of Col. Fryes Regiment, Capt. Ames, Company in the late Battle of Charleston, behaved like an Experienced Officer, as Well as an Excellent Soldier, to Set forth Particulars of his conduct would be Tedious, We Would Only begg leave to say in the Person of this Negro Centers a Brave & gallant Soldier."

Records also show that Poor served at Valley Forge and White Plains. What became of him is unknown. The conduct of most Negroes was little recorded, and their later lives were completely ignored. Any rewards Poor may have received went unrecorded. No one knows the exact year or date of his death. However, we do know that America remembers who he was by recognizing him on a postage stamp.

3/25/75. United States. 157,865,000. 29 cents. S#1560. (See color section.) *Illus. C138.*

Powell, Bud

Bud Powell was born Earl Powell in 1924 in New York City. An American jazz pianist and composer, he was the son and grandson of musicians, and is regarded today as an originator of the modern jazz piano style. He also played a significant role in developing the genre of the bebop sound. Powell played with and for such greats as Dizzy Gillespie and Billie Holiday. Unfortunately, Powell in 1946 suffered from emotional problems that kept him from working steadily. In 1956 Powell moved to France, but returned in 1964 to play at New York City's Birdland. His music can be heard on a number of recordings, including the albums *A Portrait of Thelonius Monk* and *Americans in Europe,* both released in the 1960s. Powell died in 1966.

4/3/89. St. Vincent. Quantity unknown. 5 dollars. S#1150. (Perforated souvenir sheet.) See Charlie Parker, S#1150, for the illustration of this souvenir sheet.

Powell, Colin

A stamp is said to exist recognizing General Colin Powell, secretary of state under President George W. Bush, but no information on such a stamp is available.

Powell, Mike

A stamp is said to exist honoring Mike Powell, an American track and field athlete, but no information on such a stamp is available.

Prince

Prince was born Roger Nelson in 1958 in Minneapolis, Minnesota. During his junior high school years, Prince and a friend formed Grand Central, a soul-rock group. In those years Prince was already adept at playing keyboard instruments, the guitar, and drums. By the time he finished high school Prince had mastered the saxophone and at least ten other instruments.

In 1978 Warner Records issued Prince's first album, *For You.* Subsequent records include *Prince* (1979), *Dirty Mind* (1980), *Controversy* (1981), *1999* (1982), *Purple Rain* (1983), *Around the World in a Day* (1985), *Batman* (contribution to soundtrack) (1989), *Graffiti Bridge* (1990), and *Diamonds and Pearls* (1991). Prince also produced and starred in the successful film *Purple Rain* (1984) and the less popular film *Under the Cherry Moon* (1986).

Prince is loved by many for his unique idosyncratic version of the "funk" sound. His interesting and unique live stage performance is one of his great attributes.

Issue date unknown. St. Vincent. Quantity unknown. 2 dollars. (See color section.) *Illus. C139.*

Pryor, Richard

Comedian and actor Richard Pryor was born in Peoria, Illinois, on December 1, 1940. He entered Catholic school in 1946, and his parents were divorced in 1950 and he moved in with his grandmother. In 1953 he transferred to Blain Summer Private School. He dropped out of high school in 1955, worked at a local packing company for a while, then joined the army in 1958.

In 1960 Richard Pryor made his first comedy performance at Harold's Club. At that time he married Patricia, and his first child, Richard Jr., was born. During his first marriage, he started smoking marijuana. In 1962 he performed at Collins' Corner the Black Belt Circuit, and he ended up with 35 days in jail for assault.

Richard moved to New York in 1962, and in 1963 landed comedy jobs at the Bitter End, the Living Room, and Papa Hud's.

During this time he met Comedian Bill Cosby, appeared on *Rudy Vallee Summer Variety on Broadway Tonight, Merv Griffin*, and *Kraft Music Hall*. In 1966 he appeared on Ed Sullivan for the first time and Pryor was on his way. He moved to the fast pace and glittering lights of Las Vegas. Here he started to use cocaine. His second child, Elizabeth, was born, and he was thrown in jail for drug possession.

From here on Pryor continued to get himself in trouble for drugs, assaults, and other offenses. Nevertheless, he also continued to bring color to comedy and became the funniest man from the 1970s through the late 1980s. Pryor had a keen sense of observing other people as well as himself, and he related his observations in a way to make people laugh. Many comedians took on his style, and Pryor literally changed the way comedy had been done in America. Pryor produced some 20 comedy albums (his *That Nigger's Crazy* went platinum) and starred in many movies such as *Jo Jo Dancer: Your Life Is Calling, See No Evil, Hear No Evil, Harlem Nights*, and others.

In 1986 Pryor was diagnosed with multiple sclerosis. Today he lives in Los Angeles. Pryor has lived his life in the most colorful way, played it out in movies and television. Telling stories of comic genius that also recognize and absolve the many pains of life, Richard did it his way and in most ways he did it well.

3/28/93. Gambia. Quantity unknown. Face value unknown. S#1348h. (Not pictured.) This stamp recognizes Pryor for the part he played in *Brewster's Millions* (1985).

Puckett, Kirby

Kirby Puckett was born in Chicago, Illinois, on March 14, 1961, the youngest of nine children and the son of a former Negro League player. Puckett became an outstanding outfielder for the Minnesota Twins. He averaged 200 hits per season over his first ten major league seasons (1984–1993). Puckett's distinctive, stocky build and his hustling enthusiasm on the field have made him one of baseball's most popular players.

The Twins in the first round of a free-agent draft selected Puckett in 1982. He joined the major league club during the 1984 season. He is highly respected for his offensive and defensive skills on the field of baseball. He won six Gold Glove awards (1986–1989 and 1991–1992) for his defensive skills, and in 1989 he led the American League (AL) in batting with a .339 average.

Puckett was named the AL Championship Series' most valuable player in 1991 with a .429 batting average during the series. In his appearances in the 1987 and 1991 World Series, Puckett posted a .308 average overall, but is best remembered for his wall-climbing catch of a deep hit to left-center field during the sixth game of the 1991 series against the Atlanta Braves. His 11th-inning, game-winning home run in that game locked in the winning of the World Series for the Twins. He was also named Most Valuable Player in the 1993 All-Star Game. He has been inducted into the Baseball Hall of Fame.

Following a diagnosis of glaucoma, Puckett retired from baseball in 1997.

11/28/88. Grenada. Quantity unknown. 30 cents. S#1671g. (See color section.) From the "U.S. Baseball Series 1." Tony Gwynn, S#1225 (souvenir sheet), for recognition of Puckett on a souvenir issue. His name is printed on this stamp. *Illus. C140.*

Raines, Tim

Timothy "Rocky" Raines was born September 16, 1959, in Sanford, Florida. He is an American baseball player. Tim was selected by the Montreal Expos in the fifth round of the 1977 free-agent draft. He led the National League in stolen bases four times, and won the National League batting title in 1986. Today Raines remains a reliable contact hitter who can get around on a fastball. Tim has a son (Tim Raines, Jr.) who was draft pick in June 2001 in the Orioles' sixth round. Who knows? Tim may one day get to play with or against his own son.

11/28/88. Grenada. Quantity unknown. 30 cents. S#1664f. (See color section.) From the "U.S. Baseball Series 1." *Illus. c141.*

Rainey, Ma

Ma Rainey was born Gertrude Melissa Nix Pridgett in Columbus, Georgia, on April 26, 1886. Ma Rainey is credited as the first great American female blues singer. She was introducing blues in her act by 1902. She was married to Will "Pa" Rainey in 1904, and together, as the assassinators of the blues, they toured tent shows and levee camps. They separated, but she continued as Ma Rainey. By 1923 she was recording her earthy, brooding power songs that made her most popular in the deep South. Ma recorded nearly 100 titles before 1929. She introduced such hits as "See See Rider Blues" with Louis Armstrong, "Oh My Babe Blues" with Coleman Hawkins, "Shave 'Em Dry" and "Deep Moanin' Blues" with the gospel pioneer Thomas A. Dorsey and Tampa Red. The pressings of the recordings were of poor quality. The 1930s Depression didn't help in the matter, and played a significant part in ending Ma Rainey's touring and recording careers. She retired in 1933.

Ma Rainey died on December 22, 1939. She was inducted into the Rock and Roll Hall of Fame for her early influence on Rock and Roll. Ma Rainey has also been recognized on U.S. and international stamps for her rare and pioneering contributions to the blues.

2/12/92. Gambia. Quantity unknown. 1 dalasi. S#1182. (See color section.) *Illus. C142.*

9/17/94. United States. 20,000,000. 29 cents.

S#2859. (See color section.) From the Legends of American Music series (Jazz and Blues Singer issue). *Illus. C143.*

Randolph, A. Phillip

Asa Philip Randolph was born April 15, 1889, in Crescent City, Florida. He was the son of a Methodist minister, Reverend James William Randolph. Both his father and his mother, Elizabeth Robinson Randolph, were ex-slaves.

Asa Phillip Randolp studied at City College of New York. He came to be known as "Mr. Labor Relations" and "Father of the March on Washington Movement"—an entrepreneur, socialist, civil rights advocate, teacher, singer, and actor.

A. Philip Randolph for over four decades was in the forefront of the civil rights struggle and the trade union movement in American history. He is best known for co-founding, organizing, and directing the Brotherhood of Sleeping Car Porters. This union of railroad workers was the first African American union to be recognized nationally and internationally. He was the first African American elected to the Labor Council and appointed vice-president of the American Federation of Labor/Congress of Industrial Organizations (AFL–CIO). He was also the first black American to serve on the New York City Housing Authority Board and its commission on race relations.

For a lifetime struggle against discrimination and segregation in industry, organized labor, and the United States Armed Forces, Randolph received the Clendenin Award of the Worker's Defense League; the NAACP's Spingarn Medal for advocating labor rights; and many other honors and awards.

A. Philip Randolph, the radical "Union Buster," died at the age of ninety in New York City on May 16, 1979. He has been remembered on a U.S. Black Heritage series postage stamp for his many contributions to U.S. and world humanity.

2/3/89. United States. 152,000,000. 25 cents. S#2402. (See color section.) From the Black Heritage series. *Illus. C144.*

Randolph, Willie

Larry William "Willie" Randolph is an American baseball player who was born on July 6, 1954, in Holly Hill, South Carolina. Randolph was a second baseman starting in 1975 with the New York Yankees. He spent most of his playing career with the Yankees. Willie's averages over the years are as follows: on base .366; slugging .326; and strikeout ratio 12.4.

8/31/89. St. Vincent. Quantity unknown. 60 cents. S#1234g. (Not pictured.) This stamp is found with the listing for Eddie Murray. Also see Eric Davis, S#1552b (souvenir sheet), for name recognition of Willie Randolph.

Ray, Ron

A stamp is said to exist on Ron Ray, an American track and field athlete, but no information on such a stamp is available.

Redding, Otis

Otis Redding was born in Georgia on September 9, 1941. He was considered one of the greatest exponents of soul music. He was killed in a plane crash on December 10, 1967. It has been rumored that Otis Redding's plane accident was created by an organized crime syndicate because he was one of the first African Americans during that time who wanted to take charge of producing and writing his music and controlling his own business career. Among his admirers were the Rolling Stones and Aretha Franklin, whose 1967 recording of his song "Respect" was an instant hit.

Although he achieved considerable success during his lifetime, Redding's greatest fame came after his death, with the 1968 release of his song "Sittin' on the Dock of the Bay" (1973). The U.S. Postal System

paid tribute to Otis Redding, recognizing his contribution to American music.

6/16/93. United States. 14,000,000. 29 cents. S#2728. (See color section.) *Illus. C145.*

6/16/93. United States. 66,000,000. 29 cents. S#2735. (See color section.) This is an imperforate version of the U.S. Redding stamp (no perforations on right and left sides). *Illus. C146.*

7/26/93. Gambia. Quantity unknown. 4 dalasis. S#1395b. From an issue in recognition of entertainers. See Clyde McPhatter, S#1395g, for more information.

1996. Liberia. Quantity unknown. 35 cents. S#1232c. (Not pictured.) See Jimi Hendrix, S#1232h, for more comments on this issue.

Reynolds, Harold

Harold Reynolds was born in Eugene, Oregon, on November 11, 1960. He considers Corvallis, Oregon, his hometown. Reynolds plays second base for the Seattle Mariners. He has played with more than 5 different clubs over the years. His overall average before the 1988 All-Star Game: batting .286 and home runs 2. After: batting .279; home runs 2; RBI 20.

11/30/89. St. Vincent. Quantity unknown. 30 cents. S#1271g. (See color section.) From the "U.S. Baseball Series 2." *Illus. C147.*

Rice, Jim

James E. "Jim" Rice was born March 8, 1953, in Anderson, South Carolina. Jim Rice is described as a powerful right-handed slugger. He is 6-foot-2, 205 pounds. Rice joined the AL's Boston Red Sox late in the 1974 season. The following year, he and teammate Fred Lynn staged a season-long battle for rookie of the year and most valuable player honors. Rice batted .309 with 22 home runs and 102 RBI, but Lynn won both awards.

After hitting a league-leading 39 home runs in 1977, Rice had his best season in 1978, when he won the MVP award, leading the league with 213 runs scored, 15 triples, 46 home runs, 139 RBI, and a .600

slugging percentage. He batted .315 that year.

Rice hit 39 home runs with 130 RBI and a .325 average in 1979, then was troubled by injuries for several seasons. He returned to health in 1983, batting .305 with a league-leading 39 home runs and 126 RBI. That was the last year in which he hit over .300. He retired after batting just .234 in 56 games in 1989.

In 26 seasons, all with Boston, Rice batted .295 with 2,452 hits, including 373 doubles, 79 triples, and 382 home runs. He drove in 1,451 runs and scored 1,249.

11/30/89. St. Vincent. Quantity unknown. 30 cents. S#1275b. (See color section.) From the "U.S. Baseball Series 2." *Illus. C148.*

Ritchie, Lionel

Lionel Ritchie was born in Tuskegee, Alabama, on June 20, 1949. He began a solo career in 1982 after more than ten years with the Commodores, a very popular group, during the 1970s and early 1980s. The group's first album, *Machine Gun* (1973), won immediate acclaim for its instrumental rhythm and blues–disco sound. Later, melodious ballads and a sensual vocal style grew more central to the group's appeal. In 1978 the song "Three Times a Lady" won Ritchie a country songwriter's award, exposing the common roots of soul and country music. He wrote and produced hits for other artists, notably *Lady* (1980) for Kenny Rogers and the theme for the movie *Endless Love* (1981), which he performed with Diana Ross. After leaving the Commodores, Richie wrote, produced, sang, and played piano on his solo debut, *Lionel Ritchie* (1982). That album and his second solo effort, *Can't Slow Down* (1983), sold 20 million copies worldwide combined. In 1985 Ritchie co-wrote the hunger-relief song "We Are the World" with Michael Jackson and other superstars. He wrote songs for films like *White Nights* ("Say You, Say Me") and *The Color Purple* ("Miss Celie's Blues"). Ritchie's third album, *Dancing on the Ceiling* (1986), sold over three million copies in the United States of America.

11/30/89. Grenada. Quantity unknown. 25 cents. S#1674. (See color section.) *Illus. C149.*

2/15/92. Tanzania. Quantity unknown. 75 shillings. S#811f. (See color section.) *Illus. C150.*

Roberts, Joseph J.

Born in the United States, Joseph Jenkins Roberts was the first governor and president of Liberia. His statue is a historical landmark in Petersburg, Virginia, to this day.

Joseph Roberts was born in Petersburg in 1809. During the James Monroe Administration, blacks in the United States were allowed an opportunity to settle in Liberia, West Africa, with an understanding that they would stay there for the rest of their lives. Roberts took the chance and settled in Liberia in 1829. He became a wealthy merchant in Monrovia, the capital of Liberia. Roberts became the first governor of Liberia in 1841, and in 1848 he was elected the first president of an independent Liberia. During his administration, in an 1849 letter, President Roberts appealed to the government and people of the United States for aid in purchasing the territory of Gallinas, enabling Liberia to control the West African coast from Sierra Leone to Cape Palmas. As incentive, Roberts boasted of the eradication of the slave trade in territories recently acquired by Liberia and pointed out that adding Gallinas would enable the republic to keep the whole coast "free from the demoralizing and wilting influence of the slave trade."

Roberts achieved international recognition for the new country before leaving the Liberian presidency in 1856. After many years as president of Liberia College, Roberts again served as Liberian president from 1872 to 1876. Joseph Jenkins Roberts died in 1876.

Following are those stamps paying tribute to the first African American president of Liberia. It is also of significance that the next eight presidents of Liberia were African Americans (born in the United States).

1923. Liberia. Quantity unknown. 1 cent. S#214. (See color section.) This stamp was issued as a memorial to the first president of Liberia (an African American); however, he is not pictured on the stamp. *Illus. C151.*

1948. Liberia. Quantity unknown. 1 cent. S#313. (See color section.) *Illus. C152.*

1948–50. Liberia. Quantity unknown. 1 cent. S#371. (See color section.) *Illus. C155.*

1950. Liberia. Quantity unknown. 1 Cent. S#328. (See color section.) Note the differences in Roberts's portrait on S#3113 and S#328. Subsequent stamps used the 328 portrait. *Illus. C153.*

4/10/52. Liberia. Quantity unknown. 10 cents. S#337. (See color section.) *Illus. C154.*

10/25/61. Liberia. Quantity unknown. 5 cents. S#397. (See color section.) *Illus. C156.*

10/25/61. Liberia. Quantity unknown. 10 cents. S#398. (See color section.) *Illus. C157.*

10/25/61. Liberia. Quantity unknown. 25 cents. S#C134. (See color section.) Issued in a souvenir sheet of 3. *Illus. C158.*

9/21/76. Liberia. Quantity unknown. 1 dollar. S#770. (See color section.) Celebrating the American Bicentennial Year, this stamp recognizes United States presidents George Washington and Gerald Ford, and Liberian presidents Joseph Roberts and William R. Tolbert, Jr. *Illus. C159.*

Robeson, Paul

Paul Leroy Bustill Robeson was a gentleman, scholar, athlete, philanthropist, lawyer, diplomat, actor, singer, civil rights advocate, and political activist. One of five children raised in what could be considered an upper class African American family, he was born April 9, 1898, in the college town of Princeton, New Jersey, to Robeson, Sr., a former slave turned preacher, and Maria Louisa Bustill Robeson, a schoolteacher.

Robeson was molded by his father into a scholar and athlete. He attended racially mixed schools throughout his educational experience and was loved and admired by all. His scholarly achievements at Somerville High School earned him the highest grades in the history of the school, as well as a scholarship to Rutgers University in New Brunswick, New Jersey. There he graduated at the top of his class. He also earned letters in four sports and became the first African American at Rutgers to be selected to the All-American Football Team at the position of defensive end.

Robeson's multiple talents earned him recognition as one of the first African Americans in modern times to appear in leading stage roles in New York City and throughout the world. Among his performances were leads in *Emperor Jones, All God's Chillun, Black Boys, Black Majesty, Basalik, Stevedore, Plant in the Sun* and *Othello* in which he appeared over 300 times to a total audience of around one million people. He also appeared on the movie screen in such productions as *Show Boat, Body and Soul, Jericho,* and *King Solomon's Mines,* among others.

His belief in the ideals of American democracy and the promise of the American dream made him an outspoken critic of racial prejudice and drew him into left-wing politics, especially after his visit to the Soviet Union in 1934. During the McCarthy era he was called before the House Un-American Activities Committee. When he refused to sign an affidavit disfavoring membership in the Communist Party, the U.S. State Department withdrew Robeson's passport. For almost a decade of his life he was unable to travel abroad, and access to concert halls and theaters in America was denied him, until the United States Supreme court overturned the State Department's ruling in 1958.

Due to the stress and strain placed on him as a result of his struggle with the government over his philosophy and affiliations, his health deteriorated. After returning from Europe in the early 1960s, Robeson lived in retirement until his death on January 23, 1976, in Philadelphia, Pennsylvania.

3/22/83. German Democratic Republic (East Germany). Quantity unknown. 20 pfennigs. S#2330. (See color section.) *Illus. C160.*

5/10/86. Mali. Quantity unknown. 500 francs. S#C522. Only a poor copy of this hard-to-find stamp is shown here. The stamp marks the tenth anniversary of Robeson's death. *Illus. 500.*

1989? Grenada and the Grenadines. Quantity unknown. 3 dollars. S#1113. Issued in honor of the 425th anniversary of Shakespeare's birth. *Illus. 501.*

7/26/93. Guyana. Quantity unknown. 50 dollars. S#2678g. Hard to find. Robeson's name is misspelled "Roebeson." These stamps can also be bought in souvenir sheets (9 stamps). *Illus. 502.*

Robinson, Arnie

A stamp is said to exist on Olympic long jumper Arnie Robinson, who won the gold medal in 1976, but no such information is available.

Robinson, David

David Robinson known as "the Admiral," is a professional basketball player. Robinson was born in San Antonio, Texas, on August 6, 1965. He attended the United States Naval Academy. David Robinson was named to the 1991 All-NBA First Team and All-Defensive First Team after just two seasons. He is also the only NBA player to rank in the top ten in four different areas: first in rebounding, second in blocks, ninth in scoring, and ninth in field goals. Robinson was selected a member of the 1992 Olympic Basketball "Dream Team" for the United States and helped to win the Gold Medal. His recognition on a stamp was for his participation on the "Dream Team."

12/22/92. St. Vincent. Quantity unknown. 2 dollars. S#1744f. Olympic 1992 "Dream Team." *Illus. 503.*

Robinson, Frank

Frank Robinson was born August 31, 1935, in Beaumont, Texas. Robinson was an American baseball player and manager. He played the position of outfielder from 1956 to 1976 and won the American League Triple Crown in 1966. He was the only player to be name Most Valuable Player in both leagues.

Robinson was drafted into the major league circuit in 1956. He was there because they knew he was something special. He was the National League (NL) Rookie of the Year with the Cincinnati Reds, belting 38 homers, matching the major league rookie record.

Robinson played 21 years and left a great record. He hit 586 home runs, fourth on the all-time list; played in 11 All-Star Games; and was Most Valuable Player (MVP) of the 1971 All-Star Game in Detroit.

He was inducted into the Baseball Hall of Fame in 1982.

11/28/88. Grenada. Quantity unknown. 30 cents. S#1670c. *Illus. 504.*

1/23/97. St. Vincent and the Grenadines. Quantity unknown. 2 dollars. S#2379b. (Not pictured.) From an issue in recognition of African American baseball players. See Hank Aaron, S#2379g, for more information on this stamp issue.

1998. St. Vincent and the Grenadines. Quantity unknown. Face value unknown. (Not pictured.) A gold embossed stamp done in litho.

Robinson, Jackie

Jackie Robinson was an American baseball player and all around American athlete who was the first African American to break the racial barriers in American professional baseball. He was born Jack Roosevelt Robinson in Cairo, Georgia, on Jan-

500

501

502

503

504

505

506

507

508

509

510

511

512

uary 31, 1919. Robinson went to Pasadena Junior College (now Pasadena City College) in California and the University of California, Los Angeles. He played football, basketball, and track while he was a student at the University of California. After leaving college in 1941 in his junior year, he joined the U.S. Army.

After being discharged in 1945 with the rank of first lieutenant, Robinson signed a contract to play professional baseball with the Monarchs, a Negro League team located in Kansas City, Missouri. Later in 1945 he signed with Branch Rickey, general manager of the Brooklyn Dodgers, to play with the minor league Royals in Montreal. After spending a season with the Royals, Robinson played with the Brooklyn Dodgers and became the first African American to play modern major league baseball. From 1947 to 1956, Robinson batted .311 in 1,382 games. He was also a daring base runner. In 1962 Robinson was elected to the Baseball Hall of Fame, the first black player so honored.

During Robinson's years of playing with the Dodgers he endured a lot of racial hatred and bigotry. He was called names and spit at, and in the beginning he was even rejected by his team members. Throughout these difficult years, he was always at his best on the baseball field.

When Robinson retired from baseball, he became vice president of a restaurant chain in New York City. From 1964 to 1968 he served as special assistant for civil rights to Governor Nelson Rockefeller of New York. Robinson starred in the motion picture *The Jackie Robinson Story* (1950) and was the author, with Alfred Duckett, of *I Never Had It Made* (1972).

Robinson died in Stanford, Connecticut, on October 24, 1972.

8/2/82. United States. 164,000,000. 20 cents. S#2016. Part of the Black Heritage series. *Illus. 505.*

11/28/88. Grenada. Quantity unknown. 30 cents. S#1666a. *Illus. 506.*

7/23/89. St. Vincent. Quantity unknown. 2 dollars. S#1218. *Illus. 507.*

3/25/93. The Gambia. Quantity unknown. 3 dalasis. S#1349a. Recognizes *The Jackie Robinson Story*, a 1950 movie. *Illus. 508.*

7/15/93. Tanzania. Quantity unknown. 70 shillings. S#1079d. From an issue recognizing black athletes. *Illus. 509.*

1/23/97. St. Vincent and the Grenadines. Quantity unknown. 2 dollars. S#2380q. (Not pictured.) See Hank Aaron, S#2379g, for comments.

1/20/99. United States. Quantity unknown. 33 cents. S#3186c. From the Celebrate the Century Series (1940s): Jackie Robinson breaks the color barrier in major league baseball. *Illus. 510.*

7/16/99. Senegal. Quantity unknown. 250 francs. S#1359. (Not pictured.) Color portrait of Jackie Robinson with a bat behind his back. Senegal also paid tribute to Jackie Robinson on nine other stamps with various portraits of Robinson. They are listed S#1361a–h. Muhammad Ali was also recognized under this issue (S#1360a–h).

Robinson, Smokey

Smokey Robinson has been called one of the greatest songwriters of his time. He has been described as the William Shakespeare of songwriting. He was born in Detroit, Michigan, on February 19, 1940. His songwriting skills have produced a repertoire that spans four decades and includes some of the best soul-pop songs ever written.

In 1955 Robinson formed the Miracles and with them caught the ear of Motown owner Berry Gordy, Jr., in 1957. In 1960, "Shop Around," written by Robinson and Gordy, simultaneously brought the group its first million-dollar-selling single and put Gordy's record company on its feet.

Robinson's unforgettable falsetto and his ability to meld beautiful melodies with sophisticated lyrics led to numerous hits for the Miracles. Robinson provided his group with such mid–1960s classics as "You Really Got a Hold on Me," "Ooh Baby Baby," "I Second That Emotion," and the superb "Tracks of My Tears." He has written more than 4,000 songs, many for fellow Motown artists such as the Temptations.

In 1971, Robinson quit the Miracles to become a full-time vice-president of Motown and a solo artist. After a dry spell in the 1970s, Robinson return to chart success in 1981 with "Being with You." In 1987 he struck again with "Just to See Her," for which he won a Grammy, and "One Heartbeat."

7/30/90. Tanzania. Quantity unknown. 70 shillings. S#583. *Illus. 512.*

Robinson, Sugar Ray

Sugar Ray Robinson (born Walker Smith) was born in 1920 in Detroit, Michigan. "Sugar" was a well-known professional welterweight boxer, winning one title in that class, from 1946 to 1950, and a five-time middleweight champion between 1951 and 1960. He is considered one of the greatest boxers in the history of boxing. He became known as Sugar Ray Robinson after a sportswriter described his fighting style as "sweet as sugar."

Robinson had a successful amateur boxing career even before winning the welterweight title in 1946 (his first professional championship). In 1951 he relinquished the welterweight title to assume the middleweight title he won in a 13-round knockout of Jake Lamotta. Robinson lost the middleweight title later that year to English boxer Randy Turpin. In 1952 Robinson failed in an attempt to win the light heavyweight title from Joey Maxim.

Robinson lost the middleweight title to Gene Fullmer, then regained it by beating Fullmer in a later match. Later that same year Robinson lost the title to Carmen Basilio but defeated Basilio in 1958, re-gaining the middleweight title for the last time. He subsequently lost the title to Paul Pender in 1960. He was the only boxer to win the middleweight title five times, and he retired with 175 victories in 202 professional fights.

1/10/69. Ajman. Quantity unknown. 20 dirhams. Minkus#319. Recognition of "Champions of Sports." This is a hard to find issue. It is also issued as a stamp of Manama (not shown). *Illus. 511.*

Rosetta, Sister

Rosetta Nubin was born on March 20, 1915, in Cotton Plant, Arkansas. Rosetta was the only daughter of Katie Bell Nubin, a singing and mandolin-playing evangelist in the Church of God in Christ, a Pentecostal church. The Nubins moved to Chicago around 1920, and it was there that Rosetta, known as "Little Sister," made her debut with her mother before an audience of 1,000 people, singing "I Looked Down the Line and I Wondered."

Rosetta was married three times. In 1934 she became the wife of Pastor Thoupe, an elder in the Holiness church in Pittsburgh, Pennsylvania. After this marriage ended, Rosetta kept his name but changed the spelling to Tharpe. During the 1940s, Tharpe married Forrest Allen, a New York booking agent for spiritual music. Tharpe's third and successful marriage was to Russell Morrison, her manager. They were married in 1951 in the Griffin Stadium in Washington, D.C.

The years 1921–1937 were a glorious time for gospel music, and Sister Rosetta was key to the success of it. She was the driving force that brought gospel music into the national and international limelight. She was the first gospel singer to travel extensively in Europe, and she was the first nationally known gospel singer in America. She was one of the first to be featured in *Life* magazine describing what gospel music was about, and she was also one of the first gospel singers to be recorded by a major recording company (Decca Records). She was the first to perform gospel in a theater — the Apollo Theater in New York City.

Sister Tharpe had a career span of gospel music for approximately 50 years. The last five years of her life were filled with tragedies. She suffered her first stroke in 1970 while touring Europe. On October 8, 1973, she had her second stroke while planning for a recording session. She died the next day in Philadelphia, Pennsylvania.

6/26/98. United States. Quantity unknown. 32 cents. S#3219. From the Legends of American Music series. *Illus. 513.*

Roye, Edward James

Edward James Roye is another piece to the puzzle in understanding the Liberian and American connection. Roye was the fifth African American president of Liberia. His biographical sketch helps to clarify some of the cloudy issues of that time, and offers more information about blacks settled in Liberia.

Some 160 years ago, two members of the board of trustees of the town of Newark, Ohio, met and issued an order that all Negroes should leave within twenty-four hours. A constable was sent out to the black community to inform them of the order of banishment. A young black boy ran to the home of the third member of the board of trustees, A.E. Elliot, begging him to use his influence to circumvent the order. Elliot, his son, and Eddie Roye went along to the town square where a large crowd had gathered, both blacks and whites. The entire Negro population was pleading that they should not be driven from their homes. Elliot did use his influence. He protested that such hasty action would create hardship for the blacks. His arguments proved effective, and the order was postponed until it could be given more consideration. The postponement

became indefinite and was never brought up again.

Trustee Elliot went about his affairs as usual, but young Eddie Roye walked away from the square with a determination to find a land with freedom for "men of color."

The history of Edward J. Roye and the history of Newark begin at about the same time. In 1810, just eight years after Newark was founded and surveyed, John Roye is recorded as having purchased a lot on the south side of the square. Roye was born in slavery in Kentucky, came north with his wife Nancy and became a prosperous landowner. Their son, Edward J. Roye, was born in a little house on what is now Mount Vernon Road on February 3, 1822. Later, his father sold his Newark property and went to Illinois, leaving Edward and his mother behind. A letter dated April 14, 1829, from John Edward Roye is in the courthouse in Vandalia, Illinois. The letter leaves all the property John Roye had acquired in Illinois to his son Edward.

Edward Roye had left his hometown and was enrolled in Ohio University in Athens. He went on to teach school at Chillicothe in 1836, and after that he moved to Terre Haute, Indiana, where he opened that city's first bathhouse and barbershop next door to the best hotel.

By the time Nancy Roye died and was buried in the Sixth Street cemetery in 1840, the mood of the country was changing. Colonizationists wanted to remove all blacks and send them to Africa. Whether because of the changing climate of the 1840s or because of the scene around the square that day in his childhood, Edward Roye decided to leave the United States for an African country, Liberia. On May 1, 1846, Roye sailed from New York and one month later landed in Monrovia, Liberia.

His energy and intelligence soon made him a leading merchant, and after acquiring great wealth, he returned to the United

513

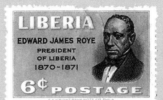

514

515

516

517

518

519

520

521

States on his own ship. It is said he visited Newark, where he was entertained at a banquet for an event for Thomas Ewin, adoptive father of William Tecumseh Sherman.

Years later Roye became chief justice, speaker of the house, and finally, president of Liberia in 1871. He began a program of reconstruction for his nation, intending to build new roads and schools. For these purposes he needed money. Roye sailed for England, where he began negotiations with London banks. The results proved disastrous. The terms of the loans were severe (a 6 percent interest rate). Roye agreed without consulting the Liberian legislature. While bonds were issued for $400,000, Liberia received only $90,000. This situation caused a powerful resentment against President Roye, and when he returned to Liberia, he was accused of embezzlement. He tried to extend his two-year term of president by edict after the people rose up against him.

In October 1871, Edward J. Roye was removed from the presidency and brought to trial, but he escaped in the night. It is believed that he drowned while trying to reach an English ship in Monrovia harbor on February 12, 1872.

After many years the nation of Liberia has taken another look at its fifth president. Was he a villain or a victim of political planning? Did he seek his own prosperity or that of the common man?

The Ohio Historical Society refers to Edward James Roye as the "ninth and forgotten president from Ohio." He is known by some as the "Lincoln of Liberia."

1948–50. Liberia. Quantity unknown. 7 cents. S#319. *Illus. 514.*

Rudolph, Wilma

Wilma Rudolph, the twentieth of 22 children, overcame scarlet fever, double pneumonia and polio to become one of America's greatest track athletes. She was born in Clarksville, Tennessee, on June 23, 1940. Rudolph attended Tennessee State University in Nashville, where she became a member of the famous Tigerbelles and was well known for her running ability. At sixteen she was a member of the women's 400m relay team that won a bronze medal at the Olympics in Melbourne, Australia. She stunned the world at age 20 winning three gold medals in Rome for her performances in 100m and 200m dashes and the 400m relay in the 1960 Olympics. Thus she became the first woman to win three Olympic gold medals. She was also the first African American woman to win the Sullivan Award.

Rudolph, during her lifetime as a track star and humanitarian, was honored with numerous awards. She became a well-known lecturer and goodwill ambassador. She was among the first track-and-field athletes to get up a charitable foundation to tutor children in academic subjects and help them participate in sports events. She was one of five athletes and the only track star recognized and honored in June of 1992 at the first annual National Sports Awards held in Washington, D.C.

The story of her life was shown in a 1977 television movie, *Wilma*. Wilma Rudolph died on November 12, 1994.

4/11/63. Niger. Quantity unknown. 25 centines. S#115. *Illus. 515.*

3/25/69. Mongolia. Quantity unknown. 30 mongo. S#519. Set Value $1.65. *Illus. 517.*

7/2/84. Liberia. Quantity unknown. 1 dollar and 25 cents. S#1004. (Perforated souvenir sheet.) *Illus. 516.*

Rushing, Jimmy

James Andrew Rushing was born in Oklahoma City on August 26, 1903. Having been born into a family of musicians made it almost impossible for Jimmy not to become a musician. Most of his family's life was centered on church music. At a very young age Jimmy had studied voice, piano and the violin. Rushing left home when he was a teenager, picking up jobs here and there as a musician. He got his first break with Jelly Roll Morton in California.

Rushing toured professionally in the Midwest and in California before joining Walter Page's Blue Devils (1927–1929) and Bennie Monten's Kansas City Orchestra (1929–1935).

Rushing's career was during a period when microphones were not plentiful or available in many situations, and a singer had to have the power to be heard above the band. Jimmy Rushing's voice was perfect and ideal for the situation without a microphone. Those who heard him said that his voice could be heard ten blocks away, ringing above the large swing bands. His style was like that of Bessie Smith. He crossed from blues to jazz. Where a blues singer would sing on the beat, Rushing sometimes anticipated it, singing as hard as any musician played in the band. He became the best of the so-called blues shouters.

Rushing was best known when he sang with the Count Basie Orchestra from 1935 to 1950. He was widely known for such great tunes as "Goin' to Chicago," "Good Morning Blues," "How Long, How Long," and "Mr. Five by Five."

He left Count Basie and from there mostly worked as soloist. He briefly led a band of his own and toured with other established jazz artists such as Buck Clayton and Benny Goodman. Jimmy was in demand for music festivals, studio sessions, and other events and appeared in several motion pictures. His music was widely recorded both with orchestras and as a featured artist.

Having the opportunity to perform with such giants as Benny Goodman, Count Basie, Walter Page, and Buck Clayton,

Jimmy established himself as one of the greatest singers in the history of jazz. He was named British jazz critics' choice as top male vocalist. Jimmy died at the age of sixty-nine on June 8, 1972.

9/17/94. United States. 20,000,000. 29 cents. S#2858. From the Legends of American Music series (Jazz and Blues Singers). *Illus. 518.*

Russ, Tim

A stamp is said to exist on actor Tim Russ, but no information on such a stamp is available. Russ is known for his role as Tuvok on the television series *Star Trek: Voyager*. A stamp depicting that character is described under African American images (S#2377a); perhaps it is the "Tim Russ stamp."

Salem, Peter

Peter Salem, an American patriot, killed a British commander at the Battle of Bunker Hill in 1775. He was born in 1750 in Andover, Massachusetts. Peter Salem was a member of the First Massachusetts Regiment, one of the better-disciplined units gathered on the hill. He had already given a good account of himself in the earlier skirmishes at Lexington and Concord. When the British launched their attack on Breed's Hill, he was in the thick of the fight. During the advance of the British soldiers the colonial officers rode in front of their troops, urging the colonials, "Don't fire 'til you see the whites of their eyes!" The British made a number of sorties under the leadership of Major John Pitcairn. It was during one of these assaults that Pitcairn fell mortally wounded, with a colonial bullet in his chest. Peter Salem is credited with having fired that fatal shot. The colonials were finally pushed from Breed's Hill, but not before the British learned that the raw American troops were willing and able soldiers.

Salem remained in the Continental army for seven years. He took part in the critical Battle of Saratoga in 1777. When the hostilities ended with the Americans victorious in 1783, Peter Salem left the army. He later married and settled in Leicester, Massachusetts, for a time. He earned his livelihood as a basketweaver. Eventually he returned to his native city, where he died August 16, 1816.

In 1882, the city of Framingham placed a memorial over his grave. The Daughters of the American Revolution purchased the land on which his home once stood in Leicester, and erected a marker with an inscription reading, "Here lived Peter Salem, a Negro soldier of the Revolution."

John Trumbull's famous painting of the Battle of Bunker Hill shows, in the lower right hand section, Lt. Thomas Grosvenor with Peter Salem just after the wounding of Major Pitcairn. In many reproductions of this painting, the right side of the picture is cropped off. In 1968 the federal government's commemorative stamp for John Trumbull used the small section which included Peter Salem, the black hero of Bunker Hill.

10/18/68. United States. 128,000,000. 6 Cents . S#1361. Salem is standing behind Lt. Thomas Grosvenor. *Illus. 519.*

2/22/73. Nicaragua. Quantity unknown. 75 centavos. S#831. "Preludes and causes of the North American Revolution." Observe picture to far right, with Peter Salem standing behind. *Illus. 520.*

2/15/76. Maldives. Quantity unknown. 5 lari. S#626. Only a poor copy of this stamp is shown here. *Illus. 521.*

Scott, Charlie

Charlie Scott is a 1968 Olympic Gold Medal winner for his role in the 1968 U.S.A Olympic basketball team. Born December 15, 1948, in New York City, Charles Scott graduated from Laurinburg Institute (a historically African American prep school noted for producing excellent basketball players as well as academic athletes) in Laurinburg, North Carolina, in 1966. He was in the 1968 All-Atlantic Coast Conference with an average of 18 points per game; his high was 34 points against North Carolina State. He helped the University of North Carolina make the NCAA finals that year.

Charlie Scott was not very well known until the 1968 Olympics. Scott, Spencer Haywood, and Jo Jo White were the stars of the gold medal winning team. Charlie Scott later signed with the Virginia Squires of the ABA and had two brilliant years with the team. He was named Rookie of the Year in 1971 and led the league in scoring to 1972. He later signed with the Phoenix Suns of the NBA and had a very good career with them.

Along with other players, Scott was recognized on a stamp for the 1968 American Olympic Team.

1969. Ajman. Quantity unknown. 15 riyals. (Perforated souvenir sheet.) This stamp is pictured with the listing for Spencer Hayward. Charlie Scott is second from the right.

Seales, Sugar Ray

Charles Augustus "Sugar Ray" Seales was born in 1953. He was an American welterweight boxer. He won the light welterweight boxing gold medal at the 1972 Olympics. His professional boxing career was curtailed by blindness resulting from boxing injuries.

Even before Sugar Ray Seales became a gold medal winner, he had won 115 fights as an amateur, against 12 losses. He won the 1972 Western Hemisphere and Olympic trials and the 1971 North American and National AAU. Sugar Ray also came in first four times in the Tacoma and Seattle Golden Gloves championships. To win the Olympic gold metal he had to win five fights by decision.

After he turned professional, Seales fought the majority of his fights as a middleweight. His first 20 fights were won

522

523

524

525

526

528

527

529

530

531

with relative ease, but he suffered defeat fighting Marvin Haggler in August 1974. He later fought a draw with Hagler and began to win again. Alan Minter knocked him out in 1976.

Seales eventually retired after becoming almost blind in both eyes as the result of detached retinas caused by heavy blows from fighting.

1972. Sharjah. Quantity unknown. 5 riyals. This hard-to-find stamp celebrates Seales as one of the winners in the 1972 Munich Olympics. *Illus. 522.*

1973. Upper Volta. Quantity unknown. 60 francs. This is a hard to find issue. Only a poor quality copy is shown here. Seales's name is in the lower left corner of this stamp. *Illus. 523.*

Sharperson, Mike

Mike Sharperson was born in Orangeburg, South Carolina, on October 10, 1961. Mike had his first National league playoff RBI at bat when he played against the Mets in 1988. He started the 1987 season as second baseman for the Toronto Blue Jays. He came to the Dodgers late in the season in trade for pitcher Jose Guzman. He won the Blue Jays minor league MVP award twice. Before the 1988 All-Star Game his averages were batting .333; home runs 0; RBIs 2. After the 1988 All-Star Game his averages were batting .192; home runs 0; RBIs 2.

8/3/89. St. Vincent. Quantity unknown. 60 cents. S#1234g. Sharperson is pictured with Mickey Hatcher, also of the Dodgers. *Illus. 524.*

9/24/90. St. Vincent. Quantity unknown. 60 cents. S#1345g. Sharperson is pictured with Roy Searage, also of the Dodgers. *Illus. 525.*

Shelby, John

John Shelby is an American professional baseball player. He was born in Lexington, Kentucky, on February 23,1958. Cockeysville, Maryland, is his present home. He plays outfield for the Dodgers. Before the 1988 All Star Game Shelby held the following averages: batting .311; home runs 5; RBIs .36.

8/3/89. St. Vincent. Quantity unknown. 60 cents. S#1234c. Shelby is pictured with Fernando Valenzuala, also of the Dodgers. *Illus. 526.*

Sierra, Rueben

Rueben Angel Sierra was born on October 6, 1965, in Rio Piedras, Puerto Rico. He considers his hometown Carolina, Puerto Rico. He debuted with the Rangers in 1986. His career highlights include the following: 5th in the American League (AL) in RBIs in 1990; first in AL in RBIs; 6th in home runs; 3rd in runs and 5th in hits in 1989. He set a Texas club record for most total bases in a season, which led AL. He was also 7th in AL in RBIs in 1987 and 2nd among the Rangers in home runs. He set the Ranger club record for extra base hits (78) in 1989. In 1987 Sierra became the youngest player in the American League to get 100 RBIs since Hall of Famer Al Kaline in 1956. He also became the youngest player in history to hit home runs from both sides of the plate in one game (9/13/86) against the Twins.

11/30/89. St. Vincent. Quantity unknown. 60 cents. S#1274f. From the "U.S. Baseball Series 2." *Illus. 527.*

Simpson, O.J.

O.J. Simpson, the American professional football player, broadcaster, actor, and football Hall of Famer (1985), was born Orenthal James Simpson in San Francisco, California, on July 9, 1947. Simpson played football at the University of Southern California, where his speed as a running back led to his selection as an All-American in 1967 and 1968. He won the Heisman Trophy as the best college football player in 1968 and was chosen first in the professional football draft in 1969 by the Buffalo Bills of the National Football League (NFL).

With the Bills, Simpson was the NFL's rushing leader in the 1972 season. In 1973 he became the first player to rush for more than 2000 yards in a single season. In 1975 Simpson broke the record for touchdowns in one season with 23, while rushing for more than 1800 yards.

Although frequently selected for the Pro Bowl team, he was frustrated by the Bills' failure to reach the finals. His request for a trade to a West Coast team was finally met in 1978 when the Bills traded Simpson to the San Francisco 49ers. He played his final two years with the 49ers, retiring after the 1979 season due to injuries. After his football career, he became a television broadcaster, actor, and lucrative endorsements for commercial products.

Simpson was depicted on a Guyanese stamp in 1993 in recognition of famous people. Only two years later, his fame turned into infamy when he was arrested and tried for the murder of his ex-wife, Nicole Brown Simpson, and her friend, Ronald Goldman. The trial was nationally televised and the center of intense media attention. Simpson was acquitted of the murder charges on October 3, 1995.

7/26/93. Guyana. Quantity unknown. 50 dollars. S#2676a. Only a poor copy of this stamp is shown here. *Illus. 528.*

Singletary, Mike

A stamp is said to exist on pro football player Mike Singletary, but no information on such a stamp is available.

Smith, Bessie

Bessie Smith was an American singer and songwriter. She sang the blues during the 1920s. Ma Rainey (a great African American entertainer and blues singer) discovered her. Smith, who was born on April 15, 1894, in Chattanooga, Tennessee, was described as the "Empress of Blues."

With the help and inspiration of Ma Rainey, Smith toured the South, and eventually ended up in New York City in 1923. There she recorded with leading jazz musicians; her first recording, made that year, was "Gulf Coast Blues." She recorded with Louis Armstrong, James P. Johnson, and Benny Goodman.

Smith was gifted with a deep, expressive voice of power and intensity. She became one of the most popular blues singers during her career. It is reported that she earned as much as $2000 a week at the peak of her career. However, when the American taste veered to radio and Hollywood movie music in the 1930s, her fan base dwindled. She also at this time became more addicted to alcohol, but she still managed to tour and fill her singing engagements.

Smith died in Clarksdale, Mississippi, in an automobile accident on September 26, 1937.

2/12/92. The Gambia. Quantity unknown. 5 dalasis. S#1187. Nos. 1178-1189 (12 stamps) valued at $7.53 *Illus. 529.*

9/17/94. United States. 25,000,000. 29 cents. S#2854. From the Legends of American Music series (jazz and blues singers). *Illus. 530.*

Smith, Jimmy

Jimmy Smith was born James Oscar Smith in 1928 in Morristown, Pennsylvania. A jazz organist and composer, he is the perennial winner of numerous jazz polls. In 1964 Smith was awarded a Grammy for his album *The Cat.* He produced many jazz hours of popularity during the '50s, '60s, and '70s.

Not much is known about what Jimmy Smith is doing today, but his music as organist during the peak of his career was the greatest.

5/17/72. Upper Volta. Quantity unknown. 500 francs. S#C104. Hard to find stamp. *Illus. 531.*

Smith, Ozzie

Osborne Earl Smith, known as the "Wizard of Oz," is an American baseball player. He was born on December 26, 1954, in Mobile, Alabama. Smith played shortstop with San Diego and St. Louis. He holds the 1978 major league record for the most assists by shortstop and is a seven-time member of the National League All Stars.

11/28/88. Grenada. Quantity unknown. 30 cents. S#1672h. See Tony Gwynn, S#1225, and Eric Davis, S#1552, for more illustrations and recognition of Ozzie Smith. *Illus. 532.*

Smith, Tim
A stamp is said to exist on Tim Smith, but no information on such a stamp is available.

Smith, Tommie
Tommie Smith is an American track and field athlete. He is considered a great sprinter. Tommie Smith was born on June 5, 1944, in Clarksville, Texas. He won the gold medal in the 200m in the 1968 Olympics. He stood on the winner's stand with John Carlos, who protested treatment of blacks in the United States by raising a clenched fist during the playing of the National Anthem and was expelled from the games.

Tommie Smith has been recognized on numerous stamps during his lifetime for his contributions to track and field.

6/30/69. Chad. Quantity unknown. 1 franc. S#199. This stamp has been overprinted several times. Not an easy stamp to find. *Illus. 533.*

1970. Chad. Quantity unknown. 50 francs. Michel#382. (Imperforate souvenir sheet.) This hard-to-find stamp celebrates three Olympic games: Tokyo 1964, Mexico [City] 1968, and Munich 1972. Tommie Smith (identifiable by the number on his uniform) is shown with his arms outstretched in victory. *Illus. 534.*

1970. Chad. Quantity unknown. 50 francs. Michel#383. (Perforated souvenir sheet with overprint). Overprinted in gold foil with the words "Munich 72" and the five-ring Olympic symbol. *Illus. 535.*

1972. Chad. Quantity unknown. 25 + 50 francs. Michel#537. (Imperforate souvenir sheet). This souvenir sheet includes two stamps, one show-

ing swimming and the other showing the Tommie Smith track event (see Michel#382 above). Hard-to-find souvenir issues. Please note these are not perforated stamps. These are perforated designs. *Iilus. 536.*

1972. Chad. Quantity unknown. 25 + 50 francs. Michel#538 (Imperforate souvenir sheet with overprint.) This souvenir sheet has the same design as Michel#537 (above) except that the words "Munich 72" and the Olympic symbol are overprinted on the Tommie Smith stamp in gold. *Illus. 537.*

Spinks, Michael
A stamp is said to exist on Michael Spinks, an African American former heavyweight boxing champion of the world, but no information on such a stamp is available.

Stargell, Willie
Willie Stargell was born Wilver Dormel Stargell in Earlsboro, Oklahoma, on March 6, 1940. Stargell is considered one of America's baseball heroes. He played his entire career with the Pittsburgh Pirates.

Stargell is described as a powerful hitter. The positions he played on the field were left field and first base. He hit more home runs (296) during the 1970s than any other major leaguer. Although he won the National League's Most Valuable Player award in 1979, he had his greatest season in 1973. During the 1973 season he led the league in slugging average (.646), home runs (44), doubles (43), and runs batted in (119). Going back to 1971 he also held his own by leading homers (48) and runs batted in (154). Stargell retired with a .282 lifetime batting average, a .529 slugging average, 2,232 hits, 475 home runs (16th on the all time list), and 1,540 runs batted in. He also struck out a lot, however; his total of 1,936 is second only to Reggie Jackson's 2,597.

Willie Stargell was elected to the Hall of Fame in 1987. He died in 2001.

11/30/90. St. Vincent. Quantity unknown. 30

532

533

534

535

can baseball player. He was born March 12, 1962, in Los Angeles, California. He started in 1983 as outfielder for the New York Mets and was National League Rookie of the Year (1983).

Strawberry is considered the best when it comes to stealing bases and hitting the ball when the team needs a hit. However, one of Strawberry's greatest setbacks as a great baseball player has been his bout with cocaine. Because of this he has been in and out for drug rehabilitation. He has also battled cancer. He is no longer with the league because of his drug problem. Nevertheless, his achievements in baseball are considerable and have been recognized on stamps.

11/28/88. Grenada. Quantity unknown. 30 cents. S#1667h. From the "U.S. Baseball Series 1." See Eric Davis, S#1552b (souvenir sheet), and Tony Gwynn, S#1225 (souvenir sheet), for further recognition of Darryl Strawberry. His name is shown on both stamps. *Illus. 539.*

Stubbs, Franklin

Franklin Stubbs was born October 2, 1960, in Laurinburg, North Carolina. He now considers his hometown Culver City, California. He most recently played with the Dodgers in 1988. Before the 1988 All-Star game his professional baseball averages were batting .197; home runs 4; RBIs 18. After the game: batting .248; home runs 4; RBIs 16.

8/31/89. St. Vincent. Quantity unknown. 60 cents. S#1234d. Franklin Stubbs pictured with fellow Dodger Jeff Hamilton. *Illus. 540.*

cents. S#1273h. From the "U.S. Baseball Series 2." *Illus. 538.*

Stewart, Michael

A stamp is said to exist on Earnie Stewart, an African American soccer player, but no information on such a stamp is available.

Strawberry, Darryl

Darryl Eugene Strawberry is an Ameri-

The Supremes

The Supremes were formed in Detroit, Michigan, and brought to full musical growth by Motown. The Supremes were one of the most popular singing groups in pop musical history. The person given most credit for the birth of this great musical group is Diana Ross.

Ross was born in Detroit and grew up there in a low-rent housing project where she played baseball, sewed her own clothes, and sang with girlfriends after school.

At the age of fourteen she failed to win a singing role in a school musical. It was at this point in her life that she and two friends, Mary Wilson and Florence Ballard, decided to form their own musical group. That group came to fruition in their senior year in high school. The three were hired by Motown Records to sing background and play record hops with Marvin Gaye and Mary Wells.

After finishing high school, the trio was named the Supremes and went on tour with the Motor Town Revue. Their first record to make the charts was "Let Me Go the Right Way." Then, "Where Did Our Love Go?" reached number one on the national charts. Over a period of ten years, the Supremes had fifteen consecutive smash hit singles, and at one point they had five consecutive records in the number one position on the charts.

In 1969, Diana Ross decided she was ready to go out on her own, but as recently as 2000 she has been able to bring the Supremes back together again and go on a world tour.

12/1/95. Tanzania. Quantity unknown. 250 shillings. S#1414d. *Illus. 541.*

Swann, Lynn

A stamp is said to exist honoring Lynn Swann, an African American professional football player, but no information on such a stamp is available.

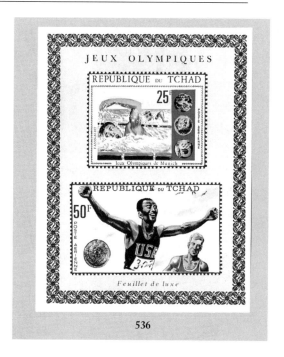

536

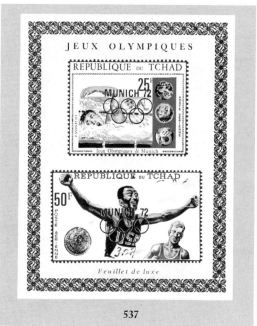

537

Tanner, Henry Ossawa

Henry Ossawa Tanner was an African American artist. Tanner was born June 21, 1859, in Pittsburgh, Pennsylvania. As a small boy Tanner wanted to be an artist, especially when he observed an artist

538

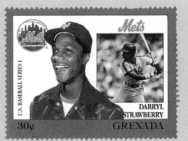

539

540

541

542

543

544

transforming a plain white canvas into a beautiful painting. To Tanner, who was then thirteen years of age, this was magic. From this point on there was no looking back for Tanner. He was destined to become an artist.

Tanner also understood the tribulations he would encounter for his love for art as a full time way of making a living. He sold several of his drawings for as low as $40, and much of the work that he submitted to publishers he never saw again. Yet Tanner continued to develop his unique style of painting. He also began to do art exhibits. He particularly went all out to exhibit in Cleveland, Ohio. At this exhibit he was in hope of raising enough money to take a trip to France. The exhibit was pretty well attended, but he didn't sell a single one of his paintings. However, his talent for painting was later recognized by Bishop and Mrs. Joseph C. Hartzell, who decided to purchase his entire collection.

Tanner sailed to Rome, and his tour continued with stops in Liverpool, London, and Paris. Being in Paris allowed Tanner the opportunity to meet and mingle with some of the best artists during this period, including Benjamin Constant, famous for his landscape paintings. Constant admired the painting style of Henry O. Tanner.

While painting in France, Tanner concentrated on developing his own technique. After five years in Paris, he also had developed a special interest in religious subjects. In 1896 his famous painting *Daniel in the Lion's Den* won him major honors. His *Resurrection of Lazarus* stunned the artistic world and was purchased by the French government. Following this, honors came one after the other. His work won the Salon Medal in 1897.

Tanner died on May 25, 1937, in France. According to Russell Adams's *Great Negroes Past and Present*, today Tanner's paintings are regarded as a successful com-bination of deep religious fervor and high artistic technique, somewhat in the manner of the master painters of the Renaissance. Tanner was recognized on a U.S. postage stamp in 1973 paying tribute to American artists.

9/10/73. United States. 146,000,000. 8 cents. S#1486. *Illus. 542.*

Tate, John

John Tate was an American boxer. He won the 1976 Olympic bronze medal for heavyweight boxing. Tate went on to win the WBA professional heavyweight boxing title (1979–80). As an amateur fighter Tate never won the big title. Even though he was the winner of 50 bouts (31 by knockouts) and lost 6, he was runner-up in the 1975 Golden Gloves and in the 1975 Pan-American Games. In 1976, at the Olympics, the Cuban Teofilo Stevenson knocked Tate out in the semifinals.

When he turned professional, Tate defeated Ken Norton in 1979 and laid claim to the World Boxing Association heavyweight title (after Muhammad Ali retired). Tate held the title for only one year before losing it to Mike Weaver in a 15-round knockout. Tate has not fought since.

6/2/79. Bophuthatswana. Quantity unknown. 15 cents. S#41. Bophuthatswana was one of the four black "homelands" designated by the government of South Africa. The state was never recognized as an independent nation by any government except South Africa's, and their stamps were not accepted for international mail. With the end of apartheid. Bophuthatswana was dissolved (1994) and reincorporated into South Africa. *Illus. 543.*

Taylor, Meldrick

Meldrick Taylor is an American boxer. He won the 1984 Olympic featherweight boxing gold medal. Taylor went on to win the International Boxing Confederation Professional Junior Welterweight boxing title in 1988.

1984. Sierra Leone. Quantity unknown. 15 leones. (Perforated souvenir sheet.) This stamp is shown in photocopy here. The souvenir sheet depicts various Olympic sporting events such as horseback riding, the high jump, and diving. "M. Taylor U.S.A. Gold Medal" is printed on the perforated stamp, which depicts a boxing match. *Illus. 544.*

Taylor, Robert

1972. Umm-al-Qiwain. Quantity unknown. 5Riyals. See Larry Black.

Terry, Sonny

Sonny Terry was born Saunders Terrell in Greensboro, North Carolina, on October 24, 1911. Terry learned the rudiments of harmonica playing from his father. Terry had all intentions of becoming a farmer like his father, but two serious accidents left him almost totally blind. Eventually he began to rely on music to make a living. Basing his style on a musical education begun in the church, he began venturing out, playing in tobacco houses, and at local events.

After his father died, Terry moved in with his sister in Shelby, North Carolina, and played for house parties and special events. He played with Bill Leach, a guitarist. Terry did his first tour with a medicine show. The man who ran the show began to cheat Terry, so Terry got his pistol and threatened the medicine man, known as Doc. Doc had no idea that Terry could see anything at all, but the man was wearing white pants, and Terry could see him well enough to shoot him in the leg.

Terry is best known for his virtuosic "cross-note" playing technique (playing in a key other than the key of the harmonica). Terry is also known for his uniqueness for executing special effects, such as animal cries, train whistles, and vocal moans, by simultaneously using his voice while he played. Terry developed a particular skill in modulating from key to key and pitch blending.

In 1934 Terry worked with Blind Boy Fuller. They played on street corners around Durham, North Carolina. Terry and Fuller recorded together until Blind Boy Fuller died in 1940.

In 1941 Terry became a part of the great black migration to the North and ended up in New York City, where he began playing with Brownie McGhee. The music style of Terry was accepted, and he even performed in Carnegie Hall, where audiences fell in love with Terry's Piedmont blues style. Terry and McGhee worked the first of their oversees tours during this period. When they returned from Europe, they were quite popular playing in white clubs.

Terry and McGhee recorded on quite a few labels. Their music appealed to both white and black audiences; in fact, they are considered one of the earliest groups who were able to cross over from one audience to the other. Although McGhee and Terry went their separate ways in 1970 due to personal conflict, they played together from time to time afterward. Terry performed solo as the leader of his own band for years. He died on March 12, 1986, from a heart attack.

6/26/98. United States. Quantity unknown. 32 cents. S#3214. *Illus. 545.*

Thomas, Frank

Frank "The Big Hurt" Thomas was born on May 27, 1968, in Columbus, Georgia. He graduated from Columbus High School. Before deciding on baseball as a professional career, Frank originally signed a football scholarship with Auburn in 1986, but he played in only one game as a freshman, catching three passes for a total of 45 yards. He quit football after his freshman year to concentrate on baseball. He set the school's all-time HR record with 49. He became the Southeastern Conference MVP in 1989, and was selected to the Southeastern all-freshman team in 1987.

545

546

547

548

549

550

551

552

553

554

555

556

557

The Big Hurt was selected by the Chicago White Sox in the first round (seventh pick overall) of the 1989 free agent draft. The 1988 season was one of the most challenging and disheartening of his career. The defending American League batting champ saw his average plummet 82 points. This lowered his career mark from .330 to .321.

Frank Thomas is very active in several charities in the Chicago area. He made an appearance in the 1992 film *Mr. Baseball* and a 1994 episode of the television show "Married...with Children."

9/6/95. St. Vincent and the Grenadines. Quantity unknown. 1 dollar. S#2204a. Recognition of American Baseball League stars. *Illus. 549.*

9/6/95. St. Vincent and the Grenadines. Quantity Unknown. 1 dollar. S#2204e. See S#2204a. *Illus. 547.*

9/6/95. St. Vincent and the Grenadines. Quantity unknown. 1 dollar. S#2204i. See S#2204a. *Illus. 548.*

Thomas, Homer Eugene

Homer Eugene Thomas was an American soldier during the administration of President Franklin D. Roosevelt. There is little information available on Thomas, though his birth date could possibly be traced through his U.S. Army records.

On a Liberian stamp in 1945, Thomas is the driver depicted in the jeep from which Roosevelt is reviewing segregated U.S. troops during a stopover in Liberia. The U.S. armed forces were segregated until 1948. It was President Harry Truman who issued an executive order to integrate the armed forces and full integration was not achieved until 1954.

Homer happened to be the driver with President Roosevelt and is credited with being the first African American to be captured on a foreign stamp.

11/26/45. Liberia. Quantity unknown. 3 cents. S#296. Not an easy stamp to find. Border art is in purple ink, while artwork in center is black and white. *Illus. 550.*

11/26/45. Liberia. Quantity unknown. 5 cents. S#297. Same art as S#296, but with blue ink for borders. *Illus. 551.*

11/26/45. Liberia. Quantity unknown. 70 cents. S#298. Same art as S#296, but with brown ink for borders. *Illus. 552.*

Tillman, Henry

Henry Tillman is an American boxer. Tillman was born in 1957 in the state of California. He defeated former heavyweight boxing champion Mike Tyson twice, earning a spot on the 1984 Olympic boxing team. He won the 1984 Olympic heavyweight boxing gold medal. Later, he lost to Tyson — one of six losses as a pro — on June 16, 1990, being stopped by Tyson in his first fight after a loss to Buster Douglas in Tokyo four months earlier. Tillman retired from pro boxing in 1992 with a 25-6 record.

At the age of 39, Tillman returned to Los Angeles in connection with a murder charge in September 1996 stemming from a murder in the California Men's Colony in San Luis Obispo, California, where Tillman had been serving a 32-month sentence for using fake credit cards.

1985. Tanzania. Quantity unknown. 1 shilling. Only a poor copy of this stamp is shown here. *Illus. 546.*

Tolan, Eddie

A stamp is said to exist on Eddie Tolan, an African American Track and Field athlete, but no information on such a stamp is available.

Truth, Sojourner

Sojourner Truth was born Isabella Baumfree in 1797 in Hurley, Ulster County, New York. She changed her slave name to Sojourner after she escaped from slavery.

She was the first African American female to speak out in public against slavery.

Even though she could not read or write, she possessed unusual oratorical capabilities that spellbound audiences in the Midwest, New England and the Mid-Atlantic states. She traveled across Connecticut, Massachusetts, Ohio, Indiana, Illinois and Kansas.

She is remembered for her efforts to gain equal treatment and human rights for African Americans to ready them to settle in the western states, away from the degrading treatment they were experiencing on the East Coast. Abraham Lincoln appointed Truth counselor to his freedmen in the capital, and she continued to work for the Freedmen's Bureau on behalf of former slaves. Truth forced a Washington streetcar company to allow blacks to ride and sued them when she received a shoulder injury.

Sojourner Truth was the mother of five children and a true champion of women's rights. She moved to Battle Creek, Michigan, after 1850. During the 1870s she promoted a plan under the federal government which was to set aside undeveloped lands in the West as farms for African Americans. Sojourner Truth died in Battle Creek on November 26, 1883, at the age of 86.

2/4/86. United States. 130,000,000. 22 cents. S#2203. From the Black Heritage series. *Illus. 553.*

Tubman, Harriet

Harriet Ross Tubman, abolitionist and daughter of Benjamin Ross and Harriet Greene, was born in 1820 or 1821 in Dorchester County, Maryland. She was one of eight children. Her sisters and brothers were Mary Ann, Benjamin, William, Henry, James, Robert, and John. She was married to John Tubman.

Born into slavery, Harriet Tubman could neither read nor write, but she escaped from slavery in her late twenties. She was a master of disguise. She used many

disguises to travel into slave territory on many occasions and helped hundreds of slaves to escape to freedom by way of the Underground Railroad network. It was for these courageous acts she earned the title "Moses of her people." She was an active Civil War participant, and assisted the Union Army as a scout, spy and nurse. Slave owners throughout the South offered heavy rewards (as high as $40,000) for her capture. It is said that she freed as many as three hundred slaves from the South.

Tubman settled down in Auburn, New York, where she established the Harriet Tubman Home for Aged Negroes. She died in Auburn on March 29, 1913. She was the first African American woman to be recognized on a United States postage stamp.

2/1/78. United States. 157,000,000. 13 cents. S#1744. From the Black Heritage Series. *Illus. 554.*

12/22/80. Turks and Caicos Islands. Quantity unknown. 1 dollar. S#461. Hard stamp to find. *Illus. 555.*

6/29/95. United States. Quantity unknown. 32 cents. S#2975k. From an issue commemorating the Civil War. *Illus. 556.*

Turner, Tina

Anna Mae Bullock (known by her stagename worldwide as "Tina Turner") was born November 26, 1939, in Nutbush, Tennessee, to sharecroppers Floyd Richard Bullock and Zelma Currie Bullock. Anna Mae had an older half-sister born out of wedlock. Tina married Izear Luster "Ike" Turner and they raised four children. Anna Mae had a son by a previous relationship, and two of the children were her husbands' from a previous marriage.

Anna Mae Bullock was a student athlete while attending Lauderdale High School in Ripley, Tennessee, and Carver High School in Brownsville, Tennessee. She was a cheerleader and basketball player and participated in track and field events. She graduated from high school in St. Louis,

Missouri. Her ambition to pursue the nursing field was abandoned when she became the lead singer for Ike Turner. Her gravelly, raspy, smoky tone of voice and torrid style was developed while singing in the church choir, during adolescence. Her first recording was "Box Top" in 1958. In 1960 her second record, "A Fool in Love," made it to the #2 spot on the rhythm and blues charts in the United States. As lead singer for the Ike and Tina Turner Revue for two decades, she toured the world, and Ike and Tina produced a string of hits during the '60s and '70s such as "It's Gonna Work Out Fine," "Poor Fool," "I'm Blue," "Tra La La La La," "Bold Soul Sister," "Nutbush City Limit," and many more.

After her separation in 1976 and divorce in 1978 from her abusive husband and partner, the pop princess, financially depressed, struck out on her own while maintaining a low profile for eight years. In 1984, at the age of 44 she was voted *Rolling Stone* magazine's Best Female Singer. From then on things were looking up for Tina Turner, who is now living a great life in Europe. She has done several movies, and her life story (*What's Love Got to Do with It*) has appeared on the screen. She has also been recognized on several international stamps during her professional career.

12/5/88. Grenada. Quantity unknown. 10 cents. S#1673. *Illus. 557.*

2/15/92. Tanzania. Quantity unknown. 75 shillings. S#811i. *Illus. 558.*

1996. Chad. Quantity unknown. 500 francs. S#669. (Not pictured.)

Vaughan, Sarah

Sarah Lois Vaughan is a native of Newark, New Jersey. She was born on March 27, 1924. Her father, a carpenter by trade, played the guitar and sang folk music, and her mother, a laundress, played the piano and sang in the Mount Zion Bap-

tist Church Choir. Thanks to the church, her musical family, and her God-given talent, Sarah Vaughan became one of the greatest jazz artists that ever lived. At the age of 12 she was accompanying the church service on organ and sang as soloist. She won the Amateur Night contest held at the famous Apollo Theater. The night she won at the Apollo she was heard by the great Billy Eckstine. He was highly impressed with her talent, and on his recommendation she won the position of pianist with Earl Hines's big band.

Billy Eckstine later decided to leave the Earl Hines Orchestra to start his own band. He took Sarah with him. Eckstine had chosen the best for his new band, including such great jazz artists as Charlie Parker, Dizzy Gillespie, Miles Davis, Art Blakeley, Budd Johnson and others. Having the rare opportunity of playing among the best of the best, and a natural voice with the flexibility of a musical instrument, Sarah Vaughan was on her way to success.

Sarah suffered several setbacks in terms of recording contracts during her early career. These early experiences in the music business provided her with strength and courage to go on her own as a soloist. She recorded such classic hits as "Lover Man," East of the Sun and West of the Moon," "Motherless Child," and other super songs.

Sarah Vaughan died at her home in Hidden Hills, California, on April 3, 1990. She has been honored with many awards for her contributions to the jazz culture, and in 1994 she was recognized on an international stamp.

1994. Mali. Quantity unknown. 240 francs. S#623. (Not pictured.) Portrait of Sarah Vaughan.

Walker, Madame C. J.

Madame C. J. Walker was born Sarah Breedlove on December 23, 1867. She was America's first black millionaire business-

TANZANIA 75/-

TINA TURNER

558

BLACK HERITAGE

32 USA

Madam C.J.Walker

559

200TH ANNIVERSARY INAUGURATION OF GEORGE WASHINGTON
1ST PRESIDENT OF THE UNITED STATES

Martin Van Buren 1837-41 50¢

TURKS & CAICOS IS.

560

ROOKIE 1989   60c

ST.VINCENT   JEROME WALTON

561

U.S. BASEBALL SERIES 2
JEROME WALTON

ST.VINCENT 30c

CHICAGO
CUBS®

562

USA   32

CLARA
WARD

563

LIBERIA

DANIEL BASHIEL WARNER
PRESIDENT
OF LIBERIA
1864-1868

3¢ POSTAGE

564

3¢

DANIEL BASHIEL WARNER

LIBERIA

565

UNITED STATES POSTAGE

10¢   10¢

566

U.S.   POSTAGE

3¢

CENTENNIAL OF BOOKER T. WASHINGTON

567

RÉPUBLIQUE DU SÉNÉGAL

100F

POSTE AÉRIENNE

BOOKER T. WASHINGTON
1856 - 1915
precurseur de la negritude

DELRIEU

568

29   USA

DINAH
WASHINGTON

569

29   USA

ETHEL
WATERS

570

woman, the child of ex-slave parents in Delta, Louisiana. Both parents died before she was six years of age, and her sister reared her. She married C.J. Walker at fourteen and was widowed at twenty.

Madame C.J. Walker began her road to success when she invented a new method of straightening black folk's hair. Negro women before Madame Walker's invention had to de-kink their hair by placing it on a flat surface and pressing it with a flat hot iron. Madame Walker invented her hair softener in 1905 along with a special straightening comb. Millions of African American women bought her products. Overnight she found herself in business, with assistants, agents, schools, and eventually an enormous manufacturing company.

Madame Walker, with her lucrative business success, was always in the headlines. She lived well, but she also shared with the less fortunate. Madame Walker donated large sums of money to charity and educational institutions. She was responsible for the founding of a girl's school in West Africa to which she donated $100,000. In New York, at her property on Irvington-on-the-Hudson, she built Villa Lewaro, a luxurious mansion furnished with a gold-plated piano, a $60,000 pipe organ, Hepplewhite furniture, Persian rugs and many huge oil paintings. African Americans from the best of America's social, educational and business quarters walked through her doors.

When Madame Walker died in 1919 she had laid the foundation of the cosmetic industry for African American women.

1/28/98. United States. Quantity unknown. 32 cents. S#3181. From the Black Heritage series. *Illus. 559.*

Walker, Moses Fleetwood

Moses Fleetwood Walker was the first black man to play professional baseball. Walker was born in Mt. Pleasant, Ohio, on May 11, 1857. As the story goes, Moses Fleetwood Walker played forty-two games in 1884 with the Toledo Blue Stockings of the American Association, which is considered a major league team. The Blue Stockings disbanded after 1884, and Walker never again reached the major league. However, he did play for several seasons at the minor league level. His brother, Welday, also played for Toledo in 1884.

11/19/89. Turks and Caicos Islands. Quantity unknown. 50 cents. S#776b. On a hard-to-find souvenir sheet of six. These stamps commemorate the 200th anniversary of George Washington and also feature various American presidents, plus pictures of events in American history. This stamp, S#776b, has a picture of the "birth of American baseball" and shows Moses Fleetwood Walker, "1st Negro professional ballplayer." *Illus. 560.*

Walton, Jerome

Jerome Walton was born in Newman, Georgia, on July 8, 1965. He led the Chicago Cubs in stolen bases in 1989 and won the National League Rookie of the Year award. He had the longest batting streak of the season (30). Walton left the Cubs for the Angels and was later signed to the Cincinnati Red in 1993.

7/23/89. St. Vincent. Quantity unknown. 60 cents. S#1224d. *Illus. 561.*

11/30/89. St. Vincent. Quantity unknown. 30 cents. S#1275. From the "U.S. Baseball Series 2." *Illus. 562.*

Ward, Clara

Singer Clara Mae Ward was born on April 21, 1924, in Philadelphia, Pennsylvania. She was the second daughter of Gertrude Mae George Ward. Clara started her singing career as a child. During the Great Depression, her mother had to provide for Clara and the rest of the children by doing domestic work for families in and around Philadelphia. In 1931 Clara's mother embarked on a career as a gospel singer. She performed for a couple of years at various churches in Philadelphia. She also included her daughters in her church performances. For the next nine years, the Ward Singers, as they called themselves, sang wherever and whenever there was an opportunity. The fees for their performances were small, but they continued to perform in these churches.

In 1943, at age 19, Clara Ward was introduced on the national gospel circuit. She performed at the National Baptist Convention, and she began to receive calls from all over the United States, particularly the southern and eastern regions.

Clara was a petite woman, about 5'3" tall and weighing approximately 108 pounds. But her height and weight had no bearing on her power, energy and charisma as a gospel musician and performer. As time passed, she would take more control over the artistic direction of the Ward Singers. She introduced striking gowns and new hairstyles. For many years, the women in the group wore their hair in ponytails. The departure from the usual concert attire gave Ward new fashion freedom.

The Ward Singers became the most popular during the 1950s. Ward started a music publishing company, and they did well. Ward herself was best known for her delivery of hymns. At her peak she had an exceptionally beautiful and clear alto voice. She also had an excellent gift for introducing new music. The Ward Singers were receiving as much as $5,000 per performance during the 1950s. The group's name was changed from the Clara Ward Singers to the Clara Ward Specials, and finally back to the Clara Ward Singers.

Clara Ward lapsed into a coma following two strokes in five weeks and died in Los Angeles on January 16, 1973.

6/26/98. United States. Quantity unknown. 32 cents. S#3218. This issue of U.S. stamps paid tribute to Clara Ward and other American gospel and folk musicians. *Illus. 563.*

Warner, Daniel Bashiel

Daniel B. Warner was born in America, either in Maryland or Virginia. He left the United States during the early or middle 1800s to settle in the country of Liberia. Little is known about his life in America.

Daniel B. Warner became president of Liberia in 1864 and served until 1868. His main concern was how the indigenous people, particularly the natives in the interior, could be brought into the larger society. He was responsible also for organizing the first expedition into the dense forest, led by J.K. Anderson.

1948–50. Liberia. Quantity unknown. 3 cents. S#315. *Illus. 564.*

1958–60. Liberia. Quantity unknown. 3 cents. S#436. *Illus. 565.*

Washington, Booker T.

Booker Taliaferro Washington was born a slave on April 5, 1856, in Hales, Virginia. Washington's mother, Jane Ferguson, was a slave on a plantation. It is strongly believed that Washington's father was a white man. With the Emancipation Proclamation in action in some states (mostly states that went against the Union), Booker T. Washington's mother took him and two other children with her to Malden, West Virginia, at the southeast edge of Charleston.

Washington, his mother, and the other two children lived in poverty. At the age of nine Booker T. had to work in the salt and coal mines of West Virginia to help support his mother and the others. He did have the opportunity to attend a school for blacks and gave his name as Booker T. Washington. He knew his name was Booker but only later did he learn his mother named him Taliaferro. He used all three names as his official name.

At the age of 16 Washington entered the Hampton Normal and Agricultural Institute (today known as Hampton Institute) which is located in Hampton, Virginia. To make his keep while he attended the institution he worked as a janitor. Within a period of three years Washington had graduated. He returned to Malden, where he taught children during the day and adults in the evening. Washington also studied at Wayland Seminary in Washington, D.C. He then returned to Hampton Normal School upon request for an experimental program to provide education to Native Americans. Soon after taking on the program for Native Americans at Hampton, Washington was offered an opportunity in Tuskegee, Alabama, to develop a school for African Americans. In 1881, Booker T. Washington founded Tuskegee Institute and became the principal.

The institute, which was begun in an old abandoned church and a shanty, offered training in farming and mechanics. The school also began to teach and train African American teachers. Years later, the school was nationally recognized, and had more than 100 well-equipped buildings, an enrollment of more than 1,500 students, a faculty of 200, and an endowment of $2 million.

There were many African Americans who opposed during this period the beliefs of Washington. Washington strongly believed blacks could benefit more from industrial training than liberal arts. As part of their training, the students actually built that institution (Tuskegee) from the ground up, providing the campus's buildings, food and other needs to make it self-sufficient. Washington's philosophy led to his establishment of the National Negro Business League in 1900.

Washington's *Up from Slavery* (his autobiography) is a classic. His birthplace was established as a national monument in 1957. Booker T. Washington was also the first African American to be recognized on a United States of America postage stamp, first on April 7, 1940, and again on April 4, 1956. He has also been recognized on an international stamp. This recognition was given for the many contributions he made to education, particularly as it related to the education of African Americans. Washington died on November 14, 1915, in Tuskegee, Alabama.

4/7/40. United States. 14,000,000. 10 cents. S#873. From the Famous Americans issue (Education). *Illus. 566.*

4/5/56. United States. 121,184,600. 3 cents. S#1074. Shows the home where Washington was born. *Illus. 567.*

4/10/71. Senegal. Quantity unknown. 100 francs. S#C98. A hard stamp to find. *Illus. 568.*

Washington, Denzel

A stamp is said to exist honoring Denzel Washington, an African American actor, but no information on such a stamp is available.

Washington, Dinah

Dinah Washington, the queen of the blues, was born Ruth Lee Jones in Tuscaloosa, Alabama, on August 29, 1924. Dinah Washington was born with a natural and versatile singing voice. She spent many years singing on the gospel circuit. In 1943 she joined Lionel Hampton to perform numbers like "Evil Gal Blues" and "Salty Papa Blues." She left Hampton in 1946 to go solo.

Washington could sing any type of tune, be it blues, jazz, Hank Williams, pop hits; you name it, and she had the voice to do it. But her specialty was blues, and Dinah Washington dominated the list of women blues vocalists during the 1950s. Her big hits were "I Only Know," "Time Out for Tears," "Trouble in Mind," "Fat Daddy," and "What a Difference a Day Makes."

Dinah's talent along with her popularity brought her riches rarely earned by African

Americans during her career in the 1950s and 1960s. As she made money, she spent it freely on cars, furs, jewels, drink, and drugs, and she had at least seven husbands.

On December 14, 1963, Dinah Washington died from an overdose of pills. She left behind a gold mine of recordings. Dinah was inducted into the Rock and Roll Hall of Fame in 1993.

6/16/93. United States. 14,000,000. 29 cents. S#2730. From the Legends of American Music series (Rock & Roll/Rhythm and Blues). *Illus. 569.*

7/26/93. The Gambia. Quantity unknown. 4 dalasis. S#1395d. (Not pictured.) In recognition of entertainers. See Clyde McPhatter, S#1395g, for more information.

Waters, Ethel

Ethel Waters was a great American singer, actress, and one of the most prominent black performers of American stage and silver screen during the 1930s and 1940s. She was born in Chester, Pennsylvania, in the year of 1900. Her parents, Louisa Tar Anderson and John Wesley Waters, were poverty-stricken. She was born out of wedlock. It was rare that enough food was available for the family. Many days the only meals that she came by were from sisters of the convent school where she attended as a child.

Ethel was married at age twelve. She worked as a maid and laundress in a Philadelphia hotel for less than $5.00 per week. Twenty-five years later Ethel had become a performing artist making $2,000 a week on stage and screen. She also became an owner of apartments in Harlem. Her first dramatic role was *Mamba's Daughters* (1938), but her most memorable role was that of the cook Bernice in the 1950 stage production and 1953 film version of Carson McCullers's *Member of the Wedding.* Waters also wrote two autobiographical works, *His Eye Is on the Sparrow* (1951) and *To Me It's Wonderful* (1972). She also

played an active part in the religious crusades of the American evangelist Billy Graham.

Ethel Waters died in the year 1977, but she will always be remembered for what she has provided to the world of entertainment.

1994. United States. 35,436,000. 29 cents. S#2851. From the Legends of American Music series. *Illus. 570.*

Waters, Muddy

Muddy Waters was born McKinley Morganfield in Rolling Fork, Mississippi, on April 4, 1915. His musical career was begun with an acoustic guitar, and his country blues were first recorded in 1941 for the Archives of American Folksong for the Library of Congress. In 1943 he switched to the electric guitar. During the 1950s he established an innovative approach to the blues by using a band consisting of amplified guitar, harmonica, piano, and drums.

Muddy Waters brought a new style of electrified blues to the world. His music inspired numerous musicians in both America and Britain, including Bob Dylan, Elvis Presley, Mick Jagger, and others.

Even though Muddy Waters was a superstar in his own right nationally and internationally, he didn't receive the kind of publicity or the monetary rewards due him. However, in the 1970s he did begin to receive some respect for being one of the pioneering innovators of rhythm and blues. He has also been recognized on U.S. and international stamps for his contributions to the blues.

Muddy Waters died on April 30, 1983.

2/12/92. Gambia. Quantity unknown. 50 bututs. S#1180. *Illus. 571.*

9/17/94. United States. 25,000,000. 29 cents. S#2855. From the Legends of American Music series (Blues). *Illus. 572.*

Watts, Quincy

There is not much information presently available on Quincy Watts. It is known that he was born on June 19, 1971 (birth location unknown). His height was 6'2" and weight 217 pounds while he attended the University of Southern California, where he participated in track and field and possibly other major sports such as football or basketball. Other brief information indicates that he also excelled in track and field events. Despite rumors to the contrary, he was never drafted by the National Football League.

Quincy Watts was recognized on a stamp issued by Equatorial Guinea for his contributions in track and field events in 1994.

1993. Equatorial Guinea. Quantity unknown. 100 céntimos. S#179. (Not pictured.) Depicts one portrait of Watts to the left of the stamp, and another portrait to the right dressed in a track outfit with the number 1772.

Wells, Ida B.

Ida B. Wells was born on July 16, 1862, in Holly Springs, Mississippi. The 13th Amendment to the Constitution was proclaimed on December 18, 1865, three years after she was born, freeing her parents and herself. Wells learned to read and write at an early age and became a country schoolteacher when she was 14 years old. She began teaching in the city of Memphis by age 22.

Wells was educated at the Holly Springs freedmen's school and continued her education at Fisk University. In 1889, she became part owner and a reporter for *Free Speech*, a Memphis newspaper. She used this paper as a tool to speak out against the lynchings of African Americans that were overtly and covertly occurring in America. In that same year, 1889, her office was ransacked, her life was threatened, and she was literally run out of Memphis. She moved to New York and started writing for the *New York Age*. Wells also was able to lecture across the United States to organize against lynching.

Ida was married in 1895 at age 33 to Ferdinand L. Barnett, a lawyer, editor and public officer in Chicago. She worked mostly in Chicago, adding the women's suffrage movement to her campaigns. Wells is credited as being one of the original founders of the National Association for the Advancement of Colored People (NAACP). She served as secretary to the National Afro-American Council in 1910 and served on the Chicago municipal court as a probation officer.

Ida Bell Wells, the fearless, militant, controversial, aggressive, courageous, determined fighter for justice and fair play, died on March 25, 1931, in Chicago, Illinois.

2/1/90. United States. 153,000,000. 25 cents. S#2442. From the Black Heritage series. *Illus. 573.*

Wheatley, Phillis

Phillis Wheatley was the first widely acknowledged African American woman poet. She arrived in America in 1761 around six years of age as a slave. John Wheatley, a prominent merchant of Boston, Massachusetts, purchased her from a slave auction block. She was taught to read and write by the Wheatley family even though to do so was unlawful. Within two years after arriving in America, she was able to speak English fluently and to write.

At the age of thirteen Phillis had written her first poem. Poetry quickly became her way of expressing her feelings about everyday life and activities that affected her and other people. At the age of 18 she had written her first book of poetry. She became internationally known for her capabilities when she was invited to England in 1773 and her first book of poetry was published there. It was not until after her death

571

572

573

574

575

576

577

578

579

580

581

582

583

that her poetry was published on American soil.

Phillis's mistress died in 1774, and her master died in 1778. Phillis became a free person, in the sense that she was not owned, but she became an instant slave of hard times, sadness, and a life of poverty. One month after the death of John Wheatley, she married a pseudo-gentleman by the name of John Peters. Peters was not a good provider, and Phillis was forced to work as a servant. She bore two children, who died almost immediately after birth. Phillis's health failed, and soon death came for her and her third child. She and the child died within hours of each other on December 5, 1784. Just before she died, she wrote a long poem titled "Liberty and Peace."

4/10/71. Senegal. Quantity unknown. 25 francs. S#C95. A hard-to-find stamp. Only a poor copy is shown here. *Illus. 574.*

5/3/82. Turks and Caicos Islands. Quantity unknown. 20 cents. S#522. Commemorates the 250th anniversary of George Washington's birth. Wheatley stands in foreground while Washington crosses in a rowboat in the background. A hard-to-find stamp. *Illus. 575.*

White, Frank

Frank White was born in Greenville, Mississippi, on September 4, 1950. He considers his hometown Lee's Summit, Missouri. He played second base for the Kansas City Royals. He led his league in fielding percentage three times. In 1988 he committed only four errors in 150 games.

11/30/89. St. Vincent. Quantity unknown. 30 cents. S#1273a. From the "U.S. Baseball Series 2." *Illus. 576.*

White, Jo Jo

"Jo Jo" (Joseph Henry) White was an American basketball player who was born on November 16, 1946, in St. Louis, Missouri. He played guard 1969–81 mostly with the Boston Celtics. He was the Most Valuable Player in the 1976 playoffs. He was also a member of the 1968 Olympic basketball team, with whom he is pictured on a stamp.

1969. Ajman. Quantity unknown. 15 riyals. See Spencer Haywood for more information and an illustration of this stamp.

White, Josh

Josh White, a blues and folk singer and guitarist, was born in Greenville, South Carolina, on February 11, 1915. As a child, White sang in churches. He left school in the 1920s to work in South Carolina, North Carolina, and Chicago, as a guide and accompanist to blind street singers. Josh worked for such singers as Blind John Henry Arnold, Blind Joe Taggart, Blind Blake and Blind Lemon Jefferson.

In 1932 White decided to move to New York to make a living as a professional guitarist and singer. By the late 1930s Josh White was well known in New York for his wide repertory of folk and blues songs. He married Carol Carr in 1934 and had five children.

In the 1940s White gravitated toward folk music and radical politics. He played with Woody Guthrie, Leadbelly, Sonny Terry, and Brownie McGhee at hootenannies, rent parties and lofts in New York, as well as at nightclubs and concerts across the United States. During World War II, Josh White appeared on radio programs sponsored by the Office of War Information and performed and recorded at the Library of Congress. By 1945 Josh White had become so popular that he performed at President Roosevelt's inaugural ball.

After World War II, White became a prominent international entertainer. In the 1960s, he turned to protest songs and recorded numerous albums. In 1966 White was forced into retirement after being involved in an automobile accident. Josh White died during open-heart surgery in

Manhasset, New York, on September 5, 1969.

6/26/98. United States. Quantity unknown. 32 cents. S#3215. From the Folk Musicians issue. *Illus. 577.*

Wilkins, Joe Willie

Blues singer Joe Willie Wilkins was born January 7, 1923, in Davenport (Coahoma County), Mississippi. Joe Willie was a local farmer and a self-taught musician. His father was the owner of a small bank, and he allowed Joe to frequently work with him to perform at local dances, etc. He also hoboed with Sonny Williamson and Robert Jr. Lockwood, working the Mississippi streets, jukes, and barrelhouses during the late 1930s. He also was in the U.S. Navy during the early 1940s.

During his time, Wilkins worked with many musicians who went on to make names for themselves in the blues arena in America. Joe went on to record as sideman for Arthur Crudup, Willie Nix, Roosevelt Sykes, and others from the 1950s into the 1970s. He settled in Memphis and traveled extensively, especially with Joe's King Biscuit Boys to festivals around the country.

2/12/92. The Gambia. Quantity unknown. 10 dalasis. S#1189. From the History of the Blues series. *Illus. 578.*

Williams, Billy D.

Billy D. Williams was born William December Williams in Harlem, New York, April 6, 1937. Billy Dee is most remembered for his suave role in *Lady Sings the Blues.*

As a youngster Williams was withdrawn and overweight. He set his future on becoming a fashion illustrator. While studying on scholarship at the School of Fine Arts in the National Academy of Design, a CBS casting director helped him secure bit parts in several television shows, including *Lamp Unto My Feet* and *Look Up and Live.* At this point Billy Dee began to study acting under Sidney Poitier and Paul Mann at the Actors Workshop in Harlem. Williams had his first film role in *The Last Angry Man* (1959), and appeared on stage in *The Cool World* (1960), *A Taste of Honey* (1960), *The Blacks* (1962) and several other popular Broadway plays, i.e., *Ceremonies in Dark Old Men* (1970). Williams's next major role was in the acclaimed movie *Brian's Song* (1970), a performance for which he received an Emmy nomination. Motown's Berry Gordy signed Williams to a seven-year contract. The contract with Motown started the ball rolling for Billy Dee with such movies as *Lady Sings the Blues* (1972) and *Mahogany* (1976) with Diana Ross. His last movie for Gordy was *The Bingo Long Traveling All-Stars and Motor Kings* (1976).

In the early 1980s, Williams appeared in two of George Lucas's "Star Wars" adventures, *The Empire Strikes Back* and *Return of the Jedi.* He has appeared in numerous television movies, including *Scott Joplin, Christmas Lilies of the Field,* and the miniseries *Chiefs.* When he was cast opposite Diahann Carroll in the prime-time drama *Dynasty,* his reputation as a romantic lead was secured. At the end of the decade, he starred in action films such as *Oceans of Fire* and *Number One with a Bullet.*

In 1995, Williams played a detective in the TV murder mystery *Falling for You.* He also hosted the Black Theater Festival in Winston-Salem, North Carolina, and the Infiniti Sports Festival. Some of Williams's paintings were featured in a computer screen-saver program, *Art in the Dark: Extraordinary Works by African American Artists.*

3/25/93. The Gambia. Quantity unknown. 3 dalasis. S#1349c. Depicts a scene from the movie *The Bingo Long Traveling All-Stars and Motor Kings. Illus. 579.*

Williams, Randy

Randy Williams was an American track and field athlete. He was a long jumper. Randy won the gold medal in the 1972 Olympics, and he won the long jump for the 1976 silver medal. He was born on August 23, 1953, in Fresno, California. He has been recognized on a number of stamps around the world for his contributions to track and field.

1972. Central African Republic. Quantity unknown. 100 francs. S#C101. A hard-to-find stamp commemorating the 1972 Olympics in Munich. *Illus. 580.*

12/29/72. Haiti. Quantity unknown. 50 centimes. S#662d. *Illus. 581.*

1973. Umm-Al-Qiwain. Quantity unknown. 1 riyal. *Illus. 582.*

1973. Umm-Al-Quiwain. Quantity unknown. 1 riyal. This is a mini version. *Illus. 583.*

1973. Umm-Al-Qiwain. Quantity unknown. 5 riyals. (See color section.) *Illus. C161.*

Wilson, Willie

Willie Wilson was born on July 9, 1955, in Montgomery, Alabama. He considers his hometown Leawood, Kansas. He plays with the Kansas City Royals. His professional baseball averages based on appearances at the plate (50 times): batting .300; slugging .358; strikeout ratio 5.4.

11/30/89. St. Vincent. Quantity unknown. 30 cents. S#1275h. (See color section.) From the "U.S. Baseball Series 2." *Illus. C162.*

Winfield, Dave

David Mark Winfield is an American baseball player, but his athletic prowess extends to many other sports. He is one of the few who have been drafted by a professional baseball, basketball, and football team. However, Dave chose professional baseball, and went with the New York Yankees to play outfield in 1973. In that year he led the National League in RBI's. Dave was born on October 3, 1951, in St. Paul, Minnesota.

11/2/87. Grenada. Quantity unknown. Face value unknown. S#1552b. (Perforated souvenir sheet.) See Eric Davis S#1552b for comments and an illustration of this souvenir sheet.

Wolf, Howlin'

Howlin' Wolf was born Chester Arthur Burnett on June 10, 1910, in West Point, Mississippi. Wolf later moved to the Mississippi Delta, known as the home of the blues. He started playing the guitar as a teenager under the training of Charley Patton, who lived on a nearby plantation, and began performing around 1920. He traveled to various plantations singing and playing at house parties and local jukes.

During the 1930s, Burnett met Sonny Boy Williamson (Alex Miller), who taught him to play the harmonica. Burnett changed his name when he learned to play the harmonica. He developed a guttural "howlin'" style. From then on he was called the Howlin' Wolf.

After serving in World War II, Howlin' Wolf relocated to West Memphis, Arkansas, where he worked as a disc jockey for WKEM radio and formed his first band. He began recording in 1951. Following the success of "Moanin' at Midnight," Wolf was signed to an exclusive contract with Chess Records and relocated to Chicago, where he remained for the rest of his life. Howlin' Wolf continued to perform and record. He also toured the United States and Europe. He helped to define the postwar Chicago blues style.

Even though Howlin' Wolf was born on a plantation in Sunflower County, Mississippi, he brought the delta blues from the South into the limelight of Chicago and London. Many of Wolf's recordings laid the foundation for the golden age of rock and roll. Howlin' Wolf died in Hines, Illinois, on January 10, 1976.

2/12/92. The Gambia. Quantity unknown. 3 dalasis. S#1186. (See color section.) From the History of the Blues series. *Illus. C167.*

9/17/94. United States. 20,000,000. 29 cents. S#2861. (See color section.) *Illus. C168.*

Wonder, Stevie

Stevie Wonder was born Steveland Judkins Morris in 1950 in Saginaw, Michigan. He was born blind. He began playing the piano at the age of four and was a proficient singer and instrumentalist by thirteen. He had his first hit, "Fingertips Part 2," in 1963. That record was released by Motown. There he was given his professional name Stevie Wonder. He produced the albums *Signed, Sealed and Delivered* in 1970 and *Where I'm Coming From* in 1970. Wonder and his wife, Syreeta Wright, solely did the latter. *On Music of the Mind* (1972) he used modern overdubbing to allow him to play most of the instrumental accompaniments. *Talking Book* (1972), a one-man album, contained the hit singles "You Are the Sunshine of My Life" and "Superstition." Wonder won five Grammy Awards for *Innervisions* in 1973 and one each for the albums *Songs in the Key of Life* in 1976 and *In Square Circle* in 1985. Other albums by Wonder include *Looking Back* in 1977, *Hotter Than July* in 1980, and *Character* in 1987. He has been active in such social causes as the anti-apartheid moment, Mothers Against Drunk Driving, and the Retinitis Pigmentosa Foundation, and other national and international organizations to help humanity.

3/30/90. Tanzania. Quantity unknown. 25 cents. S#587. (See color section.) *Illus. C169.*

Woodard, Alfre

A stamp is said to exist recognizing Alfre Woodard, an African American actress, but no information on such a stamp is available.

Woods, Tiger

When one reviews the life of Tiger Woods, it seems clear that he was destined to become a professional golfer. Between one and two years of age his father began preparing him for his destination. He has been seriously competing in tournaments since age four. At five Woods had made his first birdie, and at six his first hole in one. After graduation from high school in 1994, Woods attended Stanford University and played with the Stanford University golf team, setting records.

The most important tournament for young American golfers is the U.S. Junior Amateur Championship, which Woods won three years in a row. He won the Amateur Championship in 1994 and became the first person of color ever to win it, after making a comeback from six holes behind. Winning the Amateur Championship is almost an automatic invitation to the Master's Tournament of Augusta, Georgia — the main event for golfers from around the world. Only three other golfers of color (Lee Elder, 1975, and two others between 1975 and 1988) had ever been invited. Most African-Americans who got close to the event were caddies, cooks, kitchen and ground helpers, etc. The Masters was tacitly reserved for white males only, for the most part. Even during the early eighties and late nineties, African Americans were not a part of the Masters.

Woods's first Masters invitation came in 1996. When the tournament was finished, he came in forty-first place. His only hope for the next shot at the Masters for the following year was to win the Amateur Championship, and he did. On August 13, 1997, he became the youngest golfer to win the Masters, the ultimate win for U.S. and International golfers.

Tiger Woods was born in Cypress, California, on December 30, 1975. His mother Tida (Tee-dah) named him Eldrick, and his father Earl called him Tiger (the name of Earl's best friend, a soldier who had saved his life). Woods has set and broken some of the best records in the history of golf. Despite his youth, he has already been recognized on three international stamps.

1997. Turkmenistan. Quantity unknown. 100.00 Turkmen manata. AA#76. (See color section.) From an issue recognizing leading personalities of the twentieth century. Other personalities recognized in this souvenir issue are actors Pierce Brosnan (007) and George Clooney. This souvenir sheet comes with a total of nine stamps, with three different stamps for each person. *Illus. C163.*

1997. Turkmenistan. Quantity unknown. 100.00 Turkmen manata. AA#77. (See color section.) *Illus. C164.*

1997. Turkmenistan. Quantity unknown. 100.00 Turkmen manata. AA#78. (See color section.) *Illus. C165.*

Woodson, Carter G.

Most Americans are aware of Negro History Week, which is now celebrated during the month of February (the shortest month in the year). February is now commonly known as Black History Month. Many African Americans have researched and provided information on the role that African Americans played in the development of the United States of America and the world. For example, J.A. Rogers, William Cooper Nell, W.E.B. Dubois, William Lauren Katz, John Hope Franklin, Malcolm X and others were very significant players in presenting African American history, but it was Carter Godwin Woodson who made it a living part of the American classroom.

Now sometimes known as the father of Negro History, Woodson was born in Canton, Virginia, on December 19, 1875. Having little opportunity or money to attend school, he did not finish high school until the age of 22. While Woodson was working to complete requirements for his high school diploma he was working as a coal miner to help support his family and himself. He continued his education at Berea College in Kentucky and at the University

of Chicago. Three years later he organized the Association for the Study of Negro Life and History. Dr. Woodson firmly believed that "the achievements of the Negro properly set forth will crown him as a factor in early human progress and a maker of modern civilization." His life and work are eloquent testimony to that belief.

Dr. Woodson wrote more than 10 books referencing the history of the African American, including *The Mis-Educated Negro*; *The Education of the Negro Prior to 1861*; and *The Mind of the Negro as Reflected in Letters Written During the Crisis of 1800–1861*. He started the *Journal of Negro History*, a scholarly repository of research which is used to this day by students throughout the world.

Dr. Carter Godwin Woodson died April 4, 1950, in Washington, D.C.

2/1/84. United States. 120,000,000. 20 cents. S#2073. (See color section.) From the Black Heritage series. *Illus. C166.*

Wright, Richard

Richard Wright was a native of Roxie, Mississippi. He was born on September 4, 1908, in poverty. The first part of his life was in the South, where he got a real view of American racism. Later he spent time in Chicago and New York, where he was introduced to a less overt style of racism, and then in France, where lots of African Americans during Wright's time went to fulfill their dreams in the arts. Those varied experiences equipped him with superb inner tools to produce some of America's greatest literary works. Wright's novel *Native Son* was the first ever book by a black author, to be selected by the Book of the Month Club. Later he enjoyed further success with *Black Boy*. Some of his other literary works include *Uncle Tom's Children*, which helped to establish him as a writer.

Richard Wright died in Paris, France, on November 28, 1960. His works live on to this day.

3/25/98. Ghana. Quantity unknown. 350 cedis. S#2027d. (Not pictured.) Portrait of Richard Wright. See Maya Angelou S#2027a, for more comments.

Malcolm X

Malcolm Little, known to the world as Malcolm X (El-Hajj Malik El-Shabazz), was a civil rights activist, human rights advocate, community organizer, orator, revolutionary, and publisher. He was born on May 19, 1925, in Omaha, Nebraska, and was named Malcolm "Harpy" Little. He was the seventh child of eight children. His father was the Reverend Earl Little (a follower of Marcus Garvey) and his mother was Louise Little (a native of Grenada, South America). Malcolm was raised in Lansing, Michigan, where his family's home was burned by the Ku Klux Klan.

At the age of sixteen Malcolm moved east, first to Boston, Massachusetts, and later to New York. In Harlem, he drifted into the underworld of "numbers," bootlegging, dope, commercial sex and confidence games. By this time he had come to be known under such street names as "Detroit Red," "Big Red," and simply "Red" because of height and reddish hair. Before his twenty-first birthday he had been convicted and sentenced to prison for burglary.

It was in the state prison at Charlestown, Massachusetts, that he learned of the Black Muslim movement (the Nation of Islam) and the teachings of Elijah Muhammad. In prison from 1946 to 1952, Malcolm re-entered society a dedicated follower of Elijah Muhammad. In 1953 Malcolm X, as he had renamed himself to replace the "slave name" of Little, became assistant minister of the Black Muslims' Detroit Mosque. The Honorable Elijah Muhummad was pleased with work of his newcomer. Malcolm was transferred to Philadelphia and later assigned to Mosque Number 7 in Harlem. By the end of 1956, the New York mosque was one of the most successful in the movement under the leadership of Malcolm. By the early 1960s, Malcolm X overshadowed his nominal superior, Elijah Muhammad, and eventually the two leaders came to a parting of the ways.

In 1963, Malcolm X was suspended as a minister of the New York mosque and attempted to organize a group of his own called the Organization of Afro-American Unity. During the difficult period Malcolm traveled the nation with a strong message of black manhood and independence, and made two voyages to the Middle East and Africa. His travels had a tremendous effect on Malcolm in the way he regarded brotherhood between blacks and whites the world over.

He had made many enemies, black and white, before and after his break with Elijah Muhammad, and feared for his life. On February 21, 1965, what he feared came true. He was assassinated in the Audubon Ballroom in New York City. His death was headlined around the world. Most commentators on the life of Malcolm X agreed that his greatest contribution was "telling it like it is" in a style and manner that made Americans listen to the voice of an outraged man.

3/21/84. Iran. Quantity unknown. 5 riyals. S#2159. (See color section.) A hard-to-find stamp. *Illus. C170.*

2/1/99. United States. Quantity unknown. 33 cents. S#3272. (See color section.) From the Black Heritage series. *Illus. C171.*

Young, Lester

Lester Young, called "the Pres" or "Prez," was an American tenor saxophonist. He is regarded as one of the most significant figures in the transition from "hot" to "cool," or understated, jazz. Young was born in Woodville, Mississippi, in 1909. He played with various musical groups until he joined the orchestra of Count Basie in 1936. Within four years he established himself as Basie's leading soloist. While playing with the Count he made many memorable recordings with singer Billie Holiday. From 1940 he led his own small combo and toured extensively with Jazz at the Philharmonic, a concert group organized by the American impresario Norman Granz.

As one of the greatest tenor saxophonists of all time, Lester Young was known for his spare, laconic sound. Young died in 1959.

4/3/89. St. Vincent. Quantity unknown. 50 cents. S#1146. (See color section.) *Illus. C173.*

Young, Whitney

Whitney Moore Young, Jr., was born in Lincoln Ridge, Kentucky, on July 31, 1921, to Whitney Moore Young, Sr., and Laura. Young would become known as "Mr. Equal Opportunity." He was a low key civil rights leader, author, journalist and teacher. He was married to his college sweetheart, Margaret Buckner; they were the parents of two daughters.

Throughout his educational experiences, Young was a scholarly student and athlete whose ambition was to become a medical doctor. He received his undergraduate degree in pre-med from Kentucky State College (now Kentucky State University) in Frankfort, Kentucky, and a Master of Social Work degree from the University of Minnesota in St. Paul, Minnesota. His ambition changed for two reasons: He was not accepted by two medical schools, and while serving in the army during World War II, he envisioned being the bridge or race relations negotiator for the African American community in America. Further studies took him to the Massachusetts Institute of Technology and Harvard University.

It was while employed with the Urban League staff in St. Paul, Minnesota, that he began his career as a social worker, finding jobs for disadvantaged African Americans. He gained such renown for opening doors to corporate America that he was catapulted, at the age of twenty-six, into the position of executive director of the Omaha, Nebraska, branch office of the Urban League. He also became the University of Nebraska School of Social Work's first African American professor.

After displaying his administrative skills and capabilities in many positions (dean of the School of Social Work at Atlanta University; a leadership role in the Atlanta branch of the National Association for the Advancement of Colored People; and executive director of the Atlanta branch office of the Urban League), he was recruited by corporate America for the position of the national chief executive officer of the Urban League in New York City. It was at the national level where his administrative, community organization and fund-raising capabilities shone brightest. The Urban League's branch offices increased three-fold and its budget expanded from a $250,000 annually to well over $3 million over a period of half a decade. As a result of his agenda for African Americans and his diplomatic relationship with corporate America and presidents of the United States, job opportunities opened for African Americans that had not existed. He was a director on the boards of numerous corporations and appointed to numerous government commissions.

He was the author of two books, *Beyond Racism* and *To Be Equal*, but he was best known for his weekly column "To Be Equal," which appeared in over one hundred newspapers in the United States. He was one of the organizers of the 1963 March on Washington, D.C. Young died accidentally in Lagos, Nigeria, on March 11, 1971, at the age of 49. He was the first African American to have a president of the United States eulogize him at his funeral.

1/30/81. United States. 159,505,000. 15 cents. S#1875. (See color section.) *Illus. C172.*

Bibliography

Adams, Charles F. *Stamp Collecting: The Complete, Easy Guide to the World's Most Popular Hobby: How to Get Started, What to Buy, How to Avoid Common Pitfalls, Important Guidelines for Purchasing and Much More.* New York: Dell, 1992.

Adams, Russell L. *Great Negroes Past and Present.* Chicago: Afro AM Publishing, 1984.

"An African-American Philatelic Experience." http://www.slsabyrd.com (3/13/00).

"Alison Leland Tells of Sorrow, Gratitude." *The Houston Post,* August 16, 1989, p. A-14.

Austin, Ernest A. *The Black American Stamp Album: A Philatelic Study of Black Americans, Worldwide Topical Edition.* New Jersey: Austin Enterprises, 1988.

Babits, Lawrence E. *A Devil of a Whipping: The Battle of Cowpens.* Chapel Hill: The University of North Carolina Press, 1998.

Bears, Edwin C. *Battle of Cowpens: A Documented Narrative and Troop Movement Maps.* Johnson City, Tenn.: Overmountain Press, 1993.

"Black Memorabilia." *Black Ethnic Collectibles,* 2, no.5 (January/February, 1989).

Carnysmith, Jessie, Casper L. Jordan, and Robert L. Johns, eds. *Black First: 2,000 Years of Extraordinary Achievement.* Detroit: Visible Ink, 1994.

"Celebrating the First 150 Years of Stamps." *Meekel's and Stamps Magazine* 187, no. 6 (August 11, 2000).

Chappell, Louis W. *John Henry: A Folk-Lore Study.* New York: Washington Post, 1968.

Cunin, Bert. *Dear Rock Star Fan,* New York: Shield Stamp, 1989.

Davis, Marianna W., ed. *Contributions of Black Women to America.* Kenday, 1982.

Dennis, R. Ether. *The Black People of America: Illustrated History.* New York: McGraw–Hill, 1970.

Department of Information and Cultural Affairs, ELTV [Liberian Television Corporation], and Q.T. Vincent. *Liberia Remembers President Tubman's Diamond Jubilee 1895–1970.* Monrovia, Liberia: Author.

Dupree, Adolph. "Stamps: Ida B. Wells' Mark of Distinction." *About ... Time,* 1990, 15.

Fleishman, Henry B. "Legal Document Letter of Slaves Being Sent to Liberia." *American Philatelic Journal,* 1991, p. 339.

Fleming, Thomas J. *"Downright Fighting": The Story of Cowpens.* Washington, D.C.: U.S. Department of the Interior, 1988.

Green, Robert. *Black Courage 1775–1783.* Washington, D.C.: National Society of the Daughters of the American Revolution.

Haley, Alex. *The Autobiography of Malcolm X.* New York: Ballantine, 1965.

Harris, Middleton, et al. *The Black Book.* New York: Random House, 1974.

Hickson, R. *A Who's Who of Sports Champions: Their Stories and Records.* New York: Houghton Mifflin, 1995.

Hopkins, Claude. The *New Grove Dictionary of Music and Musicians. Vol.II: Americans.* New York: Grave's Dictionaries, 1986.

"In Step with Johnny Mathis." *Washington Post,* November 15, 1992.

"Jackie Wilson." *The African American Almanac.* Detroit: Gale Research, 1997.

Jamestown Stamp Company. *1939–1999: Our*

60th Year. Volume 59, Edition 1. Jamestown, New York: Author, 1999.

"Jazzed Up." *Stamp Collector,* August 18, 1995.

"Johnny Mathis." *Bakers Biographical Dictionary of Musicians.* Eighth edition. New York: Schirmer, 1992.

Jones, Hattie. *Big Star Fallin' Mama: Five Women in Black Music.* New York: Puffin, 1995.

Kaplan, Sidney, and Emma Nogrady Kaplan. *The Black Presence in the Era of the American Revolution.* Amherst: University of Massachusetts Press, 1989.

Kenmore Stamp Company. *Finder's Guide to Rare and Valuable Postage Stamps.* Midford, N.H.: Author, 1991.

Kirtzman, Andrew. "Probe Begins into Cause of Leland Plane Disaster." *The Houston Post,* August 16, 1989.

"Kwanzaa Holiday Celebration." *American Philatelist: Journal of the American Philatelic Society,* December 1997, 1094.

LaFontant, Jewel, ed. *A Salute to Historic Black Women.* United States: Empak Enterprises, 1984.

"Liberia from 1912 to 1930." http://www.denison.edu/~waite/liberia/history/ww1.htm (1992).

Locke, Alain Leroy. *The Negro in America.* American Library Association, 1933.

Logan, Rayford W., and Michael R. Winston, eds. *Dictionary of American Negro Biography.* New York: W.W. Norton, 1982.

McCormick, M. "Lightnin' Hopkins: Blues." New York: Jazz Panorama, 1962.

Miller, Elizabeth. *The Negro in America: A Bibliography.* 2nd edition. Cambridge, Mass.: Harvard University Press, 1970.

Minton, John. "Mance and His Music: Mance Libscomp Speaking for Himself." *Handbook of Texas Online.* Austin: The Texas State Historical Association, 1999.

Morant, Mack B. "Criteria for Evaluation of U.S. History Text Books for Black Students: A Usable Model for Other Minorities." Ed.D. diss., University of Massachusetts, 1976.

Morrison, Toni. *Jazz.* New York: Alfred A Knopf, 1993.

Moss, Bobby G. *The Patriots at the Cowpens.* Revised edition. Blacksburg, S.C.: Scotia Press, 1994.

Olcheski, Bill. "Black History Provides Collecting Focus." *The American Philatelist,* February 1993.

Page, James A. *Olympian Medalists.* Englewood, Colo.: Libraries Unlimited, 1991.

"Patriot Minorities at the Battle of Cowpens." http://www.nps.gov/cowp/minority.htm (1999).

Perry, Bruce, ed., *Malcolm X: The Last Speeches.* New York: Pathfinder, 1989.

Ploski, Harry A., and James Williams, eds. *The Negro Almanac: A Reference Work on African Americans.* Fifth edition. New York: Bellwether, 1976.

Quarles, Benjamin. *The Negro in the American Revolution.* Chapel Hill: University of North Carolina Press, 1998.

Ragatz, Lowell J. *A Guide for the Study of British Caribbean History: 1763–1834.* Washington, D.C.: U.S. Government Printing Office, 1932.

"Richard Pryor: 1940–1962." http://www.joemills.com/web/pryor/index.html (1999).

Scott 1990 Standard Postage Stamp Catalogue. 6 vols. Sidney, Ohio: Scott Publishing, 1989.

Scott Product Guide, 1995-96 Edition. Sidney, Ohio: Scott Publishing, 1995.

Scott 2000 Standard Postage Stamp Catalogue. 6 vols. Sidney, Ohio: Scott Publishing, 1999.

"Son House." *Contemporary Black Biography.* Volume 8. Detroit: Gale Group, 1996.

South Carolina Department of Archives and History. http://www.schah.sc.edu/homepage.htm.

Thornton, John. *Africa and Africans in the Making of the Atlantic World,* 1400–1800. 2nd ed. Cambridge, England: Cambridge University Press, 1998.

United States Postal Service. "The Black Heritage Series: Illuminating a People's Extraordinary Journey." *USA Philatelic: The Official Source for Stamp Enthusiasts* 5, no. 1 (Spring 2000).

United States Postal Service. *The Postal Guide to U.S. Stamps.* Washington: GPO, annually, 1985–1999.

Westminster Stamp Gallery Ltd. *Black History — M.L. King, Jr. — List # 1323.* Foxboro, Mass.: Author, 1996.

Wheatley, Phillis. *Poems of Phillis Wheatley.* Chapel Hill: University of North Carolina Press, 1966.

"Wilt Chamberlain 1936–1999." *Beckett Basketball Card Monthly,* December 1999.

Index of Countries